Land and Labor in the Greek World

*Ancient Society and History*

*Land and*
*in the*

**ALISON BURFORD**

# Labor

# Greek World

The Johns Hopkins University Press
Baltimore and London

This book has been brought to production with the generous assistance of the David M. Robinson Fund.

The Johns Hopkins University Press
701 West 40th Street
Baltimore, Maryland 21211-2190
The Johns Hopkins Press Ltd., London

Library of Congress Cataloging-in-Publication Data

Burford, Alison.
  Land and labor in the Greek world / Alison Burford.
    p.   cm.—(Ancient society and history)
  Includes bibliographical references and index.
  ISBN 0-8018-4463-0 (acid-free paper)
  1. Land tenure—Greece—History.   2. Landowners—Greece—History.
3. Agriculture—Greece—History.   4. Agricultural laborers—Greece—
History.   I. Title.   II. Series.
HD133.B87   1993
333.3'0938—dc20                                                    92-19191

A catalog record for this book is available from the British Library

# Contents

*Contents*

# Preface

The intention of this study has been to consider ancient Greek society in the context of land tenure and agriculture, and the relationships within it which were determined by landed interests in the first instance. Like Hesiod's *Works and Days,* it has never been meant to stand as a complete reference work on all legal and technical aspects of owning and cultivating the land; it does not begin to take full account of the economic factors at work, beyond suggesting ways in which they may have affected policies and attitudes of mind. Nor does it pretend to any arithmetical or statistical precision in the matter of population, acreages planted, demand, yields, man-hours expended, or productivity achieved, except in a very small way; for, as valuable as such computations can be, there is also something to be said for the argument that, so fragile and fragmentary is the evidence, so vast are the unknown entities, to focus too closely on exact figures is to go beyond the limits both of what is possible and of what is useful, and to blur rather than enhance the outlines of the subject under scrutiny.

I owe much to the numerous publications that, especially during the last few years, have contributed to the debate on these subjects. The extent of my indebtedness I have attempted to indicate by reference throughout the discussion and in the Bibliography; but inevitably in a book of this scale I have not done justice to the pioneering works of such scholars as Guiraud or Jardé. Nevertheless it should be understood that they form the foundation of my approach. The topic was originally suggested to me some years ago by M. I. Finley; this account of it sadly lacks the benefit of his criticism.

I am most grateful to the staff of the Interlibrary Loan Department of the Ramsey Library at the University of North Carolina at Asheville for help in gaining access to research material. I also wish to thank Nayyir Bayyan and, in particular, Christine Waters, for secretarial assistance of an exemplary kind.

The anonymous reader of the Johns Hopkins University Press and my husband, Guy Cooper, provided constructive comments of which I was very glad to take heed, and the editorial staff has given courteous and patient guidance at every stage.

Land and Labor in the Greek World

# Introduction

Once the cultivation of cereals and the domestication of animals had begun, two basic principles gradually became obvious: first, that in agriculture lay the foundations of a civilized society, making possible not only society's survival but also the devotion of time and energy to other things besides gathering food; and, second, that to have the land worked by someone else was the beginning of a civilized life. Landowners and laborers were the basic components of every Greek community, and preoccupation with the land formed part of everyone's thinking.[1] To a large extent this preoccupation remained beneath the surface and, considering its weight, received surprisingly little overt expression in the literature. Depictions of the Greeks show a people focused on their own participation in public life as warriors, proponents of policy, or contributors to the religious and cultural life of the city-state, as organizers of public works projects or of intellectual exercises in one or another branch of philosophy, as poets or poets' audiences. But for all that the Greeks appear to have been engrossed with the affairs of the polis, there can be little doubt that whenever a steady breeze got up about threshing time,

1

most people in the Greek world would have remarked that "here was a fine day for winnowing."

It has by now become almost a truism that a very large proportion of the population, citizen and noncitizen, free and unfree, in all Greek communities was engaged with one aspect or another of making landed property productive. Clearly the Greeks shared many points of view with other agricultural societies, and their institutions were to a considerable extent shaped by similar agrarian concerns. Yet very significant differences existed between the culture of the Greek city-states and that of all preceding and contemporary societies. The Greeks rose to greater heights above the furrowed field in more spheres of intellectual and artistic activity than other peoples; simply put, monuments in Egypt, Persia, or Assyria required for their achievement an absolute monarch's wealth and clout, whereas the great temples of Athens, Didyma, Ephesus, Samos, Selinus, Acragas, and elsewhere were put up by small-time farmers, comparatively speaking.

Whatever the Greeks thought or did, ownership and cultivation of the land were never very far out of mind. Whatever the balance of power and social prestige within a community, and however they were expressed in its constitution, landed interests played a critical role in determining political relationships and economic activities. In many places full political rights depended on the possession of a property qualification, meaning specifically the ownership of more than a certain minimum acreage of land, as at Sparta; so the *geomoroi,* or "land sharers," at many periods constituted the ruling class of Samos. Even at Athens in 403, where no such property qualification had applied for several generations, it was still possible for Phormisius to propose that the citizen body be restricted to those who owned land and for such a move to have disfranchized no more than one-fifth or one-sixth of the existing citizen body, *if the proposal had been approved,* which it was not.[2]

The answer found to the question, Who labored on the land? shaped as decisively as anything else the character of Greek society. In the case of the two most clearly distinct of all the city-states, Athens and Sparta, the answers were as different as the two

2

communities themselves: at Athens, chattel slavery became an inevitable concomitant of radical democracy, and at the same time many landowners took a hand in working their own land; in Sparta, the institution of helotry permitted the Spartans to be completely Spartan, freed of all concern with their land, and at the same time forced them to become all the more Spartan, from the necessity of keeping the helots under control. The economic value of possessing cultivated land and the political importance of having land to cultivate were powerful factors in Greek affairs. Concern for the food supply was no less pressing than in any other part of the world; indeed, the difference between "too much" and "too little" was often a very narrow one, and when crop failures occurred they could not always be met with extensive reserves. Greece has often been presented as a poor land, not least by the ancient Greeks themselves, but this does not mean that its agricultural potential was negligible, or that methods of farming the land had not been found which made the best use of what the land had to offer. But it is true that many communities had few or no alternative resources to the crops they could grow for themselves, and even those states that did have such things as mineral reserves, for instance, such as Athens, depended quite extensively on domestic food production (although the import of wheat became a matter of some moment certainly within the Classical period). Exchange of surpluses was the customary way out of a difficulty; if one crop failed, another might succeed, balancing corresponding gluts and poor harvests elsewhere. But without well-farmed land there could be no harvest, and no basis for trade of any kind. The community's abiding anxiety is expressed in Aeschylus's *Eumenides,* when Athena calls down blessings on the land of Attica: "Let there be peace and good fortune rising up from the earth and the heaving sea, and down the vaulting sky let the wind gods breathe a wash of sunlight streaming through the land, and the yield of soil and grazing cattle flood our city's life with power and never flag with time" (Aesch. *Eum.* 904–9). The Eumenides also wish to preserve Attica from "the winds that rock the olive" and their "scorching heat that blinds the buds," the "killing icy gales," and the "blight that creeps on fruit," and they pray to Pan to "make the flocks increase and the ewes drop fine twin lambs" (*Eum.* 938–46). It is exactly the reverse of all these things that many a Greek wished against his enemies, according to the formal curses that sealed soldiers' and others' oaths of loyalty to their city.

The community's existence depended on staking out and holding onto farmland that would support its members. In Greece, no less than in any other part of the world, good land was frequently the object of competition, and territorial disputes started by farmers over fertile plains, or by herdsmen in borderland grazing, contributed to the outbreak of one war after another throughout Greek history. During the seventh century the Euboean cities of Chalcis and Eretria fought over the plain land of the river Lelas, which formed a natural boundary between them; according to Thucydides, this was the first war to involve allies on either side from other parts of Greece. Cities in the island of Crete remained in almost perpetual states of war because of the continuous quarrels between neighbors over boundaries. The Megarians frequently encroached upon the borderland of western Attica, even though the Athenians had, as was so often the case elsewhere along frontiers, declared it "sacred" to the Two Goddesses of Eleusis; the Megarians' trespassing became an issue in the outbreak of the Peloponnesian War and caused further trouble in the fourth century.[3] Defense of the territory was always a major concern in the community's thinking about its military requirements; and one of the advantages of power was, as the Athenians saw it, to be able to take over land within other states' borders, which they did during their time as leaders of a great alliance, in the fifth century and then again in the fourth.

For the individual, owning land constituted in a very real sense the basis of life. It gave him economic independence and the ability to maintain a family; in many states throughout their history, and in all of them at one time or another, only a landowner could qualify as a member of the citizen body, with full political rights to protection under the law and to participation in making the decisions that affected everyone's life in the community. As a citizen he was also duty-bound to protect the community and its land when need arose. A landless man was, often enough, a man without many guarantees of a safe and prosperous life; even in democratic Athens, with all its alternative forms of wealth and economic activities, landed wealth always retained a value that went beyond the consideration of crop yields, grain prices, or rents.

Yet the ownership of land, together with its agricultural concerns, is not a subject that is much discussed as something central to the well-being or the nature of the city-state and its citizens; Pericles' funeral speech, for example, makes no reference to such matters. What attitude did the Greeks have toward farming? What value did they put on the activity beyond its capacity to produce food? The correlation between the practice of agriculture and the rudiments of civilized life appears in the earliest evidence for the Greeks' thinking, the Homeric poems: Odysseus's encounter with the Cyclopes brings civilized (Greek) man face-to-face with his opposites. They are "a fierce, uncivilized people who never lift a hand to plant or plow . . . : they have no assemblies for the making of laws, nor any settled customs" (*Od.* 9.106–12). How do they live?—by the meat and milk products of their flocks. They are merely barbarian pastoralists, who have neither the wits nor the initiative to make over a nearby island, which, Odysseus says, would be ideal for an agricultural settlement.[4] The thought that an agriculturally based society is in a fair way to be civilized recurs in Herodotus's fifth-century account of the Scythians: "The Callipidae, Greco-Scythians resembling the Scythians in their way of life, grow grain for food . . . ; further north are farming tribes, which grow grain for export, not for food . . . , and to the east of these are the nomadic Scythians who know nothing of agriculture" (4.17.1–19.1). There were also the Boudini "who are pastoralists and eat lice"; although they were in some respects culturally assimilated to the Greek communities on the north coast of the Black Sea, Herodotus carefully distinguishes them from the Greek-descended Geloni "who live among them; . . . they cultivate the soil, eat grain, and keep gardens," and were therefore to be preferred to their neighbors (4.109.1).

The concept of the Golden Age provides a different assessment of the human condition before agriculture became known—an

5

age in which people "lived like gods, with carefree heart, remote from toil and misery. . . . All good things were theirs, and the grain-giving soil bore its fruits of its own accord in unstinted plenty, while they at their leisure harvested their fields in contentment among abundance" (Hesiod *WD* 112–19). There is an ambivalence in these views; on one hand agriculture is seen as the underpinning of civilization; on the other, it imposes hard work and anxiety on man. Hesiod concludes his portrayal of society's development with the race of iron, "which will never cease from toil and misery by day or night, in constant distress, and the gods will give [men] harsh troubles" (176–78). Farming entailed wearisome labor: thus much becomes amply obvious from what Hesiod goes on to say of agriculture. It could also be seen, even in Hesiod's poem, as a right and proper occupation, even an ennobling one, but few such views of agriculture have survived, and the myth of the noble citizen farmer did not gain much currency in the Greek world—no Cincinnatus exists in the traditions of any Greek community.[5]

Xenophon does include a eulogy of agriculture in his *Oeconomicus* (on household and estate management); it provides essential nourishment and pleasant luxuries, allows the landowner to enrich and exercise himself, caters to the hunter's interests, hardens the bodies of those who may have to serve in the army or compete as athletes—all of which is rather obvious, perhaps. He concludes with a somewhat more thoughtful observation, "It has been nobly said that farming is the mother and nurturer of all the other arts. When farming flourishes, so do all the other necessary pursuits; but whenever the land lies waste, man's other skills are almost done for too" (*Oecon.* 5.1–17). Xenophon may have owed the formulation of this thought to the pre-Socratic philosopher Prodicus of Cos;[6] but it is not so very startling, and doubtless there were many similar pronouncements by men wishing to rationalize the sentiments that otherwise gave rise to a belief in agriculture as the gift to humanity of gods, demigods, or heroes.

Hesiod's *Works and Days* does not say anything quite like this. Farming for him means laboring so that the barn may be filled and the farmer may remain solvent. Yet he suggests that farming is a serious business, of cosmic importance in that the farmer works precisely according to the succession of the seasons and in direct response to the weather, the position of the heavenly bodies, and the phases of the moon; getting the process right in accordance with the established precepts is essential. His real purport is that farming is worth doing properly for its own sake, not just for the farmer's economic benefit; cooperation with nature both fills the store chamber and is pleasing to the gods.

According to both Hesiod and Xenophon, the best prescription for successful farming was a landowner with enough knowledge and experience to manage and direct work on his land and a staff of hired workers or slaves to provide much of the labor. The landowning ideal is expressed in a grant of land made by the city of Zelea in Phrygia to one of Alexander's henchmen: "It seemed good to the people, Peisitheus presided, Dromon spoke: That there should be given to Cleandrus, son of Parmenon, for being a benefactor of the city, a half allotment of forest and scrubland, a land allotment in the plain, a dwelling house, a garden, one hundred ceramic jars, [and] a resident labor force" (Schwyzer, *DGE* 734). An estate of reasonable size was best; and here the concept of a "right" amount of land is expressed in the "allotment" and "half allotment"—how much we are not told, but enough or *fair,* according to whatever criterion the people of Zelea were using in this case. As to the kind of land it was thought desirable for a man to have, the forest and scrubland would provide not only firewood but also pasture for sheep, goats, and cattle; the lot in the plain meant arable land for grain or fruit trees; and the garden provided a conveniently placed patch for the cultivation of vegetables and other plants necessary to the household. Good storage was essential to any provident property owner, hence the ceramic jars. But what made the gift really valuable was the farm staff, the "people" who went with the land.

Not all estates had labor permanently attached to them by any means, although helots were provided for Spartan holdings, and in Asia Minor the local non-Greek population had been customarily "tied" to a certain district from time immemorial. But generally owners found their own laborers. The relations between owners and workers are hard to gauge in all but a very few instances, and yet it is here that much of the day-to-day contacts within Greek society went on. To understand them a little better would be to know considerably more than we do about a large part of many men's lives; the glimpses given in the *Odyssey,* the *Works and Days,* or in Old or New Comedy are so very fleeting and partial. It is thus not at all clear for one thing who was really responsible for the effectiveness or otherwise with which farming was carried on; we would assume that the landowner always knew and said what should be done and how, but there may have been far more input by old farmhands than the evidence shows. That owners were expected to know what was happening on their estates is suggested by the references to a quite extensive agricultural literature, most of which has been lost, but which is thought to have consisted largely of farmers' manuals, written specifically to aid the landowner. Curiously enough, the two surviving works that are closest to writings of this kind, Hesiod's *Works and Days* and Xenophon's *Oeconomicus,* are neither of them concerned solely or even in the first instance with agronomy, but each author uses the subject to further other arguments.

Hesiod's poem has as its starting point the quarrel with his brother Perses over land they inherited from their father, who had migrated from Cyme in Asia Minor to the uplands of western Boeotia, at Ascra. Perses has bribed the judges at Thespiae to decide in his favor, but that has done him little good, for his shiftlessness has made him poor, so that Hesiod has the double theme of justice and providence to address. In the first part of the poem he discusses the differences between just and unjust communities, one of which is that "Famine does not attend straight-judging men, nor Blight, and they feast on the crops they tend"—that is, no enemy invader destroys or carries the crops off (*WD* 230–31). He then presents to his idle brother a series of instructions on how to cultivate the land, emphasizing the need to do things properly and at the right time in order to regain and retain wealth enough to live a respectable life. It is a didactic poem, to be sure, but its first concerns are not simply to provide a utilitarian guide to better farming; Hesiod uses the knowledge of farming, with which many in his audience would have been familiar, as reinforcement of his underlying theme, which is the proper ordering of the individual's life and his relation to a properly ordered society and to the gods. Hence the inclusion at the end of the poem of all the miscellaneous-seeming prohibitions and injunctions about what to do, and what not, and when. Efforts to show that this is a practical handbook for farmers converting from the hitherto traditional pastoralism of the Dark Age to an as yet unfamiliar system of cultivating cereal crops, with moralizing intrusions, are in vain. Not only is this *not* what Hesiod was about, there are no good grounds for supposing that there was or ever had been so big an alteration in the Greeks' use of the land.[7]

Xenophon's *Oeconomicus*, although at first sight appearing to take farm management as its central theme, may be found to have other ends in view. The discussion is presented as a Socratic dialogue, in which Socrates discovers how Ischomachus, a man who manages his household and estate very well, has set about doing so. He trains his young wife in the ways of organizing a house, dealing effectively with the servants and keeping a watchful eye on the store cupboards; he ensures the proper care of his land by training slave bailiffs to direct work on the land according to the precepts the owner has learned himself and now passes on to them. They in turn train and keep in order the slaves working under them. The dialogue certainly includes considerable discussion of how to farm, but primarily, it seems, so that Socrates may show that knowledge is innate. But the real purpose of the dialogue may rather be good government and the rule of the king: "When a sheep is ailing, we generally blame the shepherd," says Socrates (*Oecon.* 3.11). And the key to Xenophon's true preoccupation here seems to come with the discussion of the Persian king's concern to govern his empire well: one of the ways in which he checks the effectiveness of his provincial governors is to examine the agricultural standards maintained in their provinces (*Oecon.* 4.5–25). The relation between good government and proper cultivation of the land is reinforced by Xenophon's reference here to the interest of his hero, Prince Cyrus, in gardening. And so the Athenian Ischomachus, who takes up the main burden of the dialogue, is in a sense a stand-in for the Great King, or for the good ruler. He trains his deputy in the house (his wife) to look after their joint interests; he sees to the training of his agents in the field (his bailiffs) and shows them how to delegate duties to underlings and how to control them (the field hands).

Both Hesiod and Xenophon therefore demonstrate the pervasiveness of agricultural concerns in Greek thinking. Here the agricultural interests seem on first appearance to dominate, whereas in both works it is the underlying themes that should be taken as the real concerns; agriculture is treated as both subject and allegory.

There are references enough to the rural scene in other writers to give some impression of the Greeks' attitude to the countryside.[8] Many people lived in small rural communities, if not on the land itself, and many city dwellers spent much time going to and from the fields too; residence in the city did not necessarily mean a vast separation between town and country. The countryside was where many men's wealth lay, and where much of the work essential to maintaining society and the household had to be done. Aristophanes' farmers express a real affection for their country surroundings, for this reason, and Hesiod shows delight in the relaxation of a meal outdoors on a summer's day. But did the Greeks see the countryside in general as a place of beauty and intrinsic charm? The romantic appeal of landscape is probably something few people in antiquity appreciated, a view supported by the absence of rural scenery in Greek art and the small number of agricultural scenes among the subjects of Athenian vase painting.[9] Perhaps the work of the countryside was both too important and too mundane, in rather the same way as the digestive processes, to be portrayed in works of art. In poetry, however, appreciation of the grandeur of a landscape and of the charm of a rural occupation is frequently expressed.[10] Nevertheless, not all the rural similes of Homer are enthusiastic in their appraisal—some of them seem rather the cold and unromantic observations of a people for whom the countryside is often hostile, and always a place where hard work goes on: if "the south wind brings a mist over the mountain tops," it is "a mist not loved by the shepherd"

(*Il.* 3.10–11); "in winter two mountain rivers flowing in spate from the great springs higher up mingle their torrents at a waters-meet, in some deep ravine, and far off in the hills the shepherd hears their thunder"—and shudders, the tone of the passage suggests (*Il.* 4.452–55). Hesiod's northerly rainstorm is so described as to give a brilliant visual impression; however, his strategy is not to linger in admiration, but to hurry home out of the rain (*WD* 547–56.). The countryside was either alien and potentially threatening, or merely a background to the activity of the moment, and taken very much for granted; in another sense it was as much a part of the city-state as the physical structures of the city, but the Greek's sense of place, and attachment to place, was nowhere near so strong as his identification with the community, the people to which he belonged.

The period under review in this study extends from the Dark Age to the third century B.C., that is, from the time of the society reflected in the Homeric poems to the age of Alexander's successors, when the city-states were beginning to experience far greater external pressures than ever before. Most of our evidence comes from Athens, but as far as possible discussion tries to take account of conditions in other places besides Athens and Attica, for it is salutary to remember that the Athenians' experiences were not necessarily shared by other Greeks, and that evidence from elsewhere may sometimes serve to illuminate the situation at Athens; at the same time there were parallels among the experiences of all Greek communities which are reflected in some institutional similarities.

One premise of this study is that the basic framework of the city-state was laid down in the prehistoric period, that is, the Dark Age, after the collapse of the Mycenaean palaces in the twelfth century, and that the problems that Greek communities faced in and after that period gave rise to similar institutions to deal with them. Another premise has to do with what became the permanent characteristics of Greek society, and how great a degree of change took place thereafter. It is assumed here that such changes as did occur took place within the existing framework of society which was laid down in the process of the city-state's first coming into being, in response to the constriction of resources, the breakdown of security, the need for families and neighbors to consolidate in defensible groups for their survival during the bad years of the early Dark Age. The Classical city-state is, then, the developed image of the early community, not an entirely different creature.

In the same way, certain beliefs and attitudes of mind which are clearly apparent in the later periods had their origins in the Dark Age (to go no further back); there were far more constancy and consistency of concept throughout Greek history than have often been allowed, so eager have scholars been to chart a steady progress from naive and simple belief to knowledge, from "feudal" and aristocratic patronage to the political sophistication of radical democracy, from poor and mainly pastoral use of the land to a much more efficient and economically viable cereal agriculture. To take this last instance of the "rush to progress": the argument that cereal agriculture was only taken up in a big way some time about the end of the Dark Age (later eighth century) is based partly on the evidence provided by the Homeric poems for large-scale consumption of meat, a habit that is said not to be observable later.[11] Examination of the scenes in question reveals that the heroes consume meat in ceremonial or ritual circumstances, and that when traveling or in the commerce of ordinary life (which is not very often, given the heroic and epic nature of their existence) they consume such things as barley meal and red wine. The ceremonial or ritual consumption of meat continued all through Greek civilization, in connection with sacrifices at which the victim was distributed among the participants.

There were shifts of concept and alterations in practice, which cannot be denied. "Development is an important and interesting topic," so Lloyd-Jones has remarked, "but there are times when it is more rewarding to direct attention to what has remained static over a long period. By doing so, we may end by throwing fresh light even upon the development of Greek thinking."[12] This seems particularly apt with relation to land tenure and agriculture, rooted in the formation of the Greek community as they were, and integral as they remained to the fabric of Greek society.

The historical framework to which reference is made in discus-

sion stands as follows. The Dark Age followed the collapse of Mycenaean civilization. By the middle of the Dark Age (tenth–ninth
century) the Homeric poems were being composed, and so came
to reflect facets of the society of that period, which is to say, of the
early city-state. In the eighth century the Dark Age ended as lit-
eracy returned to the Greek world, and the Archaic period began,
with the start of the so-called colonizing movement (the establishment of overseas settlements in southern Italy and Sicily, the
northern Aegean, and on the coasts of the Black Sea); Hesiod's
poetry dates to about 700. During the seventh century the Spartans conquered Messenia and embarked on a long process of internal reform; elsewhere tyrants came to power, and economic
crisis at Athens brought forth the legislation of Solon around 600.
Hereafter, democratic institutions evolved in Chios; Cleisthenes
instituted democracy at Athens after 508. After the Persian War of
480–479 the Athenians became the leaders of a great alliance (the
so-called Athenian Empire); the age of Pericles ended with the
outbreak of the Peloponnesian War in 431, which did great damage to Athenian agriculture and brought down the empire. In the
fourth century warfare between cities and revolution within them
increased; after 336 the city-states were forced to look more and
more to the kings of Macedon and the successor states, while the
life and institutions of the polis continued in their accustomed
way as far as they were able. It is to the fourth century and after
that much of the evidence for agriculture and ownership of the
land belongs, including the works of Xenophon, the records of
public and sacred land tenure, and Theophrastus's scientific surveys of plants.

"Hellish dark and smells of cheese," as Jorrocks's huntsman
James Pigg remarked, when he opened a cupboard door in mis-
take for a window to look out at the weather.[13] Such is the experience all too often of those seeking to find answers to the question, What is the nature of the institutions and attitudes that
underlie the policies and events of Greek history? Much of the
evidence available to the ancient historian for the Greeks' use
and tenure of the land has been familiar long since, to scholars
such as Guiraud, whose comprehensive study, *La propriété foncière*

*en Grèce,* appeared in 1893. But the hope is that each rehandling of the sources, amplified by some fresh archaeological and epigraphic material, will provide a slightly different perspective. There are irreparable gaps in our knowledge of even the best-documented aspects and areas of antiquity; the land and its use are not included among them, so that the landowners and laborers appear only fleetingly, the half-glimpsed shadows of an ancient people better known in other roles.

Amyntichus, the subject of the following poem, is doubtless a literary invention, but the question remains, How true to life are the situation of the farmer depicted here and the sentiments toward farming and the land which the verse evokes?

Dear Earth, take to your breast the old Amyntichus, and remember his many toils for your sake. In you he always firmly set the stem of the olive tree, and decorated you with the vines of Bacchus. He made you abundantly fruitful with grain, and drawing out the channels of water he made you rich in vegetables and fruit. So in return lie gently round his aged head, and dress yourself in flowers of spring. (*Anth. Pal.* 7.321)

# One

# Ownership of the Land

At first glance the subject of landownership appears to be obscured by a paradox, in that the ancient Greek possesses no word for "landowning" or "landowner" in the modern sense of "landed proprietor."[1] The term *georgos,* "farmer," may be used of a man who farms his own land, but just as often it means "cultivator" or "agricultural laborer," a man who works on someone else's land.[2] Aristocratic landowners such as the *geomoroi* of Samos and the *gamoroi* of Syracuse are literally "land sharers," not "owners." There are various terms denoting "landholder" prefixed by *klero-* which are linked with the root-meaning of *kleros,* "land lot"; that is, land that has been allotted by the polis to a family that possesses it. Thus the *kleronomos* is a "divider of a land lot" or "inheritor," and a *klerouchos* an "allotment holder." Common usage retained the original sense to a large extent, but *kleros* could also mean "estate" or "farm" in the general sense of a piece of landed property, and was not necessarily used only of landholdings deriving from an original allotment.[3] None of these or any other terms to do with the possession of land indicate absolute private ownership; this is not to say, however, that private property rights in the Greek world actually went unrecog-

15

nized and unprotected, but that they had come into being and always existed within the context of the community, whether this was the local settlement, consisting of relatives and immediate neighbors, or the larger, more comprehensive city-state. If any entity was conceived of as the absolute owner of the land, it was the community. The question then remains about the extent to which individual members of the community held rights to the use and enjoyment of land, as *landowners* in the accepted sense.

## The Community and the Land

The polis was the proprietor in chief of all landed assets within its boundaries. Officials of the state assigned land in the newly founded settlements and to new settlers entering an established community as newly integrated citizens; it was officials of the state who intervened in the administration of property held by citizen households when circumstances warranted. So at Athens, "the *archon* has the duty of preventing citizen households from becoming extinct" and of "watching over orphans and heiresses [*epikleroi*, orphaned daughters who were the sole heir]" (Isaeus 7.30, Dem. 43.75).[4]

It is easy enough to understand the polis as proprietor in chief and creator of individual landholdings in the context of new settlements overseas, such as the Therans' foundation around 630 of Cyrene in Libya.[5] The crisis that prompted the venture—a prolonged drought, according to Herodotus—affected the whole Theran community, and in response it was the polis that organized the undertaking; the surviving version of the compact made by the settlers runs in part:

> The sworn agreement of the settlers: it has been recorded by the citizen assembly. . . . Since Apollo [the Delphic oracle] spontaneously told Battus and the Therans to settle Cyrene, it seems good to the Therans to send Battus to Libya as ruler-who-leads and king, and for the Therans to sail as his companions. On equal and fair terms are they to sail. . . . And kinsmen who later sail to Libya shall share in the citizenship and offices, and shall be given lots from the land

which has no owner [i.e., has not yet been assigned]. (Meiggs–Lewis no. 5.23–33)

The situation was that Battus as appointed leader claimed the new land for the city-to-be, and that he and his land measurers then saw to the allotment of the land, with general consent. The poet Archilochus tells a story, all the more convincing for its intrinsic triviality, about a certain Aethiops who joined the expedition from Corinth to found Syracuse, around 730, and who gave up his right to a land allotment, for the sake of a sticky bun, *on the voyage over* (fr. 216). The inference of this anecdote is that not only had the organizers already claimed the land, but everyone who went on the expedition fully expected to receive a land lot on arrival. What arrangements were made beforehand we do not know; presumably Aethiops had some token or other, perhaps indicating both his right to a land lot and the order in which he would receive his land, and perhaps *drawn by lot* in the first place.[6] (This would have occurred in the preliterate period, but we must assume that the Greeks were not only capable already of counting things but also of making marks on material suitable for tokens.) And not only must farmland be allotted to each family, but dwelling space in the city and a plot for burial too. Perhaps they were apportioned at the same time as the *kleroi*; since evidence is lacking, we can for the most part only assume that such matters were not left undefined.[7]

At first sight the question of land allotment in the communities of old Greece, in particular those where continuity of habitation and population had existed from before the Dark Age, raises more difficulties. It is less easy to imagine how or when the community became owner in chief, as opposed to individual inhabitants, whose families had existed for generations in the place where they enjoyed the use of the land. But the same sort of consideration would have prevailed there as in the new overseas settlements— the need to continue to cohere as a viable social entity; to admit new members on acceptable terms so as to maintain the settlement's numbers; to ensure that members could support themselves by income from the land as far as possible; and to safeguard against encroachment from without and ruinous exploitation from within. Pressures such as these would have provided many occasions during the Dark Age for the reassertion of the community's authority, just as much at Athens—where the inhabitants thought of themselves as "autochthonous" with some justification, in that there was continuity of population from the Mycenaean period into the Dark Age—as at Sparta and Corinth, both of which only began to come together as distinct and settled communities within their territories during the Dark Age itself.[8] Thereafter many occasions arose for rethinking the basis of society and for reallotting land—for example, the refounding of long-established communities, as occurred with Aegina, Melos, and Plataea after their sufferings in the Peloponnesian War.[9] If in the Classical period the institutional framework of land tenure varied little in fundamentals throughout the Greek world, this was due not to mere imitation by one state of another's practices or a recent coalescing of concepts, but rather to the fact that Greek societies had from their inception continued to find similar ways of dealing with similar problems, whether they were to become tightly organized city-states like democratic Athens or narrowly oligarchic Sparta, or looser confederations of smaller cities (towns and villages) like Locris and Phocis in central Greece, Thessaly to their north, or Arcadia in the central Peloponnese.

The Greek communities varied considerably in size and geography, as well as in political character. By the Classical period some city-states had absorbed the related communities in the surrounding territory into a single political unit, through the process of synoecism; Athens provides the prime example of this development, becoming one of the biggest city-states of all, with a territory of about 2,500 square kilometers. Both Corinth and Argos also became the sum of their surrounding villages, but the territory of Corinth extended only about 400 square kilometers, whereas Argos was four times this size. Synoecism continued throughout the period; Argos only took over the village of Mycenae after the Persian War, and Mantinea (150 square kilometers) and Elis (1,500 square kilometers) underwent the process at about the same time. Other city-states remained detached from their neighbors, retaining some independence within culturally related areas; examples include the Boeotians, in which Thebes, the dominant city-state, controlled perhaps 50 to 75 square kilometers of land, or the Ionians, among whom the city of Miletus may have laid claim to as much as 2,000 square kilometers, and its northern neighbor Priene a more modest 500 or so. The islands varied as much in their territorial formations: Samos made up a single city-state, but Lesbos included four separate communities within a total area of 1,300 square kilometers, and the four cities of Ceos divided not more than 150 square kilometers among them. Yet other city-states remained small in political essence but ruled over an extensive region as the Spartans did in Laconia and Messenia, which comprised a territory of over 4,000 square kilometers. Others again attempted to remain completely independent of political ties within their region; the Plataeans in Boeotia, for example, had perhaps 25 square kilometers that they could call their own, and a citizen population of one thousand, more or less. Some states on the edge of the Greek world, like Miletus and other cities in Asia Minor, on the Black Sea coasts, and in Sicily and south Italy, acquired a non-Greek hinterland and close ties of one kind or another with a non-Greek population. But despite these variations in scale and in geographic and political character, the basic institutions of the polis, including those that defined the disposition of land and the rights to its possession, persisted throughout the Greek world.[10]

The extent of the territory as a whole mattered less to individual landowners and farmers than the nature of the land available to them, and the security of their particular situation. The establishment of fixed and defensible boundaries would have been very necessary in areas where neighboring communities competed for natural assets, as did Eretria and Chalcis in the early period for the fertile plain land of the river Lelas lying between them, and Athens and Megara for their borderland or, no doubt, any of the communities with one or another neighbor in subdivided islands like Ceos, Lesbos, or Rhodes. The office of boundary commissioner must therefore have been in many places an important and onerous one; but of course no amount of boundary markers along the borders or of carefully established sacred precincts such as we know existed close to many frontiers could create unbreakable taboos, and trespass by shepherds in particular was often enough a pretext for war, if not in itself the main cause.[11]

By the Classical period most neighboring states had probably decided as far as seemed useful what should be the common border between them, but this process may never have been completed on all boundaries. For large tracts of borderland consisted of waste—rocky precipices and scrub-covered ridges where only persevering goats and dedicated quarrymen could have hoped to find anything of value; such areas could have remained truly no-man's-land for much of antiquity. Nevertheless all such assumptions are open to question, for we cannot now judge precisely what terrain was considered worthwhile in the way of grazing, cultivation, or wild herb gathering, and what was not. But where there was pasture to be got, or where strategic advantages presented themselves, then both city-states concerned with the border between them paid close attention to staking it out. The hill country between Boeotia and Attica, frequented by herdsmen, was also the region across which armies moved in either direction, especially during the fifth century and after; border fortresses were built, and the Athenians continually hoped to take permanent possession of Oropus at the northeastern end.

Land within a state's borders might also have remained unclaimed and unused, neither tilled nor grazed because it was too distant or too poor, and for the moment not considered worth anyone's while, until eventually pressure on the use of the land meant that even marginal areas came to the city's attention and were granted to private owners or retained in public ownership and leased out as required. In addition, the theory that possession is nine-tenths of the law may have been put to the test by the assertion of squatters' rights, and in some remote areas isolated hamlets or extended family households may have existed quite outside the framework of the city-state, something in the manner of the shepherd-hunters of backcountry Euboea described by Dio Chrysostom in the Roman period.[12]

The character of the city-state—an entity within which, economically speaking, member families ought to be able to be self-sufficient—meant that its territory should include adequate arable land for cereal crops, orchard land (for figs, olives, and vines in particular), and vegetable gardens. The nature of most habitable areas in the Mediterranean world was and is such that, along with cultivable land they usually included wooded hills, upland meadows, marshes, and shrub-covered mountainsides suitable for grazing.[13] Much of the cultivable land together with some pasture was given over to private exploitation, and it tended to remain in the control of citizen families for generation after generation. But the polis was not only proprietor in chief; it or its subdivisions (at Athens, for instance, the tribes, demes, and phratries) retained direct control of some of the land, both arable and pasture. There are good reasons for supposing that the polis or one of its subdivisions kept control of most of the grazing land, rather than letting private possession take over: often pasture lay in border country where quarrels between herdsmen from either side of the border tended to lead to international conflict; quarrels between herding families within the community, if left to smolder in outlying pastures, could have led to serious and long-lasting internal dissensions. By allowing no private rights to be recognized in such regions, the community maintained authority as the proprietor and arbiter in case of disputes. This public proprietorship of pastures may be discerned in the administration of their use by means of leases, for limited periods and on set terms, and in various cities' grants of *epinomia*—grazing privileges—to outsiders who had deserved well of the state.[14]

Not only the polis and its subdivisions but also the gods owned land, consisting of arable, orchard, and gardens.[15] This was so customary a part of the pattern of landholding that when, for example, the Athenians appropriated land in the island of Lesbos from their rebel ally Mytilene in 427, they devoted the revenues from one-tenth of it to Athena, while an Athenian garrison 2,700 strong benefited from the remaining nine-tenths (Thuc. 3.50.2). Every new settlement would have followed a similar course, devoting a portion of the land to the gods. All these estates, public and sacred, were handed over to private use but in the form of tenancies, usually of short duration, ten or twenty years at most, as were the estates of Apollo on the islands of Delos and Rheneia; occasionally they were leased in perpetuity, as at Heraclea in southern Italy.[16] One of the purposes of public and sacred leases was to provide income to help cover the running costs incurred by sanctuaries in maintaining the cult of the god, and by demes and other subdivisions of society in administering local affairs and sustaining the life of their organizations. Another purpose— or if it was never actually the expressed intention, this was its result—was to remind everyone that all of the land belonged in the last resort not to individuals but to the community and the gods; those who took up leases for these estates expected to serve the community and the gods as much as to benefit themselves. This is inferred from the fact that citizens of means and good standing predominate among those tenants who can be identified in any way, such as the lessees of the Delian estates, or the Athenian orator and politician Hyperides, who grew a large quantity of barley on the Rarian estate belonging to the Two Goddesses of Eleusis.[17] It is probable that members of Athenian demes were duty-bound to take up leases on deme land when required; such tenancies seem to have been restricted to demesmen.[18] And it may well be that tenants of public and sacred properties took up leases as much to assist the organization, or the god, as to boost their own incomes; in fact, evidence for the tenancies of Delian Apollo's estates indicate that some tenants did not do very well.

The scrupulousness with which these lands were administered only serves to emphasize their importance. In 338, the Athenians won back the mountainous border of Oropus from the Boeotians and divided it into five portions, each to be shared by two of the ten tribes and leased out to citizen members. But complications ensued: one and one-fifth of one tribal portion was subsequently considered to have been devoted to the local hero Amphiaraus, which necessitated official inquiry of a most searching kind. The commissioners appointed to look into the matter were directed to sleep in the hero's sanctuary, in order to obtain his answer by means of a dream as to who really owned this portion of the land. The officially dreamed response, that it was tribal land after all, was rejected, and the unfortunate dreamer was prosecuted and fined (Hyper. 4.16–17). Presumably those who had already leased land from the tribes now paid their rent to a different land-lord, Amphiaraus of Oropus.

Public and sacred tenancies were strictly regulated, if the terms of surviving leases are to be taken at their word.[19] Safeguards against default on the rent (agreed to by a form of auction that the Greeks called "sale") were set up in the requirements that lessees show evidence of financial soundness and provide guarantors for the payment of the rent in addition. Penalties for default—except in the case of war damage, when the tenant could not be expected to pay the full sum—were severe: the tenant was dismissed and obliged to pay the difference between his and the (lower) rent of the lease when it had been relet. The time limit, with the dates of entering on the lease and of paying the rent, was included in the lease agreement, together with a statement specifying who was responsible for paying whatever taxes might fall due. Treatment of the property was fully prescribed in detailed instructions as to what methods should be used, what crops grown, when certain processes should be done (sometimes even to the day of the month by which they should be completed), and in what condi-tion the land should be left for the next tenant. This was the case, whether the lease was a short or a long one, or (apart from the last item) "forever."[20] The leases also allowed for the close inspection of the estate by the officials in charge of the leasing organization, so that there was no question of their simply saving themselves trouble by letting the property to a tenant to do what he liked with it. Public and sacred estates were intended to be treated cor-rectly, and they were therefore to be worked according to the best agricultural methods available.[21]

Land owned by public bodies needed to be well marked by clearly defined boundaries. The results of not keeping them up and of letting the administration of such lands lapse are made clear by the records documenting the rescue of land belonging to Dionysus and Athena at Heraclea in southern Italy; private ex-ploitation had made serious inroads on them, the land had been badly neglected, and the sanctuary officials were obliged to renew markers along hundreds of yards of the boundary line before re-letting the estates on carefully prescribed terms so that they would be brought back into a proper state of cultivation, productive of income once more.[22]

Another feature of the ancient agricultural landscape demon-strates the state's overall proprietorship of the land. Individual trees in private estates might be designated as "public" or "sacred"; the landowner tended the trees, but the fruits went for the profit of the city or the sanctuary that owned them. "Public" pear trees and olive trees are heard of at Halaesa on the north coast of Sicily, and in Attica "sacred" olive trees were widely distributed; before the Classical period the penalty for damaging or destroying one of them had been execution, and the accusation that an owner had done harm to one could lead to serious difficulties still in the late fifth century.[23]

The city-state had charge of all the land, including that which was given over to its citizens; at the same time the city-state was the community of all its citizens. In a real sense, then, the land was communal property. In times of crisis, extreme forms of com-munal authority could have come into existence, with some inter-esting effects on land tenure, and it is not impossible that the story of how the Lipari Islands were settled has some historical validity. Diodorus says that the survivors of a failed settlement in western Sicily seized the islands in the early sixth century as a stronghold against Etruscan pirates (5.9.4–5).[24] At first they farmed the land in common, some of the settlers taking on the task of farming, while the others maintained the defenses and manned the boats; all shared in the profit of the land (and presumably of the piracy, which they must have carried on in "self-defense"). Later, the main island was divided into land lots distributed among the members of the community, but for only twenty years at a time, at the end of which they were redistributed; the other islands the settlers continued to farm in common. Finally they allotted all the land in all the islands for twenty-year periods. Diodorus's account stops here, but Thucydides goes out of his way to remark that in his time "they lived on one island and went out to farm the others" (3.88.2). Although he says nothing as to whether they still farmed

communally (or indeed ever had), or were continuing to redistribute the land every twenty years, we are left wondering why he
troubles to comment at all on what was for him a minor topic.
There was perhaps still something unusual about the Lipari islanders' management of the land, which he either misunderstood
or was pleased to allude to merely in passing.

Nothing in the Lipari islanders' story fits the pattern of land
tenure found elsewhere in the Greek world, but it is not totally
out of tune with Greek thinking on the use and enjoyment of the
land either. For although even Plato rejects the idea of working
the land in common as a feature of his ideal state, and Aristotle
only refers to barbarian people doing so, the fruits of Greek agriculture were often enjoyed communally. The sacrificial meal that
formed part of so many religious celebrations and consisted of
foodstuffs from the land—bread, cheese, honey, wine, sheep,
goats, pigs, cattle—was often shared by the general public.[25] All
Spartan citizens had to provide quotas of foodstuffs from their
estates to the common mess where they spent much of their lives.
At Athens it was customary for profits from the silver mines to
be distributed among the citizens, until Themistocles proposed
building warships with the proceeds of a particularly rich strike
in the 480s, after which they went straight into the treasury.
Wherever assets such as mines, quarries, salt pans, or other mineral resources of general utility existed, the public interest prevailed over whatever private rights there might have been residing
in the land above or surrounding them. The division of booty after
war offers an example of a comparable practice, whereby communal effort was rewarded with a share of the winnings.

Taxation such as the Greek cities knew might also be considered a form of communal or collective benefit derived in part from
the products of the land; direct taxes on property and agricultural
produce in particular were not unheard of, although at Athens the
*eisphora* was an occasional tax or contribution imposed only in a
crisis.[26] Indirect taxes on market sales, land sales, the import and
export of agricultural goods—all these would have drawn on the
product of the land for the benefit of the public treasury; similarly,
tribute paid by Athens's allies during the fifth century for their

mutual protection (in theory, at least) came in part from their agricultural wealth, and was then returned, some of it, to their own citizens in the form of wages for serving in the allied fleet or by means of the food purchases that the allied fleet made whenever it was on active duty in allied waters. The liturgies performed by the Athenian rich, by means of which the city's defenses, its religious rituals, and its cultural life were maintained, were paid for out of their private resources, which in most cases included income from the land. Similar obligatory giving went on elsewhere, and so it must always have been, wherever the rich could be made to feel that the expense was worthwhile, whether simply to avoid a penalty, or to gain popularity or power, or to render back to the community what was its due, according to the unwritten contract between the good citizen and his city.

The other feature of land management in the Lipari Islands, the short-term assignment of land, had its parallels all over the Greek world, in the public leasing of estates; but in no community was this the only form of land tenure. The island sanctuary of Delos, which (when we know it best, in the Hellenistic period) was administered by the very small city-state of Delos, presents the closest parallel in that much of the land on the island and its neighbor Rheneia belonged to the god, and was let out in the form of several large estates for ten years at a time, at the end of which the leases were relet, often to different men who were usually Delian citizens of substance and standing.[27] However, the Delian estates varied in size, and there probably was no such motive involved as *sharing* out the landed assets by redistributing estates at regular intervals. The Lipari islanders, on the other hand, would have been concerned with equality or fairness of allotment among the landholders. If this could not be achieved by assigning absolutely equal amounts of land on a permanent basis—because inevitably one hectare of land will never have quite the same qualities, or produce quite the same results as the next—differences could be evened out by redistributing the land regularly.

Fairness and equality in allotting land are themes running through the accounts of other new settlements.[28] The agreement made by the Therans when they founded Cyrene stated that they were to sail out there "on fair and equal terms": the question is, How equal? We may have a choice here between two concepts— the phrase *ep' ises* (or *peri ises*) may mean "on equal terms" in the sense of absolute arithmetical equality (as land lots of precisely equal area), or "on fair terms," fair and just in the context of the times but not necessarily equal. So it might be generally accepted that a king or founder of the new settlement, such as Battus of Cyrene, or a new settler with five sons (say) should be granted more land than a poor commoner with one daughter. When Homer compares the fighting between Greeks and Trojans to "two men with measures in their hands quarreling over boundaries in common plowland, contending for shares [*peri ises*] in a small area of land," he may mean that each man is fighting to get his due, not necessarily that each expects to get a plot of exactly the *same* size, only that it be the *right* size (*Il.* 12.421–23).

The land measurers' job in the new settlements was probably to ensure insofar as was possible that the majority of land lots were actually equal in area. This feature recurs in different settlements throughout the Greek period and is echoed in Plato's prescription for his ideal state: "We must distribute as equally as possible the land and the houses" (*Laws* 737 c). When the Thessalian city of Pharsalus admitted to citizenship 176 men who had fought alongside the Pharsalians, it granted them the same amount of land each, sixty *plethra* (fifteen acres, or six hectares).[29] The new settlement at Thurii in southern Italy, which the Athenians set up in 443, rapidly went through two stages of reorganization (Diod. Sic. 12.11.1–2). The first failed after the descendants of former inhabitants seized the chief offices and the best land, that nearest the city; this of course is a reminder that some lots would always be more equal than others, simply by virtue of their location. The second attempt to settle the place was accompanied by a division of the land *ep' ises*. One way of achieving this would have been to assign two lots of land to each citizen, one close to the city and the other toward the edge of the territory, as Plato recommends (*Laws* 745 b–e).

Many other examples of the equal distribution of land can be cited, to demonstrate that this was a widely accepted concept, if it was not always implemented; the tyrant Dionysius "selected the best land to distribute among his friends and top commanders, *and the rest* he distributed equally among aliens and citizens" (Diod. Sic. 14.7.4). That equality of holdings was much debated becomes clear from Aristotle's own discussion, together with his references to Phaleas of Chalcedon, who "was the first to propose that the property of citizens be equal," and to Pheidon of Corinth, who held that the number of households and the number of citizens should be kept equal even if at first they all had estates of varying sizes; which implies that Pheidon too thought of equality of property as the ideal (*Pol.* 1265 b 14).

But even when the land commissioners of an *apoikia* or a new allotment in an established community had measured out plots of equal area, no one could guarantee that they would be equally productive; for even in the most fertile plain, differences in the soil were undetectable until the land had actually been planted. The likelihood of such differences becoming apparent between one land lot and the next is no doubt the reason why settlers would always have been bound by oath to abide by the original settlement, as the Therans' agreement ordained.[30] So it was that the decree concerning Locrian land settlement insisted that there be no call for the redistribution of the land once the allotments had been made—no doubt so as to avoid endless comparisons and claims that the original allotments had been *unfair.*[31]

Some political theorists, combating the natural human tendency to want more land than one already has, argued that equality of property should be preserved; and this was the stated intention of many new governments. But whereas in an overseas settlement it would have been a practical concern to bring men into a new environment on (comparatively) equal terms with one another, equality of allotment surely acquired ideological significance, becoming as much a part of the ideal pattern of Greek citizenship as any other aspect. The third-century revolution at Sparta is a prime example of an attempted reversion to what the reformers presented as the old original pattern, according to which equal land lots were held by all citizens.[32] The revolutionary cry for "redistribution of the land," on the other hand, heard often in the Classical and Hellenistic periods, was less a yearning for equality for all than a popular movement against the rich; the poor wanted what the rich had, and a successful revolution usually saw the opposition dead or in exile, with no question of redistributing property equally among all citizens.[33]

In principle, land lots should have remained equal, or fair, and efforts were made to try to ensure that this was so. Within a very few years after the foundation of Thurii "the notables got hold of all the land because the state was biased toward oligarchy, but the people became stronger than the garrison, so eventually the possessors of more than their fair share gave it up" (Ar. *Pol.* 1307 a 27–33). Yet inequality was inevitable, in the nature of things; one man might simply be a better farmer or have better luck; one man might have more able-bodied family members to work the land; one man's heirs were responsible landowners, another man's might ruin the estate at once. From such beginnings great inequalities of fortune might develop, despite the installation of safeguards to preserve the principle that the land granted to a family in a new settlement was meant to form a part of the newly founded *oikos* from that time forth, as its fundamental means of support—as its "ancestral portion" to be handed down in perpetuity within the family.

The concept of "ancestral portions" was not simply an invention of the founders of the new overseas settlements. The association between the member families of the community and the land on and by which they lived must go back to the roots of communities: the whole pattern of family relationships and family inheritance, as we come to know it in the Classical period, had "always" existed (in outline if not in detail) and possession of land "had always been in the family." Whether an association between an *oikos* and any particular land had actually existed unbroken since the early Dark Age (or whenever organized settlement had begun) is impossible to say, and is perhaps beside the point; for if "always" in common parlance means little more than two or three generations back, whether it refers to coronation ritual or the placing of the tea urn at the church social, the important thing is that people tend to argue and act on the assumption that "always" means what

29

it says. The land allotments at Black Corcyra were to be preserved "forever"; at Pharsalus they were defined as ancestral.[34] These pieces of property should not, therefore, change hands except by inheritance within the family. So, says Aristotle, "in many states in early times it was laid down by law that the original estates might not be sold" (*Pol.* 1319 a 11). Few families in an agricultural society would want to do so in any case, for this meant losing the best if not the only source of income available to them, apart from the loss of status it would entail; but a series of bad harvests or pressure from a domineering neighbor might force the disposal of even the substance of the *oikos,* its land, for even if there was a law against selling, there were always men willing to buy. "Propitiate the gods," says Hesiod, so that "you may negotiate for others' allotments, not another man for yours" (*WD* 336–41).[35]

The alienation of land had always been a part of the Greek communities' internal transactions, as Aristotle suggests when he refers to ancient laws widely adopted "such as absolutely to prohibit the acquisition of land *above a certain amount,* or at any rate *to permit it only beyond a certain distance* from the central citadel and city" (*Pol.* 1319 a 8). Thus a law forbidding the alienation of the *ancestral* land lot would not in all cases have affected more than a part of the family's holdings; the ancestral lot could have been preserved while the inevitable fluctuations in a family's fortunes would have been registered in the acquisition and loss of other properties. It is therefore conceivable that some *oikoi* whose line of descent continued unbroken for several generations did hold onto land anciently acquired or allotted to them, land that was permanently heritable and thus a truly constant factor in the pattern of land tenure.[36] The question then arises how ancestral property could reliably be identified, and the answer is that it could not, other than by family tradition. As in the case of land bought and sold, no permanent records were kept of who owned what, and a check could only be provided by family members, or from the beliefs and recollections of owners of neighboring properties and fellow demesmen.[37]

The polis granted land to its citizens and ensured their rights to their property; the polis also had the power to take it back again, sometimes by compulsory purchase.[38] Public works might require a site on private land, or the opening of stone quarries to provide building material. Both quarries and mines must have access made available, often enough across private property, and in addition mining necessitated surface works—washing table, smelters, and so on.[39] But such things would have caused minor inconvenience compared with the city's power to confiscate property as part of the penalty for offenses against the state. The worst fate that could befall a citizen was political death, which involved not only his execution or exile, but also the loss of his citizenship and his property, along with the right to transmit them to his heirs. The *oikos* was blotted out, and the property sold or auctioned by officials of the state, unless the crime that had prompted the confiscation was so terrible that the landed property had to be made sacrosanct. The men accused at Athens of mutilating the Hermae in 415 were condemned as traitors, for in their presumed attack on one of the city's gods they were considered to have threatened the democracy itself; they were exiled and their properties put up for public sale, details of which, published in permanent form on stone, have survived. At Mylasa in southwest Asia Minor, those convicted of insulting the local Carian potentate Mausolus were punished with exile and confiscation of their land and houses "according to ancestral law"; and at Amphipolis the sentence pronounced on two men condemned for political crimes ran, "The land of Amphipolis is to be perpetually fled from by them and their descendants, . . . their goods are to be made public and . . . one-tenth is to go to Apollo and the river Strymon," which counted as a local deity.[40]

Property could also be confiscated for lesser misdemeanors. From Halicarnassus in the mid-fifth century we hear of property being sold off for debts outstanding to the city treasury; and at Ioulis in the island of Ceos anyone who was convicted of breaking the law that limited the export of ruddle to Athens lost his land—half of it became public property and the rest went to the person who had informed on the convicted man.[41]

In the hands of informers and unscrupulous political rivals, accusations of treason or of nonpayment of public dues, or simply the bringing of lawsuits that imposed an unpayable fine (thus constituting a debt to the public treasury) became dangerous weapons, as the evidence from Athens demonstrates very clearly. Other cities were even more badly shattered by factional fighting and wholesale revolution, and the number of exiles increased during the fourth century. Alexander's decree concerning exiles attempted to solve some of the difficulties caused when a counter-revolution or a political reconciliation meant that they might return home again—for if their lands had been sold, they must be granted other land; or if their former property was restored to them, those who had bought it at public auction must be compensated.[42] At Elis, steps were taken to reduce the chaos in such situations: it was ordained that the sentence of exile was to affect only the individual concerned, not his family or his descendants; it was forbidden to confiscate his land for public use or sale; and even the family of the exile was prohibited from disposing of his property, so that if he did return he would be able to resume his place in the community.[43] In some ways this arrangement resembles the Athenian institution of ostracism, in use from the early fifth century down to 416, according to which exile lasted for ten years only, and after which civic rights and property were recovered.

One of the effects of confiscation was to redistribute land hitherto in the possession of a rich man. No doubt other rich men often took advantage of public auctions to add to their own already substantial holdings; but the sales lists show that some big estates were split among two or more purchasers.[44] Some confiscated lands were not sold but retained by the state and leased to tenants; this practice too could be considered a form of redistribution—of the enjoyment of the land, if not its ownership, and whether or not such leases were short-term or perpetual, the fact that there was rent due at regular intervals would have served as a further reminder that the land belonged to the state.

Plato says in the *Laws* of the relationship between the lot holders and their land, "Let the apportionment be made with this intention—that the recipient of the lot should still consider it as common property of the whole state, and should tend the land which is his parent more diligently than a mother tends her children, for being as it is a goddess it is mistress over its mortal population" (740 a). The ideal he expresses here is not remote from reality, but a heightened reflection of the actual relationship between the polis and the users of the land.

### Private Possession and the Family Estate

The polis assured the vital link between its constituent *oikoi,* the citizen households, and their *kleros,* or land lot, it bestowed the rights of landownership on its citizens and saw that these rights were abused neither by the holders nor by others. While retaining overall ownership, the polis allowed the enjoyment of private possession, and it also ensured that the attachment between each household and the land was maintained as far as possible by legally protected inheritance within the family from one generation to the next. Sparse as the evidence is for most of the Greek world apart from Athens, it suggests that the subject of property ownership exercised an abiding fascination everywhere and at every level of society. If the Greek states had generally resorted to the regular reallotment of land such as the Lipari islanders are supposed to have done, they would have deprived their citizens of a major source of interest—the expectation of inheritances, the contemplation of the complex family relationships on which they depended, and the attendant discussions of the transfer of land, their own or their neighbors', to one or another member of this or that branch of the family, all of which is dramatically portrayed in the lawcourt speeches of the Athenian orators.[45]

Closely analyzed as this subject has been, the evidence is insufficient to provide a complete picture, even for Athens, of either the considerations that gave rise to the laws concerning the *oikos* and its land lot, or of actual thinking and practice. This distinction ought surely to be made, for even when we have enough evidence, such as Athenian oratory provides, to make a fairly coherent account of the way in which the law of the city ordered some aspects of the family's ownership of landed and other property, the law only tells us so much, and the episodes in which we see the law

33

invoked are only part of the total experience: what the law said
may have had little application for most families much of the time,
being referred to only in unusual circumstances, not as a consequence of the normal management of property. But given the state
of the evidence, the law is where discussion has to be centered. A
consequence of this is that it has often been persuasively argued
that when a law appears for the first time in the sources (as for
instance those associated with lawgivers of the seventh and sixth
centuries), this means that an important change in thinking and a
great move forward in practice have occurred at that time. But
the statement of a legal precept may not always reflect change and
development; it may represent simply a rephrasing or redefining
of a mode of thought deeply rooted in custom and belief. The
problem then is, whether differences of practice and concept that
are apparent in the evidence for the Classical period—for example, the contrasting approaches at Athens and Sparta to the
preservation of the *oikos* and its substance (its landed property)—
stem from very old divergences of perception or are the result of
comparatively recent social and political adjustments.[46]

There is no question that some concepts concerning land can
be traced back very far. Private possessions, especially farmland,
always conferred social worth: whatever a man was the sum of,
his wealth was an important part of it. The Homeric hero Am-
phius, slain by Ajax, was "a man rich in substance, rich in grain
land" (*Il.* 5.612–13), and the Lycians did honor to the hero Bellerophon by giving him land (*Il.* 6.194–95). Not only Hector
(*Il.* 15.498) but, at the lower end of the Homeric social scale, the
slave swineherd Eumaeus declares that a man's dearest possessions are his family, his *oikos* (his household in the sense of substance, establishment, and family past and present), and his *kleros*
(*Od.* 14.62–64). Although he does not make the point specifically, Homer surely sets the Cyclopes beyond the pale of civilized
society in yet another way (see my comments in the Introduction)
by their not needing *to own* the land that provides them with
sustenance spontaneously.

The preservation of the *oikos,* the base unit of the polis, depended on the assured transfer of inheritance within the family,

preferably from father to son. The best, simplest, and most acceptable way of becoming a landowner always remained through inheritance, and the most satisfactory arrangement was for a single surviving son to inherit the *oikos* and all the property at his father's death, and for his son to succeed him in turn, forever. Hesiod sees the happiest state of affairs thus: "Hope for an only son, to feed his father's house; (for this is how wealth waxes in the halls), and (hope) to die in old age, leaving another child within" (*WD* 376–78). If there is a grandson, the succession is assured as far into the future as most men are ever able to see for themselves, and the inheritance remains undivided.[47]

There might also be a claim on the property for daughters who must be married off with a dowry, usually in the form of movable goods—cloth, metalware (precious or otherwise), foodstuffs, or animals; if land was given for the dowry, there should have been enough left to constitute the family inheritance, shares for the sons, one of whom carried on his father's *oikos,* whereas the rest formed their own as and when they could do so.

But birth and survival rates were no more uniform in the Greek world than they were or are anywhere else. The Athenian evidence alone shows great variations, from families with several sons, all of whom had descendants, to families in which the sole heir died childless, the heir he had adopted having himself died childless in the meantime.[48] The lawgivers of the Archaic period made formulations on the problem of lack of heirs; Pheidon of Corinth held that "the number of households and the number of citizens should be kept equal" (Ar. *Pol.* 1265 b 14). One of the ways of ensuring this would have been to allow younger sons to become heirs in *oikoi* where no natural heir survived, thus distributing males of citizen birth among the existing *oikoi* and landed estates, and so allowing as many as possible to become holders of the established land lots. This was the purpose of legislation attributed to Philolaus, a member of the Bacchiad family that had ruled Corinth before the tyranny of Cypselus; he gave laws to the Thebans which they called "laws of adoption; they consisted of an enactment . . . designed to keep fixed the number of estates," whereby legitimate heirs could be provided for those houses that would otherwise die out, their landed property being merged with distant relatives' estates (*Pol.* 1274 a 31–b 4). Had Philolaus known of such a procedure at Corinth, where it had been seen to work? Or did he merely confirm a practice already informally in use at Thebes?

If the number of households and estates was to be kept fixed, often enough there would have been too many younger sons for the number of existing *oikoi* requiring heirs, so that they could presumably have become excluded from the inheritance of land and status within their community—just the sort of people to go out to a new settlement. But where was it in fact the practice that only a certain fixed number of estates could be transferred to heirs? This would have meant either strict population control, one of the most often heard of means of which was the exposure of excess children, or the acceptance by their parents of poverty and exclusion for them when they grew up. Yet severe as the crisis was on the island of Thera, the proposal for the foundation of Cyrene said that only those families *with more than one son* were to contribute members for the expedition, ensuring that an heir remained in Thera to carry on the existing *oikos*: clearly it was accepted that there were families with more than one son, and there was no question of going so far as to reduce the existing number of *oikoi,* to help deal with the famine, which presumably accompanied the drought that had caused the crisis in the first place (Hdt. 4.153). It would seem that political or legal theory, encompassing the question of the ideal size for a citizen community, did not and never could blend with the realities of variations in the birthrate or of family feeling as it shaped social behavior. But Aristotle remarks that "in present-day states the population is kept sufficiently constant, however high the birthrate, merely by the number of childless couples" (*Pol.* 1265 a 38ff). If the population tended to remain in equilibrium naturally, did the number of landholdings do so too? That is to say, did communities find it necessary to make special efforts to prevent the concentration of land in fewer and fewer hands, and the corresponding dispossession of citizen-born children? Or did devices such as adoption forestall the natural attraction of wealth for wealth, and sustain the *oikoi* from generation to generation? Athenian law was particularly concerned with the preservation of the *oikos,* whereas in other states such as Sparta the concern to maintain the number of citizen households conflicted with the desire to accumulate bigger family holdings and was badly defeated.[49]

In principle, citizens should be guaranteed proper means of support, in the form of an adequate amount of land, according to the traditional view of "proper" wealth. The rule of primogeniture would have assured this in families with more than one son, and it may have operated in some places; or a quasi rule of primogeniture may have come into play whenever an estate was small or times particularly bad, so that those sons of the family who did not care to live a poor life as poor relations helping to run a depressed farm would choose to become seafarers or mercenary soldiers, as Arcadians are known to have done, especially during the fourth century. The exposure of children would have settled some children's futures for them, at the same time (often enough) allowing the redistribution of the population by giving opportunities to childless couples to acquire an heir, or at least a young assistant in field or workshop. But given the rate of infant mortality, one imagines that the exposure of males was infrequent, for most families wanted to be sure of an heir who would live to inherit.[50]

The Greek preference was, to provide for all the children of the family as far as possible, so that primogeniture did not generally determine inheritance.[51] Property was divided equally, or as fairly as possible, according to the nature of the property and the temperaments of the heirs concerned. Hesiod's experience shows how unsatisfactory a procedure this could be, for the division of their father's land with his brother Perses led to a quarrel and a hearing before the local law lords, who decided (unjustly, of course) in the brother's favor.[52] Often enough such quarrels remained private but had even more dire results: in about 410, Thoudippus, a son-in-law as it happens of the Athenian leader Cleon, fell out with his brother Euthycrates as they were debating the division of their father's land in the deme of Araphen, and Thoudippus hit him so hard that he died of the blow a few days later, or so the son of Euthycrates' wife by her second marriage later alleged, in his claim to Euthycrates' property against Thoudippus's son and grandson

(Isaeus 9.17).[53] The contention between the two men measuring out the boundaries between them in the Homeric simile (*Il.* 12.421–23, quoted previously) might have arisen out of the division of family property too—although the poet does not say so, for all it would have sharpened the image of Greek and Trojan troops in the press of battle.[54] The unfairness of family members to one another in such situations is expressed by Odysseus in his disguise as a Cretan merchant. "My father . . . put me on an equal footing with his legitimate sons . . [but] then they split up the estate in their high-handed way and cast lots for the shares, assigning to me a meager pittance and a house to match." (*Od.* 14.207–10).

The casting of lots for shares of the property might well have been the best way of overruling arguments, for no field, sheep, stand of fruit trees, or storage vessel would quite have equaled another, especially in the eyes of family members who had known these things of old or seen them in use. But even if it was common practice, the drawing of lots would not automatically have ruled out emotional family scenes. Sometimes brothers agreed not to divide the family property but to share the estate in its existing form. Thus the brothers Diogeiton and Diodotus split the movable property but held the land in common; similarly, Menecles administered all of the landed property that he and his brother had inherited, but when he was required to mortgage it (so as to restore funds due to the orphans for whom he had been trustee), his brother inconveniently chose to claim his share of the inheritance.[55] If other forms of property could provide a perfectly acceptable means of support, such as money or other movable wealth, one brother would take the land and the other the business interests. Sometimes the estate to be divided was really large, so that there was presumably little difficulty in making a division satisfactory to all parties: in the early fifth century a certain Bouselus left property to be divided among five sons, each of whom founded his own *oikos* and lived, as far as we can tell from the status of their descendants, a reasonably prosperous life, partly supported by land.[56] Unfortunately, nothing is know of Bouselus himself, of what his wealth consisted or what position he had in the society of early democratic Athens; even his name presents an enigma—it is otherwise unknown, for it was given to none of his sons (that we know of) or to any of his descendants who are named in the sources. As to the extent of his property, it would be merely hazarding a guess to suggest that he had owned an estate of three hundred *plethra,* the largest permitted (or customary) at Athens (see chapter 2), which would have provided adequate livings of sixty *plethra* each for five sons of hoplite status.

In Bouselus's case, somehow or other, so large a number of heirs apparently presented no problems. But there were serious drawbacks for poorer families in dividing the estate among several sons, for unless each accumulated more property, his heirs would in turn inherit only a portion of that portion. Even in a wealthy family, the shiftlessness of successive heirs could drag one or another branch of a formerly rich family down to poverty, and (depending on the constitution of the polis concerned) perhaps to disenfranchisement. At Sparta an impoverished citizen lost his position as a Spartiate. What links he was able to retain with relatives who remained prosperous and within the Spartiate group is unclear: Could he or his descendants claim inheritance if a rich relative died heirless and intestate?[57] In more open societies like Athens, where property qualifications came to have very little bearing on civic status, many families may have included close relatives who belonged to quite different social and economic groups; aristocratic blood may have flowed in many a Thete's veins. Shifts of fortune could occur in the other direction too; if a rich man lacked an heir, a poor relation might step into his inheritance. How frequently this happened is another matter, but it is one of the factors to be reckoned with as regards social mobility and the redistribution of landed wealth within the community.

What happened to the property of a man who had no sons? When the hero Diomedes slew both the sons of Phaenops, the old man was left "with no other son to whom he could bequeath his wealth . . . ; it was their cousins who stepped into the estate" (*Il.* 5.155–58). We can never know how closely Homeric or Dark Age practice as regards heirless estates actually resembled that of later Greece—if the cousins simply amalgamated the property with their own, or one carried on the dead man's *oikos,* as an adopted son, giving up all claims to his paternal inheritance.

The law given by Philolaus of Corinth to the Thebans concerned adoption as a means of supplying an heir for a childless man and of preserving his *oikos,* a device employed no less at Sparta, where adoptions were overseen by the kings, than in Classical Athens. It was seemly and customary for a man to select a young male relative for adoption, although a female relative might sometimes be chosen; Dicaeogenes III had, so he claimed, been formally adopted by his first cousin on the father's side, Dicaeogenes II (Isaeus 5.6). Athenian opinion, and so the law itself, stood against the accumulation of inheritances; a man who was adopted into another *oikos* gave up his right to inherit from his own father. Thus adoption into a childless house might offer some relief to a family with more than one child.

The speaker against Phaenippus, however, held it against him that he was enjoying *two* estates, his father's and his maternal grandfather's, who had adopted him; this should have meant that Phaenippus gave up the rights to inherit his own father's estate.[58] But perhaps the position was that his maternal grandfather had no other close relative and that in addition Phaenippus was his father's only son, so that the adoption and the dual inheritance were unavoidable, while at the same time there was no one left in the family to object.

Adoption might take place in the lifetime of the adoptive father, before witnesses, or it might be instituted by will. The writing of wills must be seen as an innovation made well after the Dark Age had ended, for the techniques of writing cannot have become widespread until during the seventh century. Much has been made of the importance of written as opposed to spoken decisions about the disposal of property, adoption, and so on, but it is hard to see why the mere writing of a will would have enhanced a man's ability to dispose freely of his property, as Solon's legislation recognizing the validity of wills is supposed to have done. If there were no true heir, why should not a spoken declaration before witnesses have allowed for the adoption of an heir, or the bestowing of property as the owner saw fit at all periods, early and late, preliterate and literate? Spoken decisions remained valid throughout antiquity—one has only to think of the persistence of spoken manumissions in the Roman world. And if it is argued that witnesses to a verbal agreement might lie, "forget," or otherwise confuse the issue, the Athenian lawcourt speeches give ample testimony of written wills that were "found," "lost," altered, or forged: neither device was very reliable. Menexenus's counterclaim for part of the estate of his uncle Dicaeogenes II, against his cousin Dicaeogenes III, was based on the charge that the will by which his cousin had supposedly been adopted was forged and that it did not express the true intention of his uncle. Solon may therefore have pronounced on a technicality, rather than a legal breakthrough, regarding the writing of wills and the validity of disposal of property when there were no true heirs of the family.[59]

If a man died childless, without an adopted heir, and intestate, then the relatives weighed in to make their claims according to the established lines of succession, and the *oikos* was simply absorbed into that of the claimant who was awarded the property, as far as we can tell. In so family- and property-conscious a society, this must have been rare. The limits of relationship within which members of the wider family could qualify as heirs are known from the laws of various cities, showing that there existed a broad similarity of concept of "the wider family" where inheritance was concerned; the fourth degree of relationship was permitted, on both the father's and the mother's side of the family, that is, as far as the children of first cousins of the deceased. Known as the *anchisteia* at Athens, it seems to have comprised what an individual might normally consider his nearest relatives within the wider family. At Gortyn in Crete the line of inheritance laid down by the fifth-century code ran as follows:

> If a man or woman dies, if there are children, or children's children or their children, these shall have the property. But if there are none of these, but brothers of the dead, or children of the brothers, or their children, these shall have the property. But if there are none of these but sisters of the dead or their children, or their children's children,

these shall have the property. But if there are none of these, the next relations from wherever the property descends, these shall have the property. (Meiggs–Lewis no. 41, col. V.10–25)

The law thus allows that a family might die out, so that uncles and aunts and their descendants may be brought in to the line of inheritance.

In Locris, according to a decree establishing new land allotments in a recently integrated region,

The right of inheritance shall belong to parents and to the son; if there is no son, to the daughter; if there is no daughter, to the brother; if there is no brother, by relationship let a man inherit according to the law. (Meiggs–Lewis no. 13.3–6[60])

This would appear to be an abbreviated version of what is stated at Gortyn or at Athens, and presumably would have allowed for much the same breadth of relationships within the inheritance network.

Versions of the law quoted in the Athenian orators are in some respects less specific, leaving some room for maneuver—either by the law or by those who quote it:

When a man dies without making a will, if he leaves female children his estate is to go with them—but if not, then his brothers and their children shall take their paternal share (which means they had let their share stay with one heir when their father had died); if they are deceased, then the children of the brother's children shall inherit. . . . If there are no relatives on the father's side within the degree of children and first cousins, those on the mother's side shall inherit in the same way. If there are no relations on either side within this degree of relationship, the nearest kin on the father's side shall inherit. (Dem. 43.51)

Whatever the law was supposed to have said, however, Gernet's comment is worth considering, that "the Athenians themselves found their inheritance laws obscure."[61] They were inevitably abused or often simply overlooked. Sometimes a family might have been so curtailed by lack of heirs born to the family and by early deaths in closely related branches that there were no "children of first cousins" left; this is where an uncle's descendants would come into consideration. An even more distant cousin might cajole and wheedle a jury into granting him an estate quite beyond the bounds of the law, as the Attic orators amply demonstrate.

The case of Hagnias's estate nicely illustrates the problems and complexities of inheritance in the hands of manipulative family members (Figure 1): Hagnias was a great-grandson of Bouselus on his father's side and a great-great-grandson on his mother's side. He had no children and so adopted his niece as his nearest relative; she inherited his estate but when she died, although she had a son, the estate next went to Hagnias's half brother, who was also a great-great-grandson of Bouselus. His right to the property was challenged by Hagnias's cousin Euboulides I—whose mother's legitimacy was, however, questioned by the opposition; when he died, the claim was carried on by his daughter Phylomache (child of a first cousin of Hagnias) and her husband Sositheus, both of whom were great-great-grandchildren of Bouselus. Phylomache was awarded the estate. Six other relatives then stepped forward to challenge her possession: Hagnias's maternal uncle, his great-nephew and adopted grandson Eupolemos, his two half brothers (once more), and two first cousins of his mother. Two of the claimants died, and one of the maternal first cousins, Theopompus (who was a great-grandson of Bouselus) eventually got the estate. After Theopompus's death, his son Macartatus inherited but was challenged by Sositheus, whose wife had briefly held the estate, on behalf of their son Euboulides II, whom he registered as the adopted son of the child's own grandfather (who had challenged an early holder of Hagnias's estate). By this maneuver Euboulides II could be considered a close enough relative (the adopted son of Hagnias's first cousin) to lay legal claim to the estate. And yet Theopompus who had won it was technically outside the *anchisteia,* being only a first cousin of Hagnias's mother, whereas Hagnias's own adopted daughter's son was excluded from the inheritance. Macartatus, the last owner of the estate whom we know of, was even further outside the *anchisteia* than his father, Theopompus.

How common such involved and long-drawn-out contests for

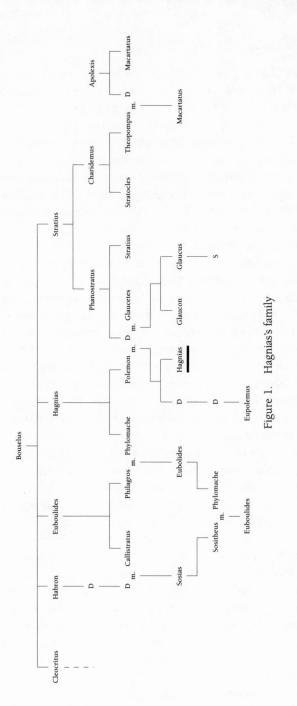

Figure 1. Hagnias's family

44

estates were, it is impossible to judge, from the incomplete record of activity even in the lawcourts of Classical Athens. No other case surviving in the Attic orators approaches anything like this degree of complexity, but for all we know there may have been even more tortuous and contentious wrangles over property. Reminiscent as the contest for the estate of Hagnias is of *Jarndyce v. Jarndyce,*[62] one can only imagine that each successive jury cheered and groaned all the more as the business entered yet another phase.

Whatever the rate of incidence of such lawsuits, the intricacies of family interrelationship which the Hagnias affair demonstrates were surely quite typical of all but the most truncated and impoverished kinship groups. The extensive network within Hagnias's family allowed for several marriages between cousins, so that many of Bouselus's descendants were related to him on both sides of their family. To what extent consolidation of property was one of the aims, we cannot be sure from the evidence available, although we might suspect that Sositheus and Phylomache were married with an eye to laying hands on Hagnias's estate. Conceivably the whole maneuver, especially on Theopompus's part, was an attempt to get hold of as much as possible of the property that had once belonged to great-grandfather Bouselus.

Hagnias's adopted daughter inherited the estate in the first instance, but under Athenian law a woman's right to administer property was restricted by her *kyrios* (literally, "lord"), her closest male relative or her husband. So for the same reason Phylomache's claim to the inheritance was made on her behalf by her husband Sositheus.

In the case of heirs left orphaned when under age, the state made it the *archon's* duty to look after their interests, insofar as he ensured that a guardian, their nearest male relative usually, took care of the estate for their maintenance, either farming the land (if there was any) himself or seeing to its proper tenancy. If a man's only heir was a daughter, she became an *epikleros* (as it were, "going along with the *kleros*"); as such she must marry either her nearest surviving male relative, who became her *kyrios* or guardian when her father died, or another relative, as her guardian or her father's will directed.[63] In fact Aristophanes shows how cavalier the popular attitude to the law and the validity of wills could be, and how peripheral the considerations on which a jury might base a legal decision: "If a father leaves a daughter as heiress and gives her to someone on his deathbed, then we tell the will it can go and boil its head . . . and we give the girl to anyone whose entreaties persuade us" (*Wasps* 583–86). At her marriage the property she had inherited went to her husband, but only for safekeeping until such sons as they had were grown and could inherit the maternal grandfather's estate. Here the preservation of the *oikos* of the *epikleros's* father was not the point at issue: the husband of the *epikleros* did not give up his own estate in order to take over his wife's inheritance (unless her father had actually adopted him as a son, to become also his son-in-law), nor did his sons carry on their grandfather's *oikos* in place of their father's. The estate went with the *epikleros,* and it stayed within the wider family, by her marriage; the concern of the law was that an orphan girl be respectably married and that the land not go outside the wider family as a result. The *epikleros* had no independent rights to the property; but even though she was not judged competent by the law to conduct business on anything but the smallest scale and was not expected to manage her father's property, this need not have prevented a strong-minded individual from taking charge, as Menander suggests—"I've married a witch of an *epikleros.* . . . We've got ourselves an outright boss of the house and the fields and everything" (fr. 334 Koerte, 403 Kock).

The importance of the proper disposal of an *epikleros* was such that the male relative designated to marry her was supposed to do so even if it meant divorcing the wife he already had. By the marriage of an *epikleros* to a relative, it was possible for sections of an estate that had been divided among heirs a generation or so earlier to come together again, until occasion arose for a later generation to divide the inheritance once more. It was also possible for the fortunes of a less prosperous branch of the family to be improved by means of marriage to an *epikleros;* the husband gained the use of the estate at least until his sons were of age, but they then might be better off than any family he would otherwise have had. The upheaval an *epikleros* could cause is remarked on in the speech for Euxitheus—the speaker's mother was divorced when her first husband had to marry an *epikleros,* and as it happened he was a poor man, who thus became entitled to "inherit" a large estate (this being the popular view of the husband's legal rights, obviously).[64] The likelihood that there were considerable differences of fortune within the immediate family is also suggested by Solon's law concerning the provision of dowries for *epikleroi* of no estate whatsoever: it prescribed the amount a member of the wealthiest census group, the *pentakosiomedimnoi,* would make available for an *epikleros* of the Thete census group (Dem. 43.54). Fluctuations of fortune within the wider family could have been corrected in some degree by such coalescence and redivision of property; large holdings acquired through inheritance may rarely have lasted more than a generation or so.

In other parts of the Greek world, women's rights to inherit were a little more positive than at Athens. At Tegea, a woman who had been an *epikleros* transmitted the property to her children, as at Athens; but a woman whose brother's heirs died could inherit his property, thus bringing together again all the property her father had left. In Locris, and perhaps Aetolia too (the evidence is very sketchy), women inherited if there were no males left to do so, as the decree on new land allotments shows.[65] How strict the rules of intermarriage were for *epikleroi* in these parts we do not know; or quite why it was that "factions arose out of *epikleroi*" in Lesbos and Phocis, as Aristotle reports (*Pol.* 1304 a 4–16). In the island of Thera, a woman who survived husband and sons took control of the whole estate, and her daughter might inherit from her in turn; and at Gortyn in Crete, too, an only daughter might inherit in her own right. The opportunity for concentrations of inherited land to grow up by means of judicious marriages was seemingly greater in these societies than at Athens, and nowhere more so than at Sparta.

The land has fallen into the hands of a small number. Here there have been errors in the legal provisions. . . . For their lawgiver [Lycurgus]

while he quite rightly made it a disgrace to buy and sell land in someone's possession, left it open to anyone to transfer it to other ownership by gift or bequest—and yet this inevitably leads to the same
thing. Moreover, something like two-fifths of all the land is possessed
by women. There are two reasons for this: heiresses are numerous and
dowries are large. It would have been better to regulate them. . . . But
as it is an *epikleros may be given in marriage to anyone whatever*. And if
a man dies intestate, *the person he leaves as heir gives her to whom he
likes*. (*Pol.* 1270 a 18–29)

Aristotle makes quite clear some of the substantial differences between Athenian and Spartan practice. The dire effects of the Spartan system he points out by reference to the decline in Spartan
citizen members by his time (the mid-fourth century). Why had
this happened? Partly because of the tendency of wealth to inter-
marry with wealth, there were fewer and fewer families able to
support the Spartan citizen life-style; land was not being redistributed by a sensibly moderate inheritance law; and the birthrate
within the remaining Spartiate group was probably static if not
itself actually in decline for one reason or another (the further
concentration of wealth being perhaps a powerful motive in this
respect too).[66]

Various questions arise, both out of Aristotle's summary of the
situation and out of the facts such as we have them. Why were
heiresses numerous? Why were not dowries limited, as elsewhere,
especially given the Spartans' official attitude to personal wealth?
Why did the kings, whose responsibility it was supposed to be to
oversee the betrothal of *epikleroi,* not prevent some of the more
outstanding instances of intermarriage between superrich families, so as to avoid the ills that must have been evident to others
besides Aristotle, and in Sparta itself? And why had not the Spartan community as a whole foreseen some of the economic and
political consequences of its inheritance practices long since? Presumably the Spartans' great love of landed property was inextri-
cably combined with the innate conviction that they could retain
both their exclusivity and the reassurance given by accumulating
land, and that few as they were they could do so forever.

## The Alienation of Land

Just as there were other ways besides dying of a man's being parted
from his land, so land could be acquired in other ways besides
inheritance. A likely source of alienable land would have been
public confiscation of properties from men condemned for treason, which were then sold at auction. The land taken by the restored democracy in 410 from the condemned oligarch Peisander
was awarded to a Megarian henchman of the democrats, for having assassinated another oligarchic leader, Phrynichus. The land
was then sold to a man who let it to tenants, before selling it in
his turn to the speaker of Lysias's oration, *On the Sacred Olive Tree.*
In the late fifth century and thereafter, as other evidence also demonstrates, land was being bought and sold with no questions
asked. This had probably always been the case.[67]

But there had been laws in various places expressly forbidding
the sale of the ancestral lot. And even if no law were pronounced
on the subject, the majority of landowners felt strongly against
parting with their land on both practical and ideological
grounds.[68] It is therefore worth considering the relevance of the
fact that the land being sold, for example, by the Megarian had
been detached from Peisander's *oikos,* and the *oikos* itself brought
to an end, by the political act of confiscation. The owner's inhibi-
tions against selling certainly were no longer a factor; and if the
buyers felt any qualms, they were assuaged by the city's action.
The purchase of land put up for sale by the state might conceivably have been regarded as something of a civic duty: thus land
that had been put out of action by its owner's malfeasance and the
city's punishment of the crime could be reincorporated into the
citizen-owned wealth of the community; at the same time the city
got a price for unused property and the purchaser took the chance
to extend his holding, at what may have been a very good price.
The punishment of crimes against the community would have
taken the form of confiscation from very early on in the existence
of the Greek states, being so clear a way of demonstrating the
unacceptability of certain behavior, and the idea of acquiring such
lands would have long been familiar.

Probably more instances than not of land actually being given up and coming onto the market, still in Classical Athens, concerned estates confiscated for political crimes or for public or sacred debt. But although public life and its results surely played a big part in putting land on the market, there were other reasons for land becoming a salable commodity. Hesiod admonishes his brother to do proper reverence to the gods so that "they may have a propitious heart and mind toward you, that you may negotiate for others' land lots, not another man for yours" (*WD* 340–41). He must have in mind the private and personal difficulties that may force a landowner to part with his fields, the chief of which is debt arising from agricultural disasters. Small and temporary difficulties could be warded off by limited borrowing and small-scale lending between neighbors. But more persistent problems—the prolonged damage done by a series of crop failures through bad weather, poor management, or the farmer's ill health, perhaps—would necessitate large-scale or extended borrowing. If better times never came, or came too late, among the last stages of indebtedness was the pledging of the land itself, and the final step was reached with the surrender of ownership of the land to the creditor. Not only the family's best means of support was thus lost but in some communities its citizen status too.

The best-documented episode of social and economic dissatisfaction stemming from agricultural debt is the crisis that brought Solon to office as reformer in early sixth-century Athens.[69] Aristotle, writing more than two hundred years later, saw the conflict as one between two sharply divided sections of society, the rich and the poor:

> The poor were enslaved to the rich. . . . (they) were called dependents and sixth-parters, since it was for the rent of a sixth that they worked the fields of the rich. All the land was in the hands of a few, and if the poor failed to pay their rents both they and their children were liable to seizure. All loans were made on the security of the person until the time of Solon. (*Ath. Pol.* 2.2)

The evidence (of which this is only a part) raises as many questions as it answers, but this much may be said: an intolerable situation had arisen in which many men had mortgaged their land for debt; some were reduced to working as tenants or sharecroppers on what had been their own farms, and some had even pledged their own persons for debt. Others, through dependence on a powerful relative or neighbor, chronic poverty, or a debt of service or protection (rather than of economic resources), were obligated to serve in return—as laborers on the land. Solon himself speaks in his poetry of calling to witness "the greatest and best mother of the Olympian deities, Black Earth, from which I removed the markers that were fixed in many places, the Earth which once was enslaved but now is free" (*Ath. Pol.* 12.4). His cancellation of debt (the *seisachtheia* or shaking off of burdens) was what freed the land; but he did not accompany it with a limitation on the amount of land that a man could put up as security for a loan, which would have prevented the loss of an entire estate in case of default.[70]

Nor did he redistribute the land, as many of his supporters would have liked, so that his constitutional reforms preserved the *thetes* (the native Athenian laborers) as the landless or almost landless poor; but he also established them as the fourth category of citizen (as Thetes), who were now qualified to exercise some of the rights of citizenship in contrast to the constitutions of many states, which excluded such people from citizenship. The significance of this change for Athenian agriculture as for Athenian society is touched on in chapter 5; suffice it to say here that in addition to Solon's restating the *thetes'* position, his laws forbade a man to pledge his person for debt, so that the debt bondsman now supposedly departed from the scene.[71]

As for the Athenian crisis, we do not know why it developed when it did—whether as the result of some recent legislation or from a long-standing set of circumstances which only gradually became intolerable. Conceivably action was only demanded when some well-connected and formerly prosperous families fell into the web of debt, and complained more vociferously than would poor men who had been entrapped long since. It is not clear how large a proportion of the population was affected, although Aristotle assumes that many families were involved. And if this crisis had close parallels in other parts of the Greek world, we can only suppose that similar remedies were sought.

Debt itself remained a recurrent problem. There is no good indication whether it was considered wiser to borrow from relatives or from independent sources, the family being only too ready to find fault or seize the farm on one pretext or another. Organizations with reserves were another source of loans, and would have had the advantage of being more detached from the borrower's immediate surroundings; the treasuries of the gods were pleased to lend, charging interest, naturally, and like all creditors demanding security in the shape of land. So at Halicarnassus, debtors who owed the gods Athena and Apollo had their lands, houses, and gardens confiscated. Commercial bankers like Pasion, former slave and freedman, subsequently a fully integrated Athenian citizen, lent money to a variety of people, but probably to merchants, condottieri employing mercenaries, and men intent on spending a lot to impress the city, not to farmers caught between one bad harvest and the next. Pasion's fortune at his death included a vast sum of money tied up in mortgaged land, something that indicates the importance of having land to pledge for a debt, still in the fourth century; money borrowed for purposes such as making up dowries or paying off money owed by guardians to their wards was secured largely by land, not cash.[72]

Despite the existence of laws and prejudices against letting one's land go, securing land for debt and selling land to raise funds were ever-present features of society. The Locrian law *forbidding* the alienation of land also *allowed* that *in cases of exceptional hardship* a man might sell his land—the law could not deny the need to do so altogether (Ar. *Pol.* 1266 b 18–21); the avoidance of total indebtedness might have been an acceptable reason, if the sale left enough over to provide a living after the debt had been repaid. But when Hesiod speaks of "negotiating for another man's land lot," does he mean that one should be in the position of the creditor to whom pledged land falls due, or simply that one should be able to buy when another man is forced to sell as the last resort before pledging his land for debt? Perhaps he envisages only the sale of part of an estate, enough to allow a family to get out of debt and carry on in reduced circumstances, with the additional disadvantage, of course, that the less land a man had, the less he could borrow on it.

Loss of the family land as a result of gambling does not figure in the evidence, although there are numerous references to young men playing dice, suggesting the possibility that patrimonies were gambled away.[73] Getting into debt through sheer extravagance is not unheard of, along with the frittering away of estates by wastrel behavior, and indulgences such as horse breeding no doubt accounted for some unnecessary expenditure, and even the collapse of some landed fortunes.

Another form of irresponsibility toward the land which would have led to its coming onto the market was the sheer distaste that some individuals had for country life and agricultural pursuits. Odysseus in his disguise as a Cretan merchant plays upon this theme: "Farming was never very much to my liking, or looking after a household. What I always loved was a ship with oars, and fighting, and polished javelins and arrows" (*Od.* 14.222–25). Aristocrats like Sappho's brother took to trading overseas, no more perhaps out of necessity or the concern to make profit from agricultural surpluses than a desire to get off the land and out of Lesbos (Hdt. 2.135). In a similar cast of mind, surely, Macartatus, the brother-in-law of Theopompus who got ownership of Hagnias's estate, sold his land and bought a trireme with the proceeds; he joined an expedition to Cyprus but drowned at sea on the way (Isaeus 11.48).

Land could also be disposed of by dedication to the gods, so as to provide a source of income from its rents.[74] Motives other than piety might have played a part, such as a wish to reduce the inheritance for a troublesome heir or to diminish one's visible wealth and avoid taxes or public responsibilities incumbent on men of a certain status. Conversely, opportunities for acquiring land arose when organizations decided that they held too much land and put property up for sale. This situation is reflected in the records of sales of land belonging to various cult and civic organizations in Attica toward or at the end of the fourth century; similar steps may have been taken elsewhere to reduce the responsibilities of the administrators by disposing of land that must otherwise be let and supervised during its leasing in order to be productive.[75]

It was sometimes possible to acquire land abroad, without becoming a citizen of another city. Athens's treatment of rebellious allies occasionally involved the confiscation of allied land, which was then allotted to Athenians (*klerouchoi*) often serving as a garrison; so it happened in Lesbos. But here the Athenians simply took an annual payment from the Lesbians who were left to work what had been their own land; the Athenians became their landlords to all intents and purposes.[76] The *klerouchiai* set up on allied land in the fourth century were more like overseas settlements, and in these cases Athenian citizens settled on the land allotted to them, while retaining Athenian citizenship and continuing to be liable for public service at Athens. Individuals also got their hands on land in other cities' territories by various means; sometimes the right to own land or even the land itself was awarded for services rendered to the city concerned, but in other cases it looks as if some political manipulation went on, whereby influential Athenians, for example, cashed in on the situation within allied cities and used opportunities to lay accusations against leaders of the opposition, gaining possession of their estates after they had been confiscated. The Hermocopid Adeimantus's vast vineyards on the island of Thasos and Oeonias's huge real estate holdings on Euboea were probably the fruits of such efforts.[77]

Sometimes deserving service to another city was rewarded by the grant of *enktesis*, the right to acquire land; at Athens a metic, or a foreigner considered as a metic for this purpose (even though he never had and never intended to reside permanently at Athens), received *enktesis*, of land and a house, but within a fixed upper limit.[78] Even for honored men there could be no uncontrolled acquisition of land. So in Xenophon's case the rights to the estate that he purchased at Scillus in the environs of Olympia were granted by the Spartans in recognition of his friendship and support on campaign.[79] But such grants were rare, and in some places the limited right of access to land, *epinomia* or grazing privilege, may have been all that was offered to outsiders; the recipient was usually expected to pay a tax for pasturing his beasts, privilege notwithstanding.[80]

Xenophon's ownership of the estate at Scillus lasted only as long as the Spartans' control of this part of Elis. In 371 the Eleans recovered the area, and Xenophon had to withdraw with his family to Corinth. Soon after, the Athenians revoked the decree of exile pronounced against him during the 390s; his family must formerly have owned land, but whether he had inherited it before he was exiled and his lands were then confiscated, now to be restored or compensated for, the evidence does not say. Because one of his sons fought and died as an Athenian cavalryman at the battle of Mantinea in 362, the assumption must be that Xenophon's fortunes recovered in some way, and that his family resumed something of its ancient status as a landowning entity under the protection of Athenian property and inheritance laws.[81]

# Two

# Landowners in Society

> For a long time . . . the Athenians had lived in inde-
> pendent communities throughout Attica . . . , both
> in earlier generations and right down to the time of
> the present war, being born and bred in the country.
> (Thuc. 2.16.1)

## Residence and Neighborhood

Because the majority of Greek landowners had good reason to take some personal interest in the farming of their land, it is natural to suppose that they mostly lived in close proximity to it, or even on their estates, and that the settlement pattern of the Greek world consisted of a few village or urban concentrations in the midst of a scatter of separate farmsteads, among which some were the residences of the great landowners whose property lay compactly round about.[1] But it is by no means clear that this was generally the case. For one thing, in Attica at any rate, large holdings tended to consist of separate plots in different regions, not single blocks of land all within the same locality, so that a wealthy landowner often enough could not have resided "on the estate," whatever his inclination.[2] Various general considerations may determine where a farming population resides, such as concern for protection, the distance between home and farmland that it is prepared to travel daily, the availability and limitation of the water supply; but the difficulty is to discern their influence on decisions made in Greek antiquity. Priorities may have altered beyond our ability to identify them properly, and physical conditions such as the accessibility of ground water and the nature of the climate may have altered in ways that cannot be gauged precisely. If most farmers did indeed live in villages, how far were they prepared to walk to and from the fields? Settlement studies in other cultures suggest an upper limit of about five kilometers; land beyond that limit would be farmed by resident farmers or by workers from another settlement within easier reach of it, whereas farmland within that limit would not have residences on it.[3] As it happens, the distribution of demes in many parts of Attica suggests a pattern of settlements roughly ten kilometers apart, each within an area of about five kilometers' radius.[4] But isolated farmsteads have been located within the five-kilometer limit, and it is not at all certain that demes were actually concentrated *settlements,* rather than communities within specified *districts.*[5] In any case, other studies of rural settlement patterns indicate that farmers may walk considerably longer distances to and from their land, and still think it practical to do so daily.[6] Landowners who were interested in living on their land would have considered the question of water supply; but how close did it have to be? Or, what distance between source and dwelling was considered impossibly far? Solon supposedly ruled that anyone within about a kilometer of a public well should use that, but if the distance were greater, he should dig his own. Even if Greece was less arid than it is now, we still cannot tell whether an absence of habitation and of wells dug in antiquity means that water was not available then or that no one cared enough to dig deep enough. A depth of sixty feet was considered the normal limit, according to another of Solon's ordinances, which gave a man the right to use his neighbor's well if he had not struck water at that depth on his own land (Plut. *Solon* 23.4).[7]

It is really only possible to sketch in some of the alternatives for place of rural residence and the relation between dwelling and farmland in Attica and other regions where the territory was not all of it within easy reach of the central settlement. For many small communities, of course, the problem of where people lived was fairly easily solved—most of them lived in the polis itself, the physical center of the *chora*.[8] But even if the question were answered with reference to landowners and their families, there is still the matter of housing for laborers and cattle. In a sense there may have been a resident population scattered over the countryside, regardless of where the citizen landowners lived.[9] The archaeological record remains very incomplete, partly because until comparatively recently little attention was given to anything in the countryside beyond sanctuaries, burials, and fortifications. But surveys have begun to reveal hitherto disregarded material; even though the nature of much rural construction—mud brick on a stone foundation course at best, the ancient habit of reusing roof tiles as well as structural timbers, and the continuous "quarrying" of building sites which has gone on ever since antiquity—means that virtually nothing survives of the rural structure itself, the scatter of pottery fragments deposited while the building was inhabited can be interpreted to locate and date a dwelling fairly precisely.[10]

Arguments may still be made either that isolated farmsteads were more the rule than the exception or that there always remained a predilection for residing where protection was available, if not actually within the confines of *the city* itself. Hesiod lived, herded sheep, and farmed "at Ascra," in the hill country of western Boeotia (*WD* 640, *Th.* 22–23). The site of the village of Ascra has been identified at the foot of a steep hill that would have provided a refuge as well as a good vantage point from which to keep watch on the valley below; the settlement itself was enclosed by a wall, and it was clearly the urban center of the district, although really an outlying dependency of the city of Thespiae, ten kilometers to the southeast.[11] In the *Works and Days* Hesiod refers to the blacksmith's, by whose fire it is tempting to loiter in the depths of winter, and to the community of neighbors, but he nowhere makes it clear whether he lives on the land or in town (493–95 and 343–56.). Whichever the case, he would not have been very far from either the pastures of Mount Helicon or his farm in the Valley of the Muses.

Thucydides' comment on the Athenians' attachment to rural Attica was made about the Athenians of his own generation, not about some long past stage of society. And when he says that they were born and bred *in the country,* he expresses it "in the fields" (*en tois agrois*), which is certainly to suggest (though not to declare unequivocally) that many of them lived not in villages but on their land. The Athenian evidence suggests that isolated farmhouses were by no means unknown, and that many landowners resided in the country, whether on their land or in small hamlets nearby. Some of the settlements were the cultural, social, and administrative centers of the *demes,* which often enough were *villages,* as the term is generally understood. But the deme was also the district or parish in the English sense, within which families owned land; and there are indications that more than one settlement might exist within them, with little or no regard for residence at a focal point. This might consist of a cult center, a meeting place, the market if there was one; craftsmen's establishments might well be somewhere else with other dwellings.[12]

The attachment to the deme was both spatial and ancestral; for many Athenians home was also where their forebears had lived and almost certainly owned land since Cleisthenes' time or long before.[13] For some Athenians, inevitably, the link between their ancestral deme and their place of residence and property had been broken, but for them, too, the deme where they were presently resident was the community that mattered most immediately, though of course their ancestral deme always remained their link with the rights of citizenship. The formation of the polis had not meant the shifting of the rural population to the central settlement, for apart from anything else the territory of Attica was simply too big to make this a feasible undertaking in a society of farmers and landowners. There was never a question of the entire citizen population becoming absentee owners of land worked by tenants or slaves. To be sure, the resident population of the city grew, particularly during the fifth century, but in many cases the move to town was either a temporary one, for the sake of education or until an inheritance came in, or part-time, the residence in the country having been retained.[14] A fair proportion of the citizen population owned no residence in the city; when the countryside was evacuated in 431, numerous families had no recourse but to camp wherever they could find space (Thuc. 2.17.1–3). Some families did give up or lose their landed interest, and take up another way of life, but for many city dwellers their contact with the land continued, and going to and fro between Athens and the country probably took up much of their time.[15] Socrates' lack of enthusiasm even for taking a walk outside the city walls was perhaps exceptional among Athenians—and therefore worthy of being dramatized in Plato's dialogue, the *Phaedrus* (230 a–e).

Attachment to the countryside is apparent in Athenian comedy and in the oratory of the lawcourts. Aristophanes' vine cultivator Trygaeus is in many ways a realistic portrayal of the citizen farmer who lives next to his plantings, suffering and rejoicing with every harmful or favorable air that blows on them, and sharing the hardships, rewards, and relaxations of rural life with his household, slaves and all (*Peace* 551–60, 571–81, 1127–71). Just such a man the speaker of Demosthenes 55 may have been, a landowner resident in the hills north of Eleusis. His place in the deme may not have dated back before his father's time, when the property was purchased; nevertheless, when his neighbor Callicles made so much trouble for him in the matter of a wall between their properties, he felt that he was being *driven out of the deme,* and this was a source of great perturbation for him (Dem. 55.35).[16] His status and wealth are unknown, but among instances of fairly well-to-do landowners residing on their estates is the trierarch who farmed near the Hippodrome and who had lived there since his boyhood (Dem. 47.53). Another affluent country resident was Apollodorus, son of the eminently successful banker Pasion; his persistence in purchasing estates and residing on one of them suggests that to do so was the norm, for he was a "new man," his father having been at one time a slave, and he wished to acquire a completely Athenian respectability by living on his land, even enduring a severe drought, which caused the field crops and the vegetable garden to fail and the wells to dry up (Dem. 50.61). As for Menander's *Dyscolus,* what makes him a misanthropist is not that he lives in the country *on his farm,* but that he lives and works almost *on his own,* with scarcely any household to support him (326–29).[17]

In rural Attica the remains of several houses have been found.

Farmhouses proper have turned up near Sounion and the mining district of southern Attica; they seem to conform with the usual plan—an enclosed yard with a dwelling and store chambers ranged along two or more sides of it, with often enough a tower (or vertical barn) either attached to one corner of the complex, or standing near but detached.[18] The farm of Timesius, including the so-called Cliff Tower, is one such; it extended over about 180 *plethra* (if its enclosure wall has been identified correctly).[19] This sort of establishment, with threshing floor nearby and an oil or wine press, or both, within the farm building or the tower, is glimpsed in both the archaeological material and the inscribed records of sanctuary estates in Delos and at Heraclea in southern Italy; extensive excavations at Chersonesus in the Crimea have also revealed versions of this layout in various sizes.[20] In addition rural residences that do not seem to have been working farmhouses have been found in Attica, two good examples being the house at Vari in the southwest foothills of Mount Hymettus and the Dema house in the uplands between the plain of Athens and the Thriasian plain.[21] Although owners of the house at Vari kept bees, there are no other signs at either site of agricultural activity in the immediate environs—no threshing floor, oil press or wine press, stables or other farm buildings, although it is possible that the enclosure in front of the house at Vari was a sheep pen.[22] The plans of these houses closely resemble those of city houses such as have been found in Athens and at Priene, Olynthus, and elsewhere.[23] But these were country residences, the Dema house one of a small group in the neighborhood (a rural settlement, then), and perhaps the working elements of the country estate that the house dwellers owned were elsewhere, but not very far away.[24]

There were close similarities between residences "urban" in style and those which were farmhouses; many urban dwellings included an elevated section or tower (*purgos*) at one corner of the structure, for much the same reasons, to economize in the use of land and structural timbers by building *up,* not *along,* and to provide security for womenfolk, valuables, and stores.[25] Often enough a garden was part of the urban land allotment, as at Tegea, for instance.[26] In this and many other ways the separation that it is natural for modern urban and suburban dwellers to assume existed between town and country was rendered meaningless: the inhabitants of small territories naturally tended to live in the central (often the only) settlement, as in Plataea, or Thebes, Phlius, or any of the four cities of Ceos. And in larger states the city, such as Athens in Attica, provided the surest refuge in time of invasion for both humans and domestic animals, and the planning of various places allowed for animal pens within the city walls.[27] Town houses in a more spacious state like Olynthus might also include agricultural equipment, just as at Athens they were as often as not the residences of active, farming landowners, whose store chambers would have contained produce from their owners' fields and orchards just as if they actually lived on their land.[28]

In many respects the city was always an enclave of citizen landowners and farmers who went to and fro frequently between their houses and their farms. Euphiletus often visited the country overnight. Returning unexpectedly, he discovered his wife with a lover; he summoned friends and neighbors to witness his punishment of the adulterer, only to find that while one of them had just returned from the country himself, others were still there (Lysias 1). These were not necessarily rich men, but they presumably had a laborer or two permanently employed if not actually resident on their land. Ischomachus on the other hand, as Xenophon presents him in the *Oeconomicus* (discussed later in this chapter), represents the wealthy landowner who has a steward to run his estate, and slaves to work under him; yet the owner still takes a personal interest in his land, visiting it regularly from the city, and remaining conversant with every detail. Because he goes and returns within a morning (mounted, of course), Xenophon means to suggest that the estate is not very far from the city (*Oecon.* 11.15–18). That the city did not even draw into it all of the immediately local citizen population appears from the recollection of a meeting of demesmen belonging to a deme about seven kilometers out of Athens; the meeting was called in the city, but it broke up early, says the victim of the convener's manipulations, because most of the members wished to get back home, out to the country, before dark (Dem. 57.10).

Even so, the Athenians' attachment to country life, to their sties, hives, vines, and barley fields, did not match that of landowners in Elis who, Polybius says, were so fond of their rustic existence that "for three or four generations many of them had taken up no lawsuits, so unwilling were they to leave the country and go into the city to prosecute them" (4.73.5). The wealthy landowners of Mantinea in Arcadia had gone along with the synoecism of about 470, when the five villages of the territory became one polis, and the population came together in one settlement; but when the Spartans broke up the city into its constituent villages again, the Mantinean aristocracy was not displeased that the Spartans were now obliging the citizen population to resume its former pattern of dispersed rural residence, because now they could live close to their own estates again (Xen. *HG* 5.2.7).

In stark contrast, the Spartans were confined to the five villages of central Laconia, separated from the land they owned not so much by distance as by the ideology that barred them from working it themselves; yet one may suspect even among the Spartans a certain tendency to creep off to see how the crops or, better yet, the horses were doing down on the farm.[29] Elsewhere, the territory of the city-state was so restricted that there would have been room for little more than a hamlet or two in addition to the central settlement of the polis itself, as at Melitea in Phthiotic Achaea, whose land was perhaps twelve kilometers across, or at places like Aphytis, Scione, or Mende, all in the Chalcidice and all pinched between coast and mountain. Much might have been decided by the state of security in the region: when the city of Priene moved to its new site, the citizens lived within the city walls for protection, leaving draught animals and laborers to take their chances on the plains below.[30] And when any new settlement was established, the scale of the threat from the hinterland would have determined the distribution of the population's dwelling places. Citizens of Olbia and Istrus, on the northern side of the Black Sea, would probably not have chosen to live very far out of the city, for Thracian and other raiders made life rather uncertain in the countryside.[31] At Chersonesus in the Crimea land west of the city was farmed and inhabited, quite densely, one farmhouse per farm;

here the distance between the city and these rural residences was under ten kilometers, but so far there is no means of telling *who* lived in them, the owners of the land, or the slaves or dependent laborers who worked the farms.[32]

As with relations between the citizen and the country, so with those between the landowner and his neighbors, Athens provides the clearest signs of the directions in which men's loyalties were drawn. They looked to the polis, which consisted in principle of the territory as a whole but which for practical purposes was embodied in the city itself, the acropolis, and the other administrative centers of the state, and which consisted politically of all of Attica's citizen inhabitants and their families. Their personal concerns were tied partly to the deme of their ancestors and partly to their extended family, not all of whose members belonged to the same deme; but what drew their attention most closely was their dealings with the immediate family and the neighbors in the district where they lived, owned land, and conducted the business of daily life.[33]

Euphiletus's neighbors in the city probably were not also his close neighbors in the country, so that although they shared the same general concerns as landowners and as residents of the same quarter in the city, they could leave behind in the country the petty annoyances and antagonisms that so often arise between owners of neighboring properties.[34] In the rural deme, virtually everyone must have known who owned what land; who had not done what he should to it, with who knew what harmful consequences for his own and surrounding properties; whose relations lived where; and how much, to within a handful of grain or a flask of oil, each of his fellow demesmen or deme residents possessed. It was just this sort of interest in others' affairs which lay at the basis of the sycophants' activities, to the ruination of many a family fortune and public career.[35] The laws ascribed to Solon concerning farming and landed property suggest the kind of conflicts which arose. For example, concerning the placing of bee hives, Solon said that each owner's hives should be set at least three hundred feet away from everybody else's. Concerning trees planted along property lines, Solon recommended that fruit trees should be no less than five feet, and olives at least nine feet in from the boundary between properties. Trenches and pits must be at least as far from the neighbor's property as they were deep; and if anyone digging a well on his own land had not struck water at a depth of sixty feet, his neighbor should allow him to draw water from the well on his land—but a fixed quantity only, not more than twice a day (Plut. *Solon* 23).[36]

Next-door neighbors could often be helpful and friendly. For a time Nicostratus kindly kept an eye on Apollodorus's farm while Apollodorus went off to perform important public duties (Dem. 53.4); and the neighboring families of Callicles and Teisias were on good terms, the women visiting to and fro (Dem. 55.23–24). But neighbors could become great afflictions: "A bad neighbor is as big a bane as a good one is a boon, nor would a cow be lost but for a bad neighbor"—so Hesiod, and so many a man must have been moved to exclaim (*WD* 346–48). Callicles decided to attribute flood damage on his property to a wall built some years past by Teisias, alleging that it stood on or even beyond the boundary of his land, encroaching on a public road that also served as a winter torrent; so he brought a lawsuit against Teisias's son, having already taken the family's trusted slave Callarus to court (Dem. 55.32). Teisias's son argued that the wall was just where it should be and that in any case the damage, according to his mother who had been across to see, amounted to no more than a spoiled jar or two of household stores (55.24). As for Apollodorus's neighbor Nicostratus, when he fell into the hands of slave traders in Aegina while pursuing some runaway slaves of his own, he asked Apollodorus to help pay his ransom, presumably on the strength of his own previous helpfulness. The matter became more complicated, and eventually Apollodorus found himself being both accused of not declaring his property in full to the state and the victim of robbery and assault—even fruit tree grafts, young vines, and olive saplings were destroyed. How close to the facts Apollodorus's story is, how guiltless he was in the affair, and how close Nicostratus actually came to waylaying him and throw-

ing him into the quarries at Piraeus are beside the point; the episode serves to illustrate the animosity that could flare up between
landed neighbors (Dem. 53.7, 13–17).

And yet true neighborliness surely endured in the form of mutual assistance, which makes the farming existence tolerable even
in bad times; if we hear little about it, the reason is partly that it
did not give rise to lawsuits. Modest borrowing is countenanced
by Hesiod, of the kind it is easy to repay, and which your neighbor
may need to do in his turn one day. "Get good measure from your
neighbor, and give good measure back, with the measure itself
and better if you can, so that when in need another time you may
find something to rely on. . . . Work . . . lest you look for livelihood among the neighbors and they pay no heed" (WD 349–51,
397–400). We do not know what the code of behavior for working farmers entailed in the way of helping one another at harvesttime, or lending draft animals in time of need, for example, although Hesiod suggests that neighbors certainly expected to be
able to borrow such things, even if he does not think this altogether a good idea.[37] "It is easy to say, 'Give me a pair of oxen and
a cart,' (but) it is easy too to refuse: 'But the oxen have work to
do'" (WD 453–54). He also says that they should in return be
ready to step forward in an emergency if the right approaches have
been made previously: "Invite above all him who lives near you;
for if something untoward happens at your place, neighbors come
ungirt, but relations have to gird themselves" (WD 342–45)—
that is to say, neighbors often lived closer than family members.
Neighbors would be the first to come to a celebration too: Chremylus, in Aristophanes' *Plutus,* wants to share out the loot of the
captured god of wealth with his friends, so he tells his slaves,
"Invite my fellow farmers; you will probably find them working
on their farms" (223–24).

## Landed Wealth

Produce from the land at all periods formed part of far more
family incomes than not, even in societies with diversified economies such as Athens or Corinth. For large numbers of households

the land was the main source of wealth—or subsistence; many men would not have called it wealth. For a comparatively small number it provided really vast riches.[38]

The amount of land that a family might own remained, to a large extent, fixed by convention and certain practical considerations, as in the case of the *zeugite* or hoplite *kleros* (see chapter 1): first, the amount of produce a single family required in order to survive from year to year; second, the amount of labor necessary to enable the householder to farm the land adequately and to serve as a hoplite when required; third, what the estate could afford in the way of working expenses—that is, how much maintenance laborers and oxen would need. According to Hesiod the "basic" farm was best worked with at least a couple of assistants and a yoke of oxen; the *zeugite* may be seen as a "one-yoke owner," and as it happens the smallest area that it is considered economically feasible to work with a yoke of oxen is one of about 5 hectares or 55 *plethra*.[39] This is what the evidence suggests was the size of a minimum hoplite land allotment; at Pharsalus, the third-century grant of citizenship to fighting men was accompanied by a land lot of 60 *plethra*, the smaller, one-family-sized farms at Crimean Chersonesus were between 43 and 55 *plethra*, and a single farm that composed part of a big estate in Attica was 60 *plethra* in extent. Plots of land this size can be detected in various parts of the Greek world.[40] The yields from a farm of these proportions would have been adequate in a good year but never princely.

We can safely assume that there were even more "basic" farms than this, of half or even one-third the size of the hoplite farm, which could also be made to produce enough to support a small family. These were the farms of households that did not, could not, own a yoke of oxen with which to work the land. At Athens the owners of such plots were Thetes, below the status of hoplite; in other less democratic states, they were those members of the citizen-descended community who did not possess full citizen rights because they were too poor. A farm of between 20 and 40 *plethra* may seem wretchedly small but if worked intensively by hand, as a garden (not as fields worked with plow animals), it would provide a living equivalent to that obtained with the use of oxen on a larger plot—but with a greater expenditure of human labor, of course.[41] If thoroughly cultivated and carefully fertilized, such a plot could produce crops annually, instead of having to lie, half of it, fallow every year, as was the established practice in arable farming on a larger scale. In the early Roman Republic it was said that "anyone for whom 7 *iugera* (about 20 *plethra*) are not enough is a dangerous citizen," which indicates that an allotment of this size was considered a viable farm plot for the lowliest of Roman citizens (Pl. *NH* 18.18).

The evidence suggests that the majority of citizens even in Attica always owned some land, not that more and more land came into the hands of fewer and fewer owners as time went on. It is therefore probable that most farms were in the range of 60 *plethra* and less. But there had always been families that owned more land than their neighbors, and there continued to be men rich enough to acquire more land; at the same time the workings of inheritance together with rates of death and survival tended to promote the consolidation of some estates for a generation or two. (See my subsequent discussion on fluctuations in wealth.) Even so, the largest holdings of land seem to have been not more than about 300 *plethra* in extent; some consisted of one continuous spread, but others were made up of several, often quite distantly separated, tracts of land (individual family farms, perhaps). Alcibiades' estate was of this size; and the Aristophanes who was condemned to death for misleading the Athenian *demos* into a disaster in Cyprus and whose property was confiscated, had purchased an estate of more than 300 *plethra*.[42] Precise figures are as always sparse, but the supposition that 300 *plethra* was accepted as the upper limit is supported, first, by the fact that, with one exception, we hear of no larger holdings than these in Attica, and second, from the consideration that good land was not boundlessly available, and that a limit to the amount that any one individual or family could own had most likely been established—when, it would be impossible to say, but perhaps at some point during the sixth century or earlier.[43] The Platonic recommendation that this should be so is then rooted in actuality, not in the fertile imagination of the political theorist; the largest estate in the ideal republic was to be not more than four times (according to Plato in *Laws* 744 e) or five times (Aristotle's version in *Pol.* 1266 b 6) the size of the smallest, so that if Plato was thinking of the *zeugite* plot as the smallest, then the largest estates were to be between 240 and 300 *plethra*.

Is it likely that such a limit would have been adhered to? The one exception would appear to be the estate of Phaenippus; he had, unusually, inherited two estates that lay next to one another (Dem. 42.21). The only dimension of which we can be at all sure is the length of their combined boundary—about eight kilometers. If the joint estate were regular in shape, it might have extended over 3,000 to 4,000 *plethra*; but various considerations, such as its location in the uneven hill country, make it likely that each of the estates fell at or just within the upper limit of 300 *plethra*.[44] Would such an upper limit have been recognized elsewhere? Farms of about 300 *plethra* are also known at Crimean Chersonesus; one even larger farm of about 360 *plethra* has been found there, too.[45] Attempts have been made to calculate the size of Spartan land allotments, based on the tradition of the contributions to the common mess which each Spartan had to make from his own *kleros*, but there are too many unknown quantities for any certain figure to emerge.[46] Spartan landowners were, as far as we know, able to own land in addition to their *kleros*, but if there ever was any upper limit set to this, the evidence does not suggest what it may have been.

Among more modest estates in Attica were Hagnias's land, valued at two talents, and large enough to accommodate one thousand olive trees; an area of 200 *plethra* might have sufficed (Dem. 43.69).[47] Timesius's farm in the mining district had a boundary of about three kilometers and stretched over 180 *plethra*.[48] And the estate granted by the city to Aristides' son Lysimachus was 100 *plethra* in size (Plut. *Ar.* 27.1).[49] Various prices or values of estates are mentioned in the sources, suggestive of dimensions within this range, but measurements are never given, and estimates of size based on prices can never be certain.[50]

Ischomachus and his father have often been pointed out as

agents of a profound change that supposedly came over Athenian land tenure during and after the Peloponnesian War, with all its disruption of the agricultural cycle and the consequent impoverishment of many families that had owned and farmed land in the traditional way. According to this view, the neglected or abandoned farms they bought up to improve and sell at a profit had belonged mostly to now dispossessed peasant farmers who could not afford the investment needed to restore their war-ravaged plots; the opportunity now arose for richer men to accumulate land.[51] Ischomachus and his father may indeed represent a certain interest in buying up property that, if it had been badly farmed, could easily be improved; but it is not necessary to suppose either that there was anything particularly new in this practice or that the war actually caused a major disruption in the traditional pattern of landowning. The evidence simply does not support such a view. That the Peloponnesian War was a profound disaster for large parts of Attica there can be no denying. But there are indications that a little farming may have gone on, even under the hoofs of patrolling Spartan cavalry after 412; and the fact that there had earlier been repeated invasions did not necessarily make the destruction worse than it would have been after one thorough ravaging.[52] A tree can be chopped down only once, after all. The Persian sacks of 480 and 479 must have dealt as deadly a blow then to many estates, and yet no one suggests that small farmers were dispossessed in large numbers after that war. It took years to recover, no doubt, as Thucydides says, for when the Athenians had to evacuate the countryside in 431, "they had only just got reestablished after the upsets of the Persian War" (2.16.1). After the Peloponnesian War the small farmers had just as much to gain as anyone else by putting their land back under cultivation, and no doubt dug their land by hand until they could find and maintain draft animals.[53]

Really large landholdings seem not to have existed in Attica; no really large fortunes were made from the land there. The very rich possessed *movable* and *invisible* wealth—derived from the silver mines by the families of such as Nicias, or Callias and Hipponicus, or from commercial and diplomatic activities abroad.[54] Thus the

Alcmeonid family's great wealth, displayed in the sixth and fifth centuries, was founded not on Attic soil but on the gold dust that Alcmeon brought out of the royal treasury of Lydia, stuffed into every hollow and crevice of his clothing and person; the families of Cimon and Miltiades and of the tyrant Peisistratus gained wealth from mining interests abroad and from useful international friendships; and the orator Demosthenes, deprived of his inheritance, which had included land, became remarkably rich by means of professional court fees and diplomatic "gifts" of one kind or another.[55] But some Athenians did own vast landed estates, and presumably grew very rich on them—not, however, in Attica, but in one or another of the allied states during the second half of the fifth century. Two of the greatest of these landowners were among the Hermocopids, Adeimantus, who had extensive interests in the vineyards of Thasos—at least 440 *plethra* according to a recent estimate, which is an awful lot of vines, considering that viable allotments of 3 to 4.5 *plethra* were given to new settlers at Black Corcyra; and Oeonias, whose holdings in various parts of Euboea fetched over eighty-one talents at the public auction of his confiscated property (where prices might have been below normal "market" values).[56]

Large fortunes rarely endured for more than a couple of generations or so. Big landholdings were likely to be dispersed by one of a variety of factors, for fluctuations in wealth were a common experience. The very rich were continually leveled down by the pressure of public obligation, litigation, manipulation of inheritances, and a tendency on the part of some men to get into debt. The challenger to Phaenippus's present immunity from the performance of liturgies says that the reason why the laws allow such challenges as his (the process of *antidosis,* to be discussed) is, quite simply, that there are fluctuations in fortunes; he must mean that these variations can only be gauged when a special investigation is carried out, such as the one he is attempting in the case of Phaenippus (Dem. 42.4).

In other parts of the Greek world, some estates were probably as big as the great overseas holdings of certain Athenians, or even larger. We do not know the size of the Sicilian tyrants' estates, but in fifth-century Acragas the private citizen Tellias was reckoned to be able to feed and clothe five hundred horsemen; his wine cellars were enormous (Diod. Sic. 13.83.1–3). Some Spartan estates had by the fourth century become very large, with the accumulation of inheritances allowed by Spartan law.[57] But the region that contained more agricultural wealth than any other was probably Thessaly, where individual holdings of land must have been vast; Menon of Pharsalus, for instance, was able to support an Athenian campaign in northern Greece not only with a large sum of money but with three hundred horses and riders from his own estate (Dem. 23.199).[58]

One of the most obvious indications of a man's wealth was given by his ability to keep horses. It was when Alcmeon brought back his Lydian loot to Athens that he could acquire a team of horses and win the chariot race at Olympia (Hdt. 6.125.3–5). Horses were very expensive; if they were pastured, they needed tracts of good grassland, which for many landowners was too valuable as grain-growing land to be spared for grazing animals. Horses were not useful, except to a limited extent in war; they were simply a glorious extravagance, and even a practical impossibility in some parts of Greece. As Telemachus says of steep-sided, narrow Ithaca, "There is no room for horses to run about in, nor any meadows at all. It is a pastureland for goats—and more attractive than the kind of land where horses thrive" (*Od.* 4.605–6). Thus the horseless comforted themselves.

Thessaly had pasture and grain to spare for horses, and this was probably one of the prime sources of both cavalry and chariot-racing horses for most of the rest of Greece.[59] Phocians and Boeotians too could raise horses, as the grant of pasture rights by the city of Orchomenus to Euboulus of Elateia suggests, for a maximum of 220 oxen and horses (and a large number of sheep and goats).[60] The breeding of horses was also possible on some Spartan estates, particularly those in Messenia; this may have been the indulgence that led to the total impoverishment of some, whereas others enlarged their estates by the acquisition of bankrupts' land and became all the more able to support racing stables.[61] One of the very few personal documents to survive from

Sparta is a long and detailed record of the many racing victories of Damonon and his son at festival race meetings all over Laconia and Messenia in the mid-fifth century: "Damonon dedicated to Athena Poliachus, having won victories in such a manner as never one of those now living. These Damonon won with his own four-horse chariot, himself the charioteer . . . and . . . seven times with colts from his own mare and his own stallion" (Schwyzer, *DGE* 12).[62] It seems that Spartan enthusiasm for horse breeding increased markedly after the Persian War, perhaps spurred by the capture of Persian cavalry chargers after Plataea.[63] Damonon boasts of rearing his own horses, and he probably devoted a large spread of land to their pasture. As Spartan women came to be great property owners in their own right too, they took up this most expensive of pastimes. The most famous of them was Cynisca, daughter of King Archidamus, who was able to enter her horses in the Olympic Games and win; she commemorated her victory with a dedication whose inscription ends, "I am Cynisca; I say I am the first woman in Greece to win this wreath" (Paus. 3.8.1, 6.1.6).

The yearning to enter a world of speed, power, and social acceptance by owning horses is mocked by Aristophanes: in the *Clouds*, Strepsiades, a "nicely comfortable countryman farmer," has married an Alcmeonid who gives their son a horsy name, Pheidippides, and encourages him to emulate the horse-owning aristocrats. This, his father says, will ruin them (*Clouds* 43–47, 60–74). Aristophanes may have had in mind his contemporary, the Alcmeonid Alcibiades, who in 416 entered seven teams at Olympia; if they were all four-horse teams, then he owned a string of at least twenty-eight animals. His estate of 300 *plethra* could perhaps have provided pasture for some of them, some of the time, but it would have produced little else. The likelihood is that he did not breed but bought them; one team we know came from Argos, and it is possible that most of Alcibiades' horses were stabled and pastured outside Attica altogether.[64] His success at Olympia demonstrates the importance of horse owning not only to the individual but to the city; he brought glory on himself and Athens by his victory, and argued this as a reason why he should be considered for the command of the great expedition to Sicily (Thuc. 6.16.2).

There were constraints set on Athenian horse owning: the Hippeis (knights who constituted the second of Solon's four property classes) owned a horse each, but usually only one, for they were not breeders of horses. Even Cimon of the rich and powerful Philaid family entered *the same team* of four mares at three successive Olympic Games; if he had been a serious horse *breeder,* he should have been able to enter other, younger horses too (Hdt. 6.103.2–3).[65] But when Phaenippus's opponent speaks of Phaenippus as a *hippotrophos* (Dem. 42.24), does he mean "breeder of horses" or merely "keeper of horses"?[66]

All but the grandest landowners who wanted to own horses were faced with a choice between giving over a lot of their land to pasture, if the horses were to graze, and using up much of it for fodder crops, if the animals were to be stabled (Ar. *Pol.* 1321 a 12). In Attica or Sparta, the choice was left to individuals. But for some communities the balance between the size of the citizen population and the land's capacity to produce food was so even that the choice could not be left to individuals. This seems to have been the case at Mantinea in Arcadia; there were strong equine associations in Mantinean cult and tradition, in particular that Samus of Mantinea had won the very first four-horse chariot race at Olympia.[67] And yet, although the terrain would have suited horses, the Mantineans are not known to have had cavalry in the Classical period, nor is there any hint that wealthy Mantineans were able to own horses for their own gratification and the enhancement of Mantinea's reputation abroad. There must have been a collective decision taken to forgo horses in favor of grain production. The small city-state of Phleius, on the other hand, where even the acropolis was planted with grain, did support a cavalry force (although no one may have owned race horses). Perhaps because Phleius was predominantly vine country, some landowners could easily afford to purchase grain for fodder from elsewhere and keep stabled horses, even if they could not pasture them.[68]

Often enough the farmer had no choice as to the use he made

of his land. Climate and geography made his decision for him. Cattle were not kept in large numbers on most estates in southern Greece because there was insufficient grazing available; dairy cattle were restricted to northern and central Greece where the land was better suited to their needs. But some cattle there always were, for plowing and for sacrifice.[69] It was not the case, as has been suggested, that Greek land use underwent a major transformation during the Dark Age from being predominantly pastoral to an arable regimen, and that the choice whether to be herders or farmers was made irrevocably then. Mixed farming to a greater or lesser degree had always been the pattern, and so it continued throughout the Greek period.[70] This generally included animals; the nature of the land as well as the pressures on its use dictated small-animal herding for most owners, just as it has ever since antiquity—sheep and goats, with mules and donkeys supplementing or substituting for draft oxen. Mixed farming ensured that "we have a little of everything," and animals were well worth the trouble of fitting them in to a narrow, predominantly arable system; they contributed something to the land's welfare, they could be nourished with less than choice grazing and vegetable waste, they provided wool, milk for cheese, meat (especially as a reserve food supply in case of a bad harvest), and skins.[71] They must also have always retained their old significance as *currency* on the hoof; if seed grain ran short, or some other vital commodity was lacking, animals could be exchanged for it and prove just as useful in the same variety of ways to their new owner. And their great value as a comparatively *durable* form of food reserve, along with their other qualities, even in an intensively arable and orchard-centered farming economy, cannot be overestimated.

The nature of the land dictated not only what animals could be kept and which were unsuitable, but also the kinds of crops to be grown, in that the competent landowner selected the crops that would do well on his land. Hence the people of Phleius, then as now, specialized in vines, as they did in the islands of Thasos, Chios, and Cos; Athenian farmers planted far more barley than wheat because it did better; Hesiod does not mention olive trees and their cultivation in the *Works and Days* because they did not prosper at Ascra. But mixed farming remained widespread, largely because much Greek farmland would support the broad range of crops found within the Mediterranean region, and because the practice accorded with the traditional concept that the household should be self-sufficient; this concept did not however negate the idea of exchange as a responsible way of filling needs, for even the most "self-sufficient" farm will have a surplus of one crop and less of another, in the nature of things and of agriculture. One need not imagine any sharp difference in thinking to have existed between the owner of a mixed farm and the man whose land was put down to one or two crops only, for each was planting what suited his land (if he was at all a competent farmer, that is), and each was prepared to exchange some of his produce, the main difference being that the man who had the specialized crop would dispose of a larger percentage of his produce in exchange for the foodstuffs he required to live on.

The proposition that after the Archaic period mixed farming tended to give way to specialization in cash crops, with concentrations of market gardening near urban concentrations as a concomitant of the "new economy," needs to be modified: there was far less change in economic thinking and agricultural practice than has been allowed in some discussions.[72] Land use in the early period did not consist of necessarily wasteful and less intensive farming practices, which changed only in response to the pressure of increasing population; what happened, rather, was not that farming methods changed on land already under cultivation but that as more families needed land to own, more land came into cultivation (by the same methods). Often it could be found within the territory of the existing community, but in some places outright economic hardship demanded that new land be sought elsewhere—Thera's misfortunes are a case in point; and in others political considerations barred the way, for the time being, to opening up the uncultivated but cultivable land on the spot. It may even be that a certain conservatism with regard to the land that had "always" been under cultivation and to those areas that had never yet seemed worth the trouble, for one reason or another, to bring under the plow prevented an easy opening up of new farmland beyond the area traditionally farmed; preparing new land for cultivation was also a hard and risk-ridden undertaking, in any case—so it might have been thought. Or the conservative attitude might have been shaped by considerations of the convenience of landowners already in long-established possession; land on which they had perhaps been used to graze their animals would be regarded as *off limits* to agricultural exploitation, and only after a few hard decisions had been taken by the community as a whole would such attitudes have given way.[73]

The land and its products constituted wealth, but more than that, they made the difference between survival and death by starvation for the major part of the population which was not engaged in alternative ways of making a living. As already suggested, the amount of land a family needed and the amount of land it could work, with a little help, were matters for careful calculation. The connection between the number of laborers needed for a farm of certain size and specified crops and the amount of maintenance they would require surely did not escape the attention of the reasonably careful landowner—or so Xenophon suggests (*Ways and Means* 4.5). Likewise the care with which estates belonging to the gods were measured and regulated reflects the prevailing concern to boost the income by obtaining the maximum from every cultivable foot of soil.[74] The instructions as to how much manure should be applied, or whether topsoil might be removed, how many trees should be planted, whether vines should be trenched, replaced, or pruned severely—all these stem from the generally pervasive idea of how things should be done in agriculture. Hence, if slave labor was employed rather than free hired workers, there must have been sound reasons for it, not just the feeling that slaves were available, or that it was fashionable to buy slaves if one could possibly afford it; nevertheless, there may well have been feckless property owners who did think along these lines, if they thought at all.

The question remains whether the ancient concept of labor use was economically sound in the modern sense, or whether labor was "chronically underemployed": Were the harvests that the land yielded worth the labor expended on them? The Greeks might have answered that the crops were essential, and that they were best obtained by certain proven methods that required a certain intensity of labor in order to be put into effect. Effectiveness, not efficiency, was the aim. The system may be said to have worked.[75]

How was land valued when it came to assessing taxes or contributions, or setting a price or rent? Presumably in much the same way as in other times and societies—partly by a businesslike consideration of the land's potential, as Socrates indicates could be the purpose of studying geometry—"to compute the yield" (Xen. *Mem.* 4.7.2); and partly by prevailing demand (if any, in the true market sense).[76] When the Spartans were trying to persuade the Plataeans to give up the struggle peacefully in 429, King Archidamus suggested that they hand over their city to the Spartans: "Show us the boundaries of your land and your trees by number, and anything else it is possible to reckon in numbers. . . . We will hold it in trust for you, seeing that the land is cultivated and paying you a regular allowance" (Thuc. 2.72.3). The Plataeans refused this offer, understandably perhaps; nevertheless it prompts certain considerations. The grainland and the orchards were presumably under as intensive cultivation as possible, according to the long-established agricultural practices familiar to all—no more trees could have been added to the stock already planted, but losses could be replaced so as to maintain the correct number.[77] The value of the land was calculable—it could be *measured* and *counted up*. What, we might ask, was in it for the Spartans? In this episode they seem to demonstrate a nose for business which usually only appears in individual attempts to amass personal fortunes unbeknownst to the authorities. But land and its management were of particular importance to all Spartans; we can assume that they would have rather relished organizing the leasing of the Plataeans' land (no doubt to surrounding Boeotians, especially Thebans), devoting most of the rent to their war chest while sending off a pittance to the Plataeans. Rents would perhaps have been established as they were for public and sacred leases elsewhere, by "sale" or auction to the highest bidder; if there was only one bid per rental, the leasing officials might have set a minimum below which the bidder could not go.[78] The value of an estate lay in its productive units—not only the number of *plethra* under the plow but the number of trees; hence the stipulation in some leases that the lessee leave as many fruit trees in the estate as there were when he took up his lease. Some landlords cared not how the trees were treated, so long as there were the right number of what would appear to be mature and productive trees in the new tenant's eyes.[79]

Could the Plataeans have put a price on their land? They would have considered not what the land was worth (to them it was beyond price), but what they could get for it. When the Samians were casting round for something profitable to do with the money they had taken from the Siphnians, they lit upon the island of Hydra and bought it from the city of Hermione for one hundred talents (Hdt. 3.58.4–59.1); the Eleans offered thirty talents for the territory of Epeum, a little place on the Arcadian border (Xen. *HG* 3.2.29–30). Were these purchase prices of large tracts of land *real,* in the sense that the parties to the sale took account of the current state of the land market locally? Was there enough of a market in land anywhere to provide such a basis for calculation? Or were they *conventional* payments, and like so many international loans asked nowadays, assessed according to what either side thinks the other will countenance? The prices paid by Samos and Elis had to be satisfactory, in that the buyer had the price in his hand and the seller accepted it as a proper recognition of the seriousness of the deal and an adequate recompense for letting the land go; but assessment of every fig tree, furrow, or pig trough may not have come into question at all. So what price did the people of Hermione agree to?—the very amount, which everyone in the western Aegean must have known quite well, that the Samians had in hand. And so the owners of Epeum calculated not what the land was worth, but what they could expect the Eleans to be willing to pay.[80]

It is possible that a base or conventional price might have been applied to the land, at a higher rate for arable and a lower one for uplands and scrub. The existence of a base price per *plethron* has been detected in some Athenian records of public sales during the later fourth century.[81] Almost all the prices are divisible by 12.5, and the explanation has been put forward that these lands were offered at a starting price of 50 drachma per *plethron* for farmland, and 12.5 drachma per *plethron* for *eschatiai* or upland not under cultivation. The evidence shows that many of the properties went to administrators of the organizations that were selling them off, which suggests an arranged sale. One or two prices, however, do not fit the pattern; perhaps they were the result of the few sales in which some competitive bidding did go on, so that the base price was surpassed.[82]

Wherever there was competition for land at public sales, then of course the base price would have become ineffective, but the use of some set figure as a conventional basis for calculation might have been adopted everywhere in assessing properties to be taxed. If such assessments turned out inaccurate and unfair, it was up to the individual to raise objections, as men assessed for liturgies at Athens were wont to do, by charging that someone else was in a much better position to be able to afford the liturgy in question. (See Phaenippus's case, discussed in the next section.)

At the other end of the scale of landowners from Aristophanes, with his large estate and his expensive house, who within four or five years was *choregos* twice and trierarch three times, besides making various other public contributions to the city, was the farming Thete who owned no slaves but who could just get by on his one-family small holding if his health held out, or if his son was old enough to take on some of the labor of working it.[83] Above him was the hoplite farmer, working his farm on a slightly grander scale, but who was not necessarily very much better off otherwise except that he could afford to employ a laborer or two. The difference between those who considered themselves rich and those who were counted as poor was in most cases very much slighter than one is accustomed to think. Xenophon puts it that the poor (*penetes*) are those who do not have enough to pay for what they want, and the rich (*plousioi*) are those who have more than enough (*Mem.* 4.2.37). There is really no middle group that has just about enough. In such a society, although the (few) very rich owned many quite unnecessary possessions or luxuries, many of those who had more than enough for their needs were only just over the divide, no doubt living about as simply as the poor, which was the only way that they could afford anything in addition to the necessities of life; many a horse owner in Athens may still have eaten exactly the same things for dinner as his poorer neighbor. The *plousioi* and the *penetes* were united at least in this, that they were better off than the needy (*endeeis*) and the indigent (*ptochoi*).

The needy and the indigent were presumably the people who had very little or no land, and no good alternative livelihood, or who failed through ineptitude or disability to make anything out of their land, just the sort, surely, whom Herodotus describes as "the needy" who were prevented by their poverty (and a lack of charity among their relatives and neighbors?) from gaining shelter on Salamis with other Athenians during the Persian invasion (8.51.2).[84] Out of this group would have come many of the hired laborers and part-time tenders of other men's crops, the sellers of wild herbs in the market, the small-time local herdsmen who worked for poor but solvent families that had no children available for such jobs—the subclass, living on the fringes of an agrarian economy. In times of famine especially they would have been joined by poor farming families, which usually got by, as they combed the wasteland and woods for edible wild plants.[85] But it is not unlikely that even in good times smallholders still needed to find supplementary food of this kind, even if they had farmed their land well and the harvest had been satisfactory; death from malnutrition was doubtless not considered very remarkable, and the proverbial greed of women, against which Hesiod warns, no doubt had its roots in the traditional meanness of the poor majority in a society which had to reckon up every piece of bread, every fig, and every olive (*WD* 373–74).[86] The old joke about the land giving a fair return—"it repays exactly what was put into it, and no more," meaning that the yield of the grain crop is very low—might make a prosperous landowner smile at the farmer's traditional disparagement of his land, but it could never have seemed very amusing to the poor, or those poorer than poor.[87]

*Social Status and Economic Attitudes*

Xenophon's Ischomachus, the main speaker and subject of his dialogue, the *Oeconomicus,* is a landowner and a *kalos k'agathos,* or what is generally defined as a "gentleman farmer." His is the most detailed portrayal of a landowner in all of Greek literature except for Hesiod's farmer in the *Works and Days,* who is drawn from life if not exactly Hesiod's own in every respect; and it purports to be the portrait of a real person, the Ischomachus living during the last part of the fifth century, who became connected by marriage to two of the best families in Athens.[88] Xenophon, who presumably knew him as an acquaintance of Socrates, presents him as a rich man, a *hippeus* or knight and therefore a horse owner, whose status laid various obligations of public expense on him, the owner of land and field slaves as well as a residence in Athens; he has so arranged the management of his affairs that he can spend much of his time on public business in the city, as all citizens who could do so were expected to do. The Ischomachus of the dialogue is an idealized or stylized character; the question is, How far Xenophon has taken his stylization from real life, either as to the facts or the circumstances of Ischomachus's experiences, or as to the kind of interests he represents in the *Oeconomicus?* Xenophon clearly has several axes to grind, among them the art of dialectic as displayed by himself, agriculture as an illustration of the proposition that knowledge is innate, and the principles of royal government on the Persian imperial model, but he must also have intended Ischomachus to be *lifelike*—the ideal landowner, yes, but not so removed from the range of interest of his public as to make the argument at either the agricultural or the philosophical level unconvincing.[89]

Ischomachus, the good manager of his household and his estate, takes a close interest in the work being done there; this is the intelligent and proper course for all landowners, in order to ensure as good harvests as possible and to preserve or even enhance the value of the property. He visits daily, relishing the exercise as well as the interest of seeing how things are coming along, and he keeps in close touch with the bailiff who now runs the farm for him, a man dependent on him for all his knowledge of farming and estate management, and with the field hands, who must be made aware of his authority as well as his benevolence to those who have earned reward.[90] He has acquired his knowledge of farming from watching his father in action and then, presumably, by working the land himself; his father is said to have been an active owner of land, buying neglected or abandoned property in order to bring it back to a fully productive condition before re-selling it (*Oecon.* 20.26). Ischomachus now owns several farms but appears no longer to be so deeply involved in buying new ones to improve as his father has been (*Oecon.* 20.22); perhaps his father was not a *kalos k'agathos* and had less time for the finer things of life which Ischomachus is now able to enjoy.[91] But like his father, Ischomachus knows just what should be done in the fields, the orchards, and the vineyard.

A natural extension of the proposition that Ischomachus is a gentleman farmer is that Hesiod's farmer is his antithesis, a peasant. And yet their points of view, such as we have basis for comparing them, are not so very different, for all that Ischomachus simply rides out to see how things are on the farm, returning home to a light lunch, whereas Hesiod's farmer shares some of the work with his laborers and dressed accordingly. Both look on the land as the basis of their wealth, both employ others to work it, and both are (in differing degrees, to be sure) personally concerned with the operation of the farm. They are united by more than what separates them, either socially or ideologically. They share the same practical morality, that hard work is the secret of success in agriculture—"Gods and men disapprove of that man who lives without working, like . . . the blunt-tailed drones. . . . Work is no reproach. . . . Whatever your fortune, work is preferable, that is, if you turn your blight-witted heart from others' possessions toward work, and show concern for your livelihood as I tell you," so Hesiod admonishes his indolent brother (*WD* 303–16). For Ischomachus, "Land responds to good treatment. . . . No one persuades himself that man could live without bread; therefore if a man will not dig and knows no other profit-earning trade, he is clearly minded to live by stealing or robbery or begging"

(*Oecon.* 20.14–15). Ischomachus's father was a land speculator, and Hesiod's (here the poem is surely autobiographical) an immigrant who carved out the family property at Ascra, leaving enough property to make worthwhile farms for both his sons.

There are of course obvious differences. Hesiod's farmer belongs to a small Boeotian community of the early Archaic period, whereas Ischomachus is a citizen of Classical Athens where the quality of life might be thought to have been better in many respects. But in some ways it was much the same; and the points of view of Hesiod's farmer and Xenophon's Ischomachus were perhaps even closer than has just been suggested.

How does Xenophon's Ischomachus, wealthy, horse-owning, busy with many undertakings, a man who has delegated the care of his estate to a bailiff, compare with other landowners who can in any sense be identified in the sources as more than a name or a mere statistic? There is the man accused of rooting up a sacred olive tree on his land; he speaks first of purchasing the estate, then of letting it to tenants, and finally of farming it "myself" (Lysias 7.10–11). He is the kind of landowner whom his accuser can describe as being seen supervising the destruction of the tree, while his slaves (allegedly) did the actual digging (7.18–19). What he had done while the land was let to a tenant, there is no indication; perhaps he was in the Athenian army or navy, for this was still wartime, or was trading overseas, but he eventually decided to work this estate himself. Perhaps Ischomachus would have found some of the Bouselids congenial, Hagnias for instance, but not his cousins, Theopompus and his son Macartatus who, according to another cousin, rooted up more than one thousand trees in order to sell the stumps, even as the neighbors watched (Dem. 43.69–70). Although they must have had some help in this laborious undertaking, the picture their opponent wants to represent is that of greedy and unscrupulous men grubbing for profit with their bare hands, quite against the best interests of the estate itself. This portrayal cannot have been altogether farfetched, indeed it might have been true, and was in any case calculated to appeal to the jurors' reason as well as their prejudices. And yet these were not poor men. Among other property belonging to

Theopompus and his brother Stratocles were two estates, valued at two and two and a half talents, as well as two smaller farms, three houses, farm equipment, animals, and cash in the form of dowries and loans (Isaeus 11.41–44); they were rich, but their behavior as their opponent presents it calls to mind the pejorative use of the term *peasant,* and contrasts sharply with the manners of Xenophon's Ischomachus.

It has long been customary to refer to the less distinguished and less affluent citizen landowners, Hesiod's farmer included, as "peasant farmers," but the validity of this description is questionable.[92] The term *peasant* may denote status within a political and social system, or it may indicate attitude of mind, in particular toward wealth and the use of resources. As for the first, a peasant is someone who lives on and by the land with, at best, limited rights of ownership, who farms it by his own labor (with or without assistance), and who is under obligation in a greater or lesser degree to men of higher status within a hierarchical society of clearly distinguished gradations.[93] Greek society always included greater and lesser men, the democracies no less than the oligarchies, in the sense that some men were richer and some poorer, some possessed of a considerable following, others of no political account at all. But although there were certainly episodes in which one group exerted domination of an extortionate kind over other groups within the citizen community, for example in pre-Solonian Athens, the process by which the polis came into being involved a rejection, not an integration, of the practices they had involved. Feudalism had never existed within the Greek world, for even though there are incidental parallels to be found in some Homeric relationships, they were not institutionalized; no overlordship came to be imposed on the Greek world whereby a hierarchical society with the definite aim of creating a peasantry arose. It might be argued that oligarchies that imposed property qualifications for full citizenship created an underclass of those who belonged to the citizen community by relationship but who were debarred from full participation in decision making, and that the rule of Alexander's successors exacerbated this state of affairs by frequently discouraging democracies, so that lesser men may have fallen into dependency and indebtedness to greater and richer men. But this still does not mean that it is historically correct to call Hesiod's farmer or an Athenian *zeugite* landowner a peasant.[94]

Some Greek societies included noncitizen, dependent, or subordinated populations, such as those at Sparta or Thessaly, and they may be thought of as possessing something approximating to a peasantry in the social and political sense of the word. Even so, it is less helpful to our understanding of these groups' situation to think of them as *peasants* than to consider their particular circumstances in the communities where they existed, and the reasons for their coming to be helots, *penestai*, Killyrioi, *klarotai*, and so on.[95]

The epithet *peasant*, meaning peasantlike, to indicate an attitude of mind, may more aptly be referred to persons or groups in Greek society. In a good or neutral sense the peasant point of view is conservative, traditional, and limited in outlook economically speaking, because economic opportunities are limited; in a bad sense it is narrow, dominated by self-interest, ungenerous and grasping, boorish, and reflecting all the other qualities associated with country and village life at its nastiest. The *kaloi k'agathoi*, the "brightest and best" or upper-class citizens, were always ready to describe the less rich and less well connected of their fellow citizens as *the mass, the low, the bad, the poor, the resourceless;* but since they were members of a society in which many resources were limited, all Greeks, well born or otherwise, wealthy or impoverished, shared some peasantlike attitudes of mind. Hesiod, so often presented as the peasant poet as distinct from Homer, the spokesman for the aristocratic and heroic point of view, addresses the interests not only of the commons, the lower-class farmers, but of all heads of households who own land. For whom was the *Works and Days* composed? Its audience would have included people of a wide variety of statuses and outlooks, none of whom nevertheless would have found anything surprising or unfamiliar in the economic details of the poem, or in the moral and ethical concerns that it was Hesiod's purpose to discuss. The dimensions of the life he depicts are modest, but even if some of Hesiod's first hearers were prosperous enough not to have to dig in the manure heap themselves, so to speak, all would have found quite credible the farm establishment of a yoke of oxen and two or three hands, and have approved completely of the need he states to work steadily at tasks in their proper order, and to be careful of one's resources. No one would have denied the importance of maintaining good relations with neighbors, of avoiding debt and of not lending too generously either, of getting an heir who would inherit. Few would have quarreled with the concept that there were lucky and unlucky days for performing certain tasks, or taboos that should be observed. As for Hesiod's central theme, the quarrel with a close relation over an inheritance, this would have struck a responsive chord in most of those who heard the poem.[96]

Nothing in Hesiod's world would have seemed at all out of the way to a Homeric hero, either, except for the scale of the estate, perhaps. There is much emphasis in both the *Iliad* and the *Odyssey* on agricultural wealth of the kind that will give a man the standard of living he requires: Bellerophon's gift from the Lycians consists of "a fine orchard and plowland for him to possess" (*Il.* 6.194–95); the Aetolians promise Meleager "a vineyard and fallow grainland" (9.577–80); "a man's dearest possession" is "his family, his household and his land inheritance" (15.498). And in the great importance attached to the gifts given between heroes, and the prizes won on the battlefield and in various contests, the dividing line between the altruistic sense of honor that is catered to by the acquisition of these objects and the sheer materialism of owning valuable objects is a fine one. The whole practice of gift exchange, so vital a part of the heroic code, yet has something very practical and down-to-earth about it; when Glaucus and Diomedes exchange armor, to acknowledge their paternal guest friendship, Glaucus goes "witless," and gives golden armor for bronze—"a hundred oxen's worth for the value of nine"; *he did not get a fair exchange* (*Il.* 6.234–36). The Homeric heroes are certainly not *peasants,* but neither are they romantics detached from practical concerns; possessed of a lack of sentimentality, even a certain hardheadedness, they are not totally unpeasantlike in some of their attitudes.[97]

Touching the agricultural aspects of the *Works and Days,* Hesiod may be described as "peasant" in a good sense, a prudent man fully aware of the limitations of his resources, who believed that self-sufficiency should be the rule by which to live. Aristotle, like many others in later antiquity, refers to Hesiod in such a way as to suggest close familiarity with his poetry; he subscribes to the same belief, that "wealth in the true sense . . . is property which gives self-sufficiency for a good life" (*Pol.* 1256 b 26–40).[98] Exchange that contributes to the supply of what is necessary for the good life (not that which is made simply for the sake of accumulating unnecessary wealth) "serves only to satisfy the normal requirements of sufficiency" (1257 a 28–30). There may be more than mere distaste for seafaring in Hesiod's admonitions on trading abroad (*WD* 618–34), and it is tempting to read into them a principled disapproval of anything more than the exchange of goods for the commodities that are essential to the household's maintenance.[99] Hesiod believes in enlarging one's property in accordance with prudence and justice only, not in working hard in order to get more wealth without limit and for its own sake. Aristotle for his part views *chrematistike,* which is moneymaking by means of exchange (or trade), as the unnatural form of wealth, distinct from the supplying of needs, which is the natural form (*Pol.* 1256 b 40–1257 a 5).[100]

Xenophon's Ischomachus (Xenophon himself, in this regard?) does not perhaps subscribe to these views of economic activity, but the concern in the *Oeconomicus* is certainly less with creating more wealth than with good management, and with the proper treatment of the land to achieve agriculture's true end. The impression is given that although in his youth Ischomachus has followed his father in buying up properties to improve and sell at a profit, he is now content with the farms he has (*Oecon.* 20.24).

Ischomachus knows how to earth up vines so that drought will not debilitate them; he is aware of the value of compost; he rejoices in seeing his land well worked and the crops prospering. In these ways he differs little from Hesiod's farmer or from Trygaeus, the vineyard owner of Aristophanes' *Peace.* Trygaeus looks forward, in the midst of the Peloponnesian War, to the time when he can return home to see his dear vines and fig trees again and the tools glittering in the sun all ready for clearing out the vine rows (*Peace* 551–70), and to the pleasures of the old way of life—"the pressed figs and the fresh figs, the myrtle berries and the sweet new wine, the bed of violets near the well, the olive trees that we yearn for" (571–80). Peace is the "greatest benefit to all of us who spend our life in working the land . . . , for to the country folk you mean grits and security. And therefore all the vines and the young fig trees and all the other plants will welcome you with smiles of delight" (587–600). Aristophanes expresses in one way the value put on the land and its cultivation, and the pleasure taken in it, which Ischomachus speaks of in another: "Agriculture is such a humane, gentle art that you have but to see her and listen to her, and she at once makes you understand her. The vine climbs the nearest tree and so teaches you that she needs support. When her clusters are still tender, she spreads her leaves about them, and teaches you to shade the exposed parts from the sun's rays during that period" (*Oecon.* 19.17–19). Trygaeus is a countryman engrossed in farming, he has chosen not to let his land to someone else, put in a bailiff, or sell it and live a quite different life in the city. Ischomachus is an urban man of affairs who includes landowning and farming in his scheme of things, but who has chosen *not* to live in the country. Yet there need be no greater social or economic distance between them than between Tolstoy's Nikolai Rostov who works with his serfs on the land and his brother-in-law Pierre Bezukhov who pursues politics in the capital and leaves his serfs to work the estate.

The historical Ischomachus (Figure 2) was said to have been rich enough to leave his two sons substantial inheritances (ten talents each).[101] Furthermore, two rich men in succession sought Ischomachus's daughter in marriage—Epilycus, who was connected with the leading families at Athens, and Callias, inheritor of one of the biggest mining fortunes in Athenian history.[102] Ischomachus, like his father before him, had accumulated land and profited from improving and selling off properties. Xenophon's Ischomachus is efficient and careful, but a contemporary of the historical Ischomachus, the comic poet Cratinus, speaks of him as "mean";[103] perhaps he did continue to deal in property, not (as

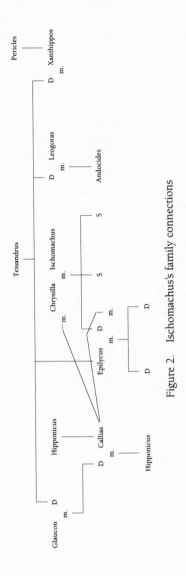

Figure 2. Ischomachus's family connections

Xenophon seems to suggest) being satisfied with the gains of his youth, and by dint of carefully arranged sales was able, for example, to conceal the full extent of his wealth when assessments were being made, thus avoiding some of the public expenses for which he was strictly liable and so calling down on himself the accusation of meanness. His marriage to Chrysilla—her name is only known from Andocides' speech against Callias—would appear from Xenophon's account to have accorded entirely with the Athenian ideal, the older husband successfully educating the young wife in the ways of good conduct and seemly housekeeping (*Oecon.* 7.4–10.13). The impression we gain of Chrysilla in later life is rather different; Andocides alleges that she became the mistress of her own son-in-law Callias, some time after Ischomachus's death, and eventually supplanted her daughter as Callias's third wife (1.124).

Andocides had strong personal reasons for wanting to put the worst interpretation on everyone connected with Callias, for among other things he had been a rival of Callias's son (by his first marriage) for one of Ischomachus's granddaughters (a child of Epilycus). But whatever the rights and wrongs of the situation, and however exaggerated the account of Ischomachus's daughter's despair and flight while her mother was in the house, it may be that Xenophon was moved to make a defense of Ischomachus's memory against the taint of scandal attaching to his widow's subsequent alliance, and so he portrayed Chrysilla as having had an ideally dutiful first marriage in the *Oeconomicus*.

If *property* had not been in the picture, Callias would hardly have become involved first with Ischomachus's daughter and then with his widow. The tendency of wealth to attract wealth presumably played some part, as usual where marriage connections were concerned. Whether or not the family's mining fortune had declined badly by the end of the Peloponnesian War, it would have been entirely in accordance with accepted practice that Callias seek to improve his finances by suitable marriages. For one thing, and this was one of the points of enmity with Andocides, he claimed for his son a marriage with Ischomachus's orphaned granddaughter on the basis of kinship; Callias's first wife was a niece of the girl's father Epilycus, and so Callias's son was the son of the girl's first cousin, within the *anchisteia* and therefore eligible to marry an *epikleros,* which she now was. Andocides, however, was a first cousin, and so even more eligible; but other difficulties, including his supposed involvement in the affairs of the Hermocopid sacrilege and the pollution of the Mysteries, outweighed this consideration. Epilycus had been both well connected and well-off, so that Callias as the husband of his widow would have had the opportunity to manage the daughters' inheritances until they were married (to his son or whoever it might be); as the husband of her mother, Ischomachus's widow, he could also expect to become guardian of Ischomachus's sons if they were not yet of age, and to look after their inheritance too.[104]

Callias may have acted quite unscrupulously, with profit to his own family foremost in his mind.[105] On the other hand, his maneuvers may have been dictated, partly at least, by social custom and the intricacies of Athenian family law.[106] His ability to safeguard any land still left among the property of his wards would have depended not only on his honesty but on his competence as a landed proprietor. Silver mining, not farming, was the basis of his ancestral wealth; but the family no doubt owned land too, as did the family of Nicias, another mining magnate, although none of these owners may have taken any more active interest in their farms than they did in the working of the silver mines.[107]

As the Athenian forensic speeches make clear, greed, envy, and the natural dislike of relatives played their part in motivating many actions, claims, and counterclaims connected with property.[108] Was this especially "peasant" behavior? If it was, it was also a manifestation of human nature as it has always been, the desire to protect the interests of the immediate family coupled with sheer acquisitiveness. Then again, how often might Hesiod's farmer have been tempted to refuse a loan to a neighbor, not out of prudent regard for his own resources but from malice? If it meant that without the seed grain for the next season's sowing the neighbor would have to let go some of his land, Hesiod's farmer would "be in a position to buy up someone else's land" (*WD* 340–41), and to leave an enlarged inheritance to his heir.

From a variety of motives, property owners often went to great lengths to cheat: the state, if they were rich enough to qualify for liturgic service; and members of their own families, if they became guardians of minors or unmarried heiresses. As regards liturgies and the concealment of wealth, a certain conflict entered in; for the valuation made of a man in society's eyes depended to some extent on his possessions and what he did with them, what display he made by expending some of his surplus on conspicuous consumption, such as keeping horses. By this means he could gain social prestige and political influence, as did Alcibiades, and also Nicias, who chose to dedicate a huge bronze palm tree and a profit-bearing estate to Delian Apollo and put on a very showy choral festival in the Delian sanctuary.[109] And yet it might be to his advantage in other ways to conceal the extent of his wealth from taxmen and jealous relatives. Liability for liturgies, which might entail equipping a trireme, backing the performance of a comedy or tragedy, or going on an embassy, depended on what a man's wealth was perceived to be; cash, jewelry, gold and silver plate, ivory-inlaid furniture, textiles, and so on could easily be kept hidden or dispersed, but fields, like flocks and herds, needed a certain amount of manipulation before they would disappear when required to do so.[110] However, because the value of a farm reposed not only in its extent and the mere numbers of its component parts but also in its productivity, an owner could always make out that the last harvest had been particularly poor; for once the crops were harvested and ready to store they too could be spirited away into friendly barns or simply sold, and no one the wiser.

One way of avoiding a liturgy was to challenge someone else to take it on, under the proceeding of *antidosis* (discussed in the next section). Phaenippus was so challenged. His opponent claimed that the property consisted of two estates, each of which had been considered liturgy-worthy, and the income included a substantial grain harvest, a large vintage, and steady profits from the sale of firewood. Phaenippus, as noted previously, was also a keeper of horses. He had attempted concealment: he delayed in handing over the inventory of the property and tried to take barley and other things out of buildings that had been sealed for the purpose of checking what he actually owned; furthermore, he was claiming that there were debts outstanding against the estate and that it was mortgaged—but there were no mortgage markers to be found. Phaenippus is supposed, in turn, to have asserted that his opponent had not made out his own inventory correctly (Dem. 42).

Who would know what Phaenippus was worth? Neighbors would have been able to assess the size of the harvest he was going to get, while those who purchased produce from him would know how much they had bought and how much they paid, but even with the best record keeping possible, it was all too easy for errors or alterations to creep in, let alone the tendency for witnesses to take sides and shape their testimony accordingly.

Damages awarded in court cases, even fines imposed by the state for political offenses, could also be evaded by various means—by sales or gifts on a temporary basis to friends or relatives, which could be reversed once the moment of crisis had passed. The story of Demosthenes' inheritance shows how all this might be done, as his guardians evaded their duties and misappropriated funds, which they should have been protecting for his majority.[111] His cousin Aphobus, having omitted to marry Demosthenes' widowed mother as a guardian should, failed to restore to Demosthenes the property he had been overseeing. When the court judged against Aphobus, he first argued that whatever had been done with Demosthenes' inheritance so that it had now evaporated had accorded with the intentions of Demosthenes' father, who had wished the fortune he was leaving to be concealed, so as to avoid the payment of a debt to the state owed by Demosthenes' maternal grandfather; the grandfather Gylon had been accused of betraying an Athenian outpost in the Tauric Chersonese, but Demosthenes argued that the fine had been paid long ago. When Aphobus's argument collapsed, he proceeded to get rid of his own property, so that it could not be awarded to Demosthenes in recompense; he gave an apartment house to his brother, and his farmland to his brother-in-law Onetor, withdrawing to Megara where he settled as a tax-paying metic, against the time when he could safely return to Athens and resume ownership of his estate (Dem. 29.3).

Demosthenes then tried to get the land away from Onetor, who alleged that it had now been mortgaged as security for the dowry of Aphobus's wife, to be paid back to her family now that Aphobus was divorcing her. The divorce turned out to be a fiction, and it appeared that the whole idea had been simply to put the land out of Demosthenes' reach. Indeed, neighbors were said to have observed Aphobus himself "in possession of and cultivating the land," although it was supposed now to belong to Onetor (Dem. 30.26). And so the maneuvering went on, through yet another stage of trumped-up mortgage so as to freeze Aphobus's assets, as far as Demosthenes' ability to get at them was concerned.

These too were hardly poor men. Onetor's fortune was valued at thirty talents, so Demosthenes says, and that of his sister's first husband (Aphobus being her second husband) at ten talents, so that Aphobus himself must have had substantial means of his own, originally. Greed, extravagance, or incompetent management, perhaps succeeded by guilt for the loss of the estate, which then led to an attempted cover-up, could well have prompted these devious proceedings. The guardians of orphans with smaller inheritances than Demosthenes' (worth fourteen talents, according to his reckoning) could not cheat their wards on so grand a scale, and a poor man's heir had little to lose. Even so, a little was considerably more than nothing, and it may be that there were reduced versions of the cases involving the estate of Hagnias and Demosthenes' vanished inheritance being heard wherever judges sat, all over the Greek world.[112]

## Attachment to the Family Estate

The man who challenged Phaenippus to an *antidosis,* claiming that Phaenippus could far better afford the cost of a liturgy, did so in the expectation that if he won his claim, Phaenippus would either take on the liturgy, or *exchange properties* with him. In the latter case he would then enjoy Phaenippus's double estate and all its assets, less the cost of the liturgy, which he could now afford to undertake, while Phaenippus went away from his father's and his maternal grandfather's estates, to grapple with his challenger's less opulent property: so one interpretation of the device of *antidosis* would have it. The other interpretation prefers to see the whole proceeding as a means simply of deciding *who is the richer,* and who shall therefore take up the liturgy; the matter is never supposed and was never intended to come to an actual exchange of properties (this being a logical conclusion to which no one was expected to rush).[113]

The first interpretation requires us to assume, among other things, that an exchange of properties actually took place as a result of successful challenges. This would suggest that wealthy landowners maintained a rather cavalier attitude to their estates, regarding them purely as an economic resource, like cash reserves, slaves in workshops, or mining concessions, in accordance with a meanly calculating view of their own and their opponents' wealth, and their own duty as prosperous citizens to sustain the city's costs. There is much to be said for this view; yet the evidence for actual exchanges of property is slight. The only instance in which *antidosis* is better understood as "exchange," not "comparison," as the second interpretation would see the term, seems to have been prompted by rivalry for a slave woman (Lysias 4).[114]

In this case, apparently, only the movable property was made subject to *antidosis,* not the land itself, but it would appear that the participants were both landowners. The man (B) who initiated the process of *antidosis,* considering himself unfairly subject to a liturgy, owned a slave woman on whom the man (A), whose property he challenged, had his eye. Instead of accepting the liturgy that was adjudged to him when the *antidosis* went against him, (A) preferred to exchange properties for the sake of getting the girl. "If he made the exchange, he did it for her" (Lysias 4.2). It had proceeded so far as for the yoke of oxen, the slaves, and various other items belonging to (B), and presumably similar items belonging to (A), to have been transferred from one estate to the other, when the two men became reconciled, the goods were returned, (B) performed the liturgy after all, and they agreed to share the slave woman. Unfortunately, (A) then refused to abide by their agreement, and so there was an altercation in which (B) blacked (A)'s eye with a piece of broken pot, as a result of which (A) claimed that he had been half-murdered.

The silliness of the story strengthens the impression that few if any exchanges of property actually took place, and that the threat of having such a thing happen had originally been included purely as a safeguard against the obdurate evasion of public duty. To lose in this or any other way the very property acquired by inheritance or by one's efforts through purchase was surely regarded as a disgrace, and something to be avoided as far as possible.

Property need not have been in the family very long for it to seem a part of the ancestral heritage. Land was the means by which a new settler in an overseas foundation was able to become and remain a vital part of the community; it was the means by which the nouveaux riches like Apollodorus found themselves a place in society. Devotion to the land of one's ancestors could, however, have a very real meaning, particularly if they had been buried there. The question is whether this commonly occurred at any period.[115] Burials found in the countryside during the Dark Age and Geometric periods, removed so far as we can tell from the environs of settlements and not located in public cemeteries, suggest that it was a long-established practice; later evidence indicates that it was still subscribed to in the Classical period, but yet all the signs are that this was never a widespread practice anywhere in the Greek world.[116] The usual places of burial were the public cemeteries or along frequented roadsides. Candidates for the office of archon at Athens were asked whether they had family tombs, and if so where they were, *not* whether they were situated on family land (*Ath. Pol.* 55.3). When we hear of Aristides being buried on his estate at Phaleron (Plut. *Ar.* 1), there is no indication that his grave was included in an established family burial plot; even if it were, this would not have been *ancestral* land of any long attachment, for Aristides' deme lay elsewhere (in Alopece, not far away, as it happens). Burial sites in the countryside of Attica which include several graves may have been reserved to a single family, not to unrelated local residents, but it is impossible to tell from the present state of the evidence whether they were on private land belonging to one family or constituted small public cemeteries.

What seems certain is that no family could claim an unbroken line of connection with either an ancestral burial site, either public or private, or a particular piece of land from the Dark Age or even the early Archaic period. Family piety always remained very strong, but in every age it was directed to recent generations only.[117] The son of Teisias mentions the existence of family tombs on the land that his father bought; they are not connected with his own family but are important because their presence proves that the land the neighbor alleges is public property, onto which Teisias encroached when he built his wall, was always private land—"a place full of trees, and some tombs and other things that are to be found in most private estates" (Dem. 55.12–15).[118] No reference is made to the ownership of the tombs, and probably Teisias's son did not even know whether they belonged to the family of the previous owner, who disliked the country and had removed to Athens, or dated back to owners of the land long gone and forgotten. The only clear indication of an expressed wish to be buried on family property is the reference to Timarchus's unfortunate mother; she begged her son not to sell the property at Alopece, so that she might be buried there, but he disregarded her request (Aeschin. 1.99). Was it an unusual one, for the mid-fourth century or any other period? And what prompted it? Had the Alopece estate been in her family for many years, had she grown up there, or did she simply become attached to the location in later life?[119]

Timarchus is described as having been a gambler and a wastrel in his youth, and a neglectful landowner thereafter; the *eschatia* that he sold, to a man of trierarchic standing, had been let go to waste (Aeschin. 1.42, 98). Not for him the pleasure taken in work well done on a prospering and fruitful farm, or the homesick yearning of the country dwellers trapped in Athens by the war, as Aristophanes expresses it:

My desire is marvelously strong
to go back to the countryside.
For you (Peace) were the greatest benefit to us all,
to all of us who spent
our life in working the land, for
you alone were a help to us:
for many things came to us
in former days, in your time, that were sweet,
and without cost and to be cherished.

(Peace 585–94).

# Three

# Farming the Land

> About each procedure (of agriculture) there is the
> account that gives its reason, and the reason must
> not escape us. For the man who carries out the pro-
> cedure in ignorance of the reason, guided by habit
> and by the event, may perhaps succeed, but he does
> not *know* (just as in medicine); and complete pos-
> session of the art comes from both.
> (Theophr. *CP* 3.2.3)

*Causes of plants*

The expertise that landowners and their laborers
brought to bear on the cultivation of the land
emanated from a farming tradition continually re-
taught with each fresh transmission, and revised
as and when circumstances dictated. If the right
procedure were followed, then with good fortune—the will of the
gods and favorable weather—the fields, orchards, and vegetable
plots would bear well. In order to make the best use of the traditional precepts of farming, a good farmer must continually exercise the capacity for observing and remembering minute details of
plant behavior from one season to the next, adding his own stock
of information to what he had learned. Blind obedience to accepted practice could only go so far and might even be detrimen-
tal if standard procedures were applied without adaptation to land
acquired in a different region. But in order to achieve the desired
result there was no absolute need to find out in addition *why*

certain processes produced certain results, or even to understand *how,* that is, the nature of the link between action (plowing, manuring, weeding) and result. The experienced farmer, like the good craftsman, came to know almost instinctively what must be done in order to make his materials—the soil, the seed, the saplings, the infant vines—behave in the way he intended; and every landowner who cared about his land could say with very little hesitation what each section of his property would or would not bear, and give a reason, such as that one area was too steep-sloping for some crops, another too wet, and yet another too sour or too rich, even if he could not explain *why* one kind of soil suited some crops better than others.

The main literary sources for our knowledge of Greek agriculture and what the Greeks thought about its whys and wherefores are Xenophon's Socratic dialogue *Oeconomicus* (on household and estate management), Hesiod's *Works and Days,* and Theophrastus's two philosophical surveys, *History of Plants* (or, more accurately, *inquiry* into plants) and *Causes of Plants.* They all demonstrate both the importance and the widely prevailing habit of making close observations within the agricultural landscape. Xenophon does so in the first instance because of his concern to argue that knowledge is innate, merely needing to be brought forth in response to the right question, but that does not in any way invalidate his testimony to the popular interest in farming, or the kind of knowledge in general circulation.[1] His expert landowner Ischomachus says, for instance, that the nature of a farm's soil is best judged by examining the crops on it, and that wasteland too can reveal its potential by the wild plants growing on it to "even the novice who has no experience of farming"; Socrates, representing the complete layman, is able to reply that "fishermen, though their business is on the sea, and they do not stop their boat or slow down to take a look, nevertheless do not hesitate to say which land is good and which bad, when they see the crops as they sail past. . . . And . . . they generally agree very closely with the experienced farmers" (*Oecon.* 16.4–7). Further on, Socrates admits to having heard about fallow land and the preparation it requires before being sown, and has actually observed the hand sowing of grain (16.10–15, 17.7). When Ischomachus asks him if he can distinguish between wet and dry ground by using his eyes, Socrates offers the obvious contrast between the dry land about Mount Lycabettus and the coastal area of Phalerum; he can also state with assurance that the hole for a new tree should be dug deeper in dry than in wet ground (*Oecon.* 19.6–7). Ischomachus points out that the correct way to plant olive trees can easily be seen along the roadsides, to which Socrates replies that "of course there is nothing in what you have said that I don't know" (19.13–14).

Xenophon is making a philosophical point here, but it is a practical one as well. The precisely observed countryside appears here and there throughout Greek literature from Homer to Theocritus in such a way as to suggest that it has not become an artificial and conventionalized landscape but always remains very close to the real thing. Various Homeric similes depend for their effect on arousing a response in the audience by recalling farmers' and herdsmen's experiences—the death of Euphorbus at the hands of Menelaus is compared for its tragic impact with the disappointment of "a gardener (selecting) an olive shoot and planting it in a place of its own where it can take up plenty of moisture: it grows into a fine young tree swayed by every breeze, and bursts into white blossom. But a gusty wind blows up one day, uproots it from its hole, and stretches it on the ground" (*Il.* 17.53–58). Aristophanes surely draws on a quite extensive familiarity with wild birds for the details he includes of nomenclature and behavior—the *Birds* are not merely cartoon creatures but are also meant to impress the point of the play by means of their heightened realism.[2] Theognis's shriek of agony at the memory of his lost land is prompted by "the fall bird's shrill alarm . . . that call which bids the farmer plow his fields. My heart was shattered by the crying bird; my fertile pastures lie in other hands" (*Elegies* 1197–1202). For all his other preoccupations, the poet is tied by unbreakable bonds to the natural rhythms of the farming year. In Hesiod's case, of course, agriculture constitutes a major theme of the *Works and Days,* and the natural world is discussed in practical and graphic terms, with perceptions that foreshadow those of the Ionian philosophers: it is time, he says, for men to sail in spring "as soon as the size of the crow's foot is matched by the aspect of the leaves on the fig branch" (*WD* 678–81). Or again,

> The morning is cold when the north wind comes down. In the morning, from the starry sky to the earth, a mist extends over the wheat fields of the fortunate; it draws from the ever-flowing rivers, rises high above the earth on the wind squall, and sometimes rains toward evening as the Thracian northerly scurries the clouds on in dense tumult. (*WD* 547–53)

This is not mere romantic admiration of the grandeur of nature, but the observation of an all-too-real world, the natural environment in which the farmer had to work with, and often against, the elements.

Taking note of the seasonal indications that it is now time to perform prescribed tasks is the beginning of successful farming. Xenophon's Socrates would doubtless have agreed, while pointing out that no secret skill is required to master this technique. Did Xenophon have in mind not only the inherited or traditional knowledge of farming, handed down by word of mouth and example, but also the treatises of experts who dealt with the problems of land management? There can be no doubt that there were works of this kind, and not only because of what Aristophanes has to say about such publications: in the *Frogs,* Euripides says that "the public has learned from me how to think, how to run its households, to ask, 'Why is this so? What do we mean by that,'" to which Dionysus replies, "That's right; whenever an Athenian comes home nowadays, he shouts at the slaves and starts asking, 'Why is the flour jar not in its proper place? What do you mean by biting off the head of this fish?'" (971–85). Aristophanes seems to be parodying, and Xenophon echoing (if not also mildly mocking, in the *Oeconomicus*) very much this kind of treatise.[3]

In his poem Hesiod alludes to many aspects of farming and often in some detail: he clearly possesses all the practical information that the composer of a manual for landowners would have required, but this is not his purpose. The subject of the *Works and*

*Days* is, rather, the proper ordering of social and economic relationships, part, but only part, of which entails being a responsible
farmer.[4] If this poem were intended solely as a cereal grower's
companion, the information it provides is curiously incomplete or
at best allusive; the fallow land is, he says, to be plowed at least
three times (as was generally agreed), but we are not told what
other preparation it requires, such as being dug over or fertilized.
He makes no recommendations as to what size a viable estate
should be, the quantity of seed grain that should be sown in this
or that type of soil, or the variety of crops that a self-sufficient
household should cultivate. Viticulture is mentioned but only in
passing, as is the keeping of livestock.[5] And when he discusses the
construction of carts and plows, he simply evokes their wholes by
alluding to some of their parts—the "three-span wheel" of the
"ten-palm cart," or the "plow-tree . . . of holm-oak, for that is the
firmest for plowing with oxen" (*WD* 426–29). His hearers knew
exactly what he meant, for the agricultural context of these structures was one with which they were all familiar.

For Hesiod the causes of plants reside in the farmer's performing the right task at the proper time, in cooperating diligently with
the divinely ordered cycle of the seasons. In order that his efforts
not be wasted, he must know *what* to do and *when* to do it. But
can the conscious and physical encouragement of plants to produce food be considered a skill or *techne* in the same sense as the
craft of the sculptor, silversmith, or potter? Agriculture, like warfare, was an activity in which very few men could avoid taking
part, one way or another, and Xenophon certainly sets out to show
that it is indeed of a different order from *techne*: far from being a
question of arcane processes handed on within a closed circle during years of training in which the apprentice is initiated into the
craft's mysteries, agriculture is accessible to all.[6] "It is not *knowledge* or *want of knowledge* which causes one farmer to do well while
another is poor," it is "because he takes no trouble" to do what he
knows should be done (*Oecon.* 20.2–3). He surely forces the argument, however; for there is a considerable difference between
being aware of the need to let land lie fallow, of when to plow
and how to sow, and actually making use of one's knowledge. In

fact he himself has a great deal to say about how the landowner first gains experience by watching and doing, and then is able to transmit his knowledge to the slave whom he has selected to be his bailiff, who in turn instructs the other workers under him (12–14).[7] Just as in any craft, so in farming the best results are achieved by applying the right method and steady effort. So says Hesiod, "A man of ineffectual labor, a postponer, does not fill his granary; it is application that promotes your cultivation" (*WD* 411–12).

Theophrastus sees the cultivation of plants as both a natural process and an intervention in it; nature tries to achieve what is best, and

> what proceeds from husbandry does this too . . . the nature of the plant is fulfilled when it obtains through *techne* what it happens to lack—the right food, the removal of impediments and hindrances, all of which are provided by the regions appropriate to a given plant, regions where we assert that the nature of plants should be studied.

The region gives external help, whereas *georgia* (cultivation) stirs things up within the plant, so that if the nature of the plant requires the external modifiers, "it would accept also those internal modifiers as appropriate to itself" (*CP* 1.16.11–12). His approach to agriculture is clearly of a different order from Xenophon's.[8] He stands in the direct line of inquiry into the nature and origin of things in which *precise observation* of the natural world, as exemplified by the meteorological similes of Homer or Hesiod's description of a winter rainstorm, opened the way to speculation as to the *reasons* for the phenomena, and eventually to the scientific classifications (demonstrated in his biological works) of Aristotle, who was Theophrastus's teacher.[9]

The distinction between pure and applied science cannot be drawn very exactly in the case of many of the authorities whom Theophrastus quotes and on whom he based much of his own thought; for like Theophrastus himself, though they may not all of them have had the practical concerns of the agriculturalist foremost in mind, they took their material from the natural world and from field, orchard, and garden. How far the objective analysis of plant physiology and speculation on the origin of things appealed to landowning members of the general public, we can only guess; Anaxagoras's statement, that "the air contains the seeds of all things, and these carried down by the rain, produce the plants" (*HP* 3.1.4), may have seemed eminently reasonable to many thoughtful men, even if it was of no particular help to a farmer considering the layout of a new orchard. But surely Diogenes' hypothesis that plants come into being "when water decomposes in some way with earth" (*HP* 3.1.4) could have accorded well with the watchful agriculturalist's observation of wet farmland after planting. The inevitable overlap of theoretical with practical concerns in the consideration of the causes of plants appears in Theophrastus's quotations from Cleidemus, who supposed that "plants are made of the same elements as animals, but . . . they fall short of being animals in proportion as their composition is less pure and as they are colder" (*HP* 3.1.4), and also included in his writings some consideration of when to sow and what the condition of the soil about to be planted should be: sowing at the winter solstice he thought was risky, for the soil is damp and apt to become lumpy "like badly carded wool" (*CP* 3.23.2).

Democritus the atomist (with whose theories on the growth of trees both Aristotle and Theophrastus disagreed—*CP* 2.11.7) also wrote a study of agriculture (or land measurement, it is not clear which—Diog. Laert. 9.48). And Empedocles, to whose views as a vegetable behaviorist Theophrastus refers several times—for instance, "the tall trees lay their eggs" (*CP* 1.7.1)—included among his various achievements of a practical kind a method of controlling wind damage to crops which required bags made of donkey skin to be distributed about the countryside (Diog. Laert. 8.60). Leophanes and Chartodras, on the other hand, are only known for their statements on practical matters: Leophanes recommends black soil "because it can withstand both rain and drought" (*CP* 2.4.12), and Chartodras lists manures in the order of decreasing pungency—human, pig, goat, sheep, cattle, horse-mule-donkey (*HP* 2.7.4). But in Androtion, who is quoted on fruit trees—although myrtle and olive like to grow together, nothing else likes to grow next to the olive (*CP* 3.10.4)—we seem to find a literary man of affairs who, like Xenophon, also took an active interest in farming.[10]

Theophrastus gives no hint that he himself ever farmed, for all his close attention to the minutiae of plant behavior under cultivation. Much of his information is attributed to anonymous sources, presumably including the farmers whom he or his assistants questioned directly; thus "they say" that monk's rhubarb may live for any length of time (*HP* 7.2.7), or that the flowering period of the bean is longer than that of vetch or chickpea (8.2.5).[11] There can be little doubt that the accounts he gives of cultivated plants in his study of plant life in general are based on real farming experiences. But his primary, indeed his only object is to describe the characteristics of plants as a whole; the importance of cereals and of their reactions to one or another circumstance for him lies not in the questions about how valuable they are as a source of food (although the answer may contribute to the overall picture of their behavior), or how they are best cultivated, but *of what nature they are and why*.

The separation between Theophrastus's concerns and those of the working farmer is apparent in the passage quoted at the beginning of this chapter, and is well exemplified in the scientific as opposed to the popular understanding of the problem why fig trees often drop their fruit before the fruit has ripened. For the farmer it was enough to know that figs could be encouraged not to do this by having wild figs with galls on them planted nearby, or by attaching galls taken from wild trees to the branches of the cultivated fig early in the fruiting cycle; this is the process known as caprification. The ostensible reason why wild figs did not drop their fruit before they were ripe was that gall wasps from inside the galls penetrated the fruit and benefited it in some way; Herodotus in the mid-fifth century understood the matter thus: when the fruit of the male fig (the gall) was attached to the female tree, the gall wasps in the fruit of the male fig entered the fruit of female fig, somehow preventing it from detaching itself from the tree (1.193.4–5).[12] Theophrastus's view in the later fourth century was that the wasp, which was *engendered* from the seeds of the male gall, got into the female fruit and *drained and ventilated* it, thus allowing it to ripen properly (*HP* 2.8.1–3, *CP* 2.9.5–6). The fact that it was the wasp's pollination of the cultivated fig which allowed the flower to set and the fruit to mature was not fully recognized until well after the end of antiquity.[13] That the matter was quite widely and earnestly discussed Aristophanes suggests by his echoing and mocking the controversy in the *Birds*: the thrushes will eat up the enemies of the fig, among which he includes not only the *knips* but the gall wasp too, before they eat up the fruit (588–91). He deliberately muddles things, for neither insect actually consumes the fruit, but it is the *knips* that kills the gall wasp, on whose agency the fig depends for its development.[14]

Theophrastus subscribed to other theories that were erroneous, such as that wheat and barley could deteriorate into darnel (*CP* 4.1.7, *HP* 8.7.1). But when he relates instances of what we would consider irrational or superstitious beliefs current within the farming community of his time, it is probably safe to say that he puts little credence in them and includes them perhaps for their anthropological interest, or to point a contrast with his own analysis of cause and effects. Thus the common belief was that the herb cumin would grow better if the sower cursed the seed as he planted it (*HP* 7.3.2–3), and that the ill effects of salty sea mists on flowering olive trees, such as were experienced at Taras, would be mitigated if diviners offered sacrifice (*CP* 2.7.5). The ordinary farmer combined the practical and the irrational, seeing no need to make any formal distinction; the rational perception that cereals must be cultivated by certain methods in order to stand a chance of producing good harvests did not necessarily rule out the belief that the gods were ultimately responsible for the creation of barley, wheat, and other edible plants, or that magic practice or religious ritual would assist the process or at least not hinder it in any way. "Avoid the thirteenth of the standing moon for beginning sowing," so Hesiod advises (*WD* 780–81); a one day's delay could have done no harm. Hard work at the appropriate times should be supplemented by ritual observance and prayer—"Naked sow and naked drive the oxen and naked reap, if you want to bring in Demeter's works all in good season" (*WD* 391–93), and "Pray to Zeus of the earth and pure Demeter for Demeter's holy grain to ripen heavy. . . . Good order is best for mortal men and bad order is worst" (465–66).

## Farming in Its Setting

> The Aetolian elders promised Meleager that he could
> choose an estate of fifty *gyai* for his own use, half
> vineland and half open plowland, to be carved out
> of the richest part of the Calydonian plain.
> (*Il.* 9.577–80)

Theophrastus and Xenophon argue that location and climate are the two determining factors in a plant's development, and that the farmer's function is to help each cultivated plant to pursue its natural course. The Mediterranean region includes most of what made up the Greek world in antiquity; its soils, climate, and latitudes have always made possible the cultivation of barley, wheat, vines, pulses, and olive, fig, pear, and other fruit trees, and the grazing of sheep and goats, all of which constitute the staples of the Mediterranean diet, ancient and modern. All tolerate the combination of wet winters and hot dry summers with a largely limestone-based soil, while the geography and geology of the area usually provide a variety of terrains within short distances of one another—from low-lying coastal plain and fertile or comparatively well watered valley land to inland plateaus and uplands that are suitable for some fruit trees and cereal cultivation or offer at least woodland and hill pasture conveniently close at hand.[15] Cultivation generally does not extend very far above the valley floor or the plain, for the mountains tend to rise rocky and abrupt from them, but farmers have always succeeded in creating pockets of land on hillsides by means of terracing if the need for land warranted it. Other techniques for remedying the inadequacies of the land included draining marshy areas so as to bring them into cultivation or to make them accessible to grazing cattle, and irrigating sections of the farm too dry for the crops intended; a commoner alternative to irrigation was to dry-farm, that is, to treat the soil in certain ways so as to preserve as far as possible throughout the growing season the moisture that the winter rains bestowed.[16]

Some plants do better in one area than another. The range of olive trees, for example, is restricted to fairly low-lying places and southerly latitudes; so it is that of the estates belonging to Delian Apollo the only one that included olive trees was located on Myconos, which happens to include the only location in all three islands, of Delos, Rhenea, and Myconos itself, where olives have been cultivated in modern times.[17] And thyme, a herb sought out for export in Attica, will only grow in regions where sea breezes penetrate, so that it was unknown in Arcadia (Theophr. *HP* 6.2.4). But mixed farming remained as far as possible the general rule in antiquity, which enabled men to be self-sufficient (in principle at least) by providing them with a wide range of the foodstuffs they required to live on; it was made feasible by the small-scale variations occurring within the territory of almost all communities, if not each individual estate. Some regions by the Classical period had become more specialized: the plains of Thessaly were devoted largely to grain, the islands of Thasos, Chios, and Cos to vines, as much because vines did well there as because in these places the landowners or the community had decided for *other* reasons to specialize in this type of cultivation rather than another. Even so, mixed farming can never have been completely set aside. In Elis, flax was an important crop, but there seems to be no question that Elis ever became anything remotely resembling a one-crop region. It is possible, however, that mixed farming was maintained in areas where the better policy would have been to specialize more, and that what had become *customary* militated against what would have conformed to sound *economic* farming principles as they might be formulated today.[18]

The way in which Greek farms were laid out must in many areas have resembled that of a dense patchwork, each subdivided by its plantings of vines, its rows of trees, its grain and bean fields and gardens. It would have appeared that, when the seasonal plowing and sowing of grain had to be done, the whole valley or plain was being worked as a continuous unit, the plowland of one farm running alongside part of the arable belonging to the neighboring estates, the farmers each with their draft animals working the land to and fro. If the plowing scene on Achilles' shield

(*Il.* 18.541–49) seems more appropriately related to the large-scale grain production of Thessaly than to the little fields of Athenian or Peloponnesian estates, nevertheless it was repeated in every small section of farmland. Thus the fatal quarrel between the brothers Thoudippus and Euthycrates was witnessed by "many Araphenians [fellow demesmen] who were working their land at the time," each visible to his neighbor (Isaeus 9.17–18).

Cultivation extended from the plains and the valley floors into the *eschatiai,* the "more remote" regions round about and above the old-established farmlands. These hillsides, once cleared of scrub and stone, could provide a basis for crops with the aid of terrace walls built from the stones that had been cleared off the land to make it workable in the first place. Landowners must often have found it useful to take in even uncultivable woodland and scrub-covered hillside, which could provide firewood, range for bees, and grazing for animals, not to mention the chance of game to supplement the frequently meatless table.[19] Estates in this sort of country would have been quite irregular in outline, their boundaries determined by the vagaries of the landscape in which they lay, as the so-called Table of Halaesa suggests. This survey describes, with some difficulty, the boundaries of a group of estates in northwestern Sicily, which lay as it appears in very uneven territory; numerous landmarks are mentioned, so that assuming that the boundary turned slightly at each point described, the properties can in no sense have been rectangular:

> [Estate] A. From the Halaesus stream up to the boundary marker on the rock, by the ?feeding troughs [or tombs], and along the wooded ridge up to the rock on which is a marker, and to the road, and along the road to the rivulet, and along the rivulet to the ditch below the marker, and then beyond the ditch from the marker toward the threshing floor, and beyond the threshing floor along the ditch up to the olive tree, and beyond the olive tree along the path and ditches to the olive tree marked "of the city of the Halaesans," and from that olive tree to the ditch, and then to the prickly shrubs round the boundary marker, and along the ditch to the marker on the stone, and the boundary marker below the threshing floor [?mentioned above?],

and to the marker on the tower, and from the tower down to the rivulet below the hill spur at [?by, ?above] the tower, and down the rivulet
to the Halaesus stream, and along the Halaesus stream to the beginning of the "enboundariment" [*perioresia*]. This contained the property [or lease] of Agrias.[20]

Phaenippus's double inheritance somewhere in the *eschatiai* of Attica (see chapters 1 and 2) produced a considerable amount of
grain requiring two large threshing floors; it also included woodland and vineyards.[21] As a way of indicating that his estate was
extraordinarily large, so that he could and should have under-
taken large public expenses, rather than give its area Phaenippus's
opponent merely states the length of its boundaries, 40 stades or
nearly 7.5 kilometers; if they had run smoothly round a regularly
shaped plot, the estate might have measured 3,000 to 4,000
*plethra,* ten times the size of the largest estates heard of otherwise
in Attica. But if the estate took in the kind of terrain suggested by
the Halaesa record, its boundary might have made innumerable
turns and jogs round an area not much over 600 *plethra* in
extent.[22]

The geography of Greece being what it is, there must have been
many such estates. But the preference was for *rectangular* plots,
and not only where they might most easily have been laid out, in
flat or evenly sloping terrain unbroken by roads or watercourses.
The way in which the sales lists of the Athenian *poletai* describe
properties suggests that they were generally thought of as more or
less rectangular, implying that they generally were so indeed; they
are defined by the neighboring features of estates lying north,
south, east, and west, just as Plato is supposed to have described
his estates in his will:

> The estate in Iphistiadae, bounded on the north by the road from the
> temple at Cephisia, on the south by the temple of Heracles in Iphistia-
> dae, on the east by the property of Archestratus of Phrearrhion, and
> on the west by the property of Philippus of Cholleidae . . .
>
> The estate I bought in Eiresiadae from Callimachus—bounded on
> the north by the property of Eurymedon of Myrrhinous, on the east
> by the property of Eurymedon of Myrrhinous, on the south by the

property of Demostratus of Xypete, and on the west by the river Ce-
phisus. (Diog. Laert. 3.41–42)[23]

Rectangular plots made life much simpler for everyone involved, not least the organizers of new settlements and the administrators of public and sacred estates. The boundary surveyors of
the estates of Dionysus at Heraclea in southern Italy had a comparatively easy task for this reason:

> We measured together, beginning from the boundary road above Pan-
> dosia and cutting between the sacred lands and the private property,
> as far as the boundary road making the line between the estate of
> Dionysus and the land that was owned by Coneas son of Dion. We
> cut it up into four plots—the first—as to its width: from the boundary
> road passing the Herodian property toward the thirty-foot [road] go-
> ing across the sacred lands, and in length—from the springs down to
> the river Aciris. And there were measured in this section 201 *schoinoi*
> of plowland, and of scrub and unplowed land and woodland, 646.5
> *schoinoi*.[24]

This land did not, then, consist of level arable alone. But if these
estates were four-sided, were they truly rectangular or only approximately so? The fact that the unit of areal measure used here
was rectangular, 100 by 120 feet, and the one most commonly
used elsewhere was the 100-foot square *plethron* (10,000 square
feet) does not of itself indicate a preference for overall rectangu-
larity, but the archaeological evidence does.[25] For while the fact
that ancient terracing on the lower slopes of Mount Hymettus in
southwest Attica was set in parallel lines may only mean some
regularity *within* an irregularly shaped farm, there are hints in various places of rectangular allotments and furthermore of a close
relation between the squared grid plan of the city itself and the
rectangular divisions of the land outside it.[26]

Perhaps the most striking example of the application of square
and rectangle to the layout of estates comes from Crimean Chersonesus in the Hellenistic period; there excavations have revealed
a series of large farms, several of them about 630 by 415 to 420
meters in dimension, and others 420 square meters, or 300 and
200 *plethra* respectively.[27] The larger estates seem to have been

measured out in three pairs and the smaller in two pairs of 50-*plethra* squares, a unit also employed in the layout of some city sites.[28] A square measuring 50 *plethra* can be quite simply measured out by using the method referred to in Plato's *Meno* (826–85 c), which is to take the diagonal of a 100-*plethra* square, halve it, and use that as the measurement of the side of the 50-*plethra* square—that is, a length of about 720 meters.[29] The choice of a 50-*plethra* unit must have something to do with the fact that this was the accepted norm for the basic land allotment, which ranged between 40 and 60 *plethra*.[30] But rectangular plots of various measurements would have been very easy to calculate, and probably were generally preferred to squares, not only for mathematical reasons but because many aspects of farming tended to be dealt with in strips or rectangles, not squares, such as plowing, vineyard terraces, and rows of vines and vegetables; and irregularities in the lie of the land could have been more easily compensated for by adding onto the short end of a rectangle than by trying to expand a square.

The need to adjust dimensions so as to allow for physical variations in the land, and for making allotments as equal as possible may be part of the reason why land was measured in such small units as the *plethron* and the *schoinos*. The modest scale and intensive nature of much Greek farming may explain the rest. A larger unit was also known, the *gyēs;* but although at Heraclea its value was 50 *schoinoi*, so that it approximated the standard family land lot, the *gyēs* figures only occasionally in the evidence for measurement of land and its dimensions elsewhere are unknown.[31] The smaller units, the *plethron* and the *schoinos*, allowed for small-scale adjustments in the overall dimensions of an estate; they also represented a useful amount of land in themselves, for much could be done with a *plethron* of vineyard or garden, and at least four olives could be planted within a *plethron* plot.[32]

It should be borne in mind that we cannot be certain when or how these measures ever became truly standardized, if ever, and that in talking of the smallest unit, the foot, we are dealing with a measure that varied from place to place, or even from one surveyor to another, depending on the length of his own foot—as in the case of architects' feet in temple and other architecture.[33] But local standards must have been enforced to some extent, otherwise arguments about areas and boundaries would have flared up with every change of owner, each claiming that his neighbor had encroached on his property. When it came to dealing with estates like Phaenippus's, where the opponent signally did *not* estimate the area but only the boundary, or the properties at Halaesa, or the sacred estates of Delian Apollo, the difficulties presented by the terrain would have meant that each section could only be measured in small units such as the *plethron,* or even subdivisions thereof. Fractions of the *plethron* and the *schoinos* are heard of, and their existence points to the value attributed to literally every square foot of land; but these fractions so far have only appeared in two sets of records. One is from Larisa in Thessaly, where the *pelethron* was subdivided into a *pelethraia,* probably a strip 10 by 100 feet, and a *kapbolaia,* a 10-foot square; both measures could have been usefully applied to plantings of vines or vegetables, and the *kapbolaia* may originally have had some connection with the rate at which a grainfield was sown.[34] The *schoinos* at Heraclea was subdivided into *paces* and *feet;* the anxiety to register every clod of earth on the estates is reflected in the measurements of the properties: one estate of Athena measured 138 *schoinoi* and 8 paces, of which 133 *schoinoi,* 26 paces, and 1 foot were planted in grain, and 4 *schoinoi,* 11 paces, and 3 feet in vines.[35]

The arrangement of the Chersonesus farms revealed by excavation suggests all the neatness of a very large kitchen garden, and this is probably what smaller Greek farms resembled even more closely, everything set out as far as possible in rectangular beds and straight rows, pruned, trained, or propped up each according to its requirements. "There is nothing, not a green thing in the whole enclosure, not a fig, olive, vine, pear, or vegetable bed that does not show signs of your care"—so says Odysseus to his father Laertes, and so it could have been said of every well-tended farm (*Od.* 24.245–47).

The neatness of the agricultural landscape would have been enhanced by the subdivisions within each plot, between one planting and another; one of the Chersonesus farms contained forty such subdivisions.[36] They were defined by the terraces and walls that held soil and moisture in and, on the outer edges of the estate, kept trespassers and voracious animals out. Field walls were simply constructed, often enough, on a lower course or two of stone with mudbrick on top. Just such a wall had Teisias built at the edge of his hill farm above Eleusis, to stop passing herdsmen taking a shortcut with their hungry charges across his land (Dem. 55.11). The lease terms of a public estate on Amorgos instructed the lessee to repair fallen walls round the vineyard and to reinforce the field walls, even to the extent of plastering them.[37]

Irregularities in the pattern of basically rectangular farm plots would have come about because of the presence of roads, wherever the lie of the land determined that they run a certain course, or wherever they had been in use since long before the farmland had extended so far. Areas prone to flood and water courses, both rivers and streams that flowed the year round and those that drained the winter torrents but dried up in the summer (like the one that lay between the farms of Teisias and Callicles), were even more important factors in determining the layout and dimensions of estates. Irrigation channels would sometimes have formed part of the divisions within a farm, and perhaps existed cross-country in certain areas; for instance, Xenophon speaks of their presence in Greek millet-growing regions (*Anab.* 2.4.13).[38]

Sometimes there were encumbrances on the land, such as family tombs, which must be respected, and to which relatives (if not of the family that now owned the land) must have access. But the evidence suggests that burial on private land was not the general practice, although no one expressed any surprise that it occurred at all, either.[39] Public or sacred trees belonging to the city or a sanctuary were also to be found on leased or privately owned land; public olive, fig, and pear trees are heard of at Halaesa, and sacred olives at Athens. Rights of way to shrines and *temena* of the gods might also have interfered with the rational arrangement and normal comings and goings of a farm, but who would have questioned their preeminence? As for fortifications and their impact on agricultural interests, fortresses in the borderlands would generally have affected only pasture, and then not very seriously, but structures such as the Long Walls between Athens and the Piraeus or Megara and Nisaea must surely have cut through some prime farmland, if they did not also disrupt the movements of grazing sheep and goats in the district.[40]

The industrial use of the land for mining also created a certain competition of interests with agriculture; but despite the existence of numerous roadways, mine entrances, smelting works, slag heaps, and the mining communities, farming continued in the Laurium district of southern Attica close to the mines themselves. The same close coexistence of mining and agriculture presumably was to be found in the heavily mined island of Thasos; but Thasian concentration on viticulture was surely due as much to the island's suitability for vines as to the fact that farmland was so reduced by the presence of many mines that landowners turned to a form of cultivation which could produce adequate profit from a small plot.[41] Quarrying on a regular basis went on in only a few places, and large-scale extraction of stone only happened occasionally; most quarries were situated in cliffs or mountainsides and did not in themselves disrupt farming, although the roadways for transport might have done so, especially if the organizers of public works were seeking the shortest or gentlest route for the carts and other stone-moving devices, and the large teams of draft animals which hauled them.[42]

Farming was impinged on by the other interests that made use of the countryside. In turn it imposed, within the pattern of its estate and field boundaries and the placing of the crops, its own structures upon the landscape—threshing floors, storage places, and farm dwellings. Threshing floors were permanent fixtures, with hardened or even pebble-paved surfaces; Phaenippus's estate included two, each measuring about a *plethron*—unless the opposition was exaggerating this aspect of his riches too, for threshing floors found in south Attica measure only twelve to eighteen meters across. Storage might include small barns for straw and hay, as at Heraclea in southern Italy (where a lessee was directed to build a house, a chaff store, a stable, and a granary), and accommodation for wild herbs gathered for winter feeding, and rooms or lofts in the farm dwellings and residences in the countryside for the dried fruits, olive oil, preserved olives, wine, grain, beans, nuts, flour, and so on.[43] The most prominent storage compartment would have been the tower built at one end or corner of the residence, which also served as the refuge for womenfolk and the most precious possessions of the household.[44]

Numerous towers now standing in isolation about the countryside have been identified as combined refuges and store places, to which field workers could run in case of pirate or other attack, and in which field crops could be laid up until needed elsewhere or sold. There are good reasons for supposing that some such purpose was the reason for their existence; the absence of evidence for other structures close to them is one.[45] But these isolated towers raise more questions than they provide answers, and it seems better to suppose that some were built strictly as defensive or lookout towers, and that others are *the only surviving element* of a regular farmhouse complex and were not originally intended to serve as isolated tall barns. Their use as safe havens for the rural population would have been limited, except in the face of the most transient threats or preoccupied invading forces. Among the various problems they raise is the fact that the dating of many of these "agricultural" towers can only be very approximate; another is that, although such towers have been found on many of the islands, they are not reported in any number from Chios, Samos, or Lesbos, or on the mainland apart from Attica, the Argolid, and one or two other places—and this cannot be due entirely to the accident of survival.[46] Records of property purchase on the island of Tenos mention a tower shared by several owners; it and others among the properties sold are listed in close conjunction with houses, so that they may actually have been within the farmhouse complex, not standing away in the countryside somewhere.[47] If storage towers were within the farmyard, they would surely have been much more secure than if they had been off on their own, where anyone with determination and a ladder or a crowbar could have broken in, however sound the lock.

The question of security brings up once more the question how densely the farming countryside was inhabited. Some landowners had land in several lots, often at some little distance one from another. How were they to keep an eye on their interests, since they themselves could at best reside on only one of them at a time? They either let to tenants, who resided on or close to their tenancy or had slaves do so, or depended on bailiffs with slaves, who resided on the land; for there was no better security than the constant presence of persons *in residence,* along with a guard dog or two, like the ones kept by Eumaeus which rush at Odysseus as he approaches the farmyard (*Od.* 14.21–34). The safeguards the Athenian general Epichares provided for farmers during the Chremonidean War included watchdogs.[48]

It has often been argued that split holdings were preferred because advantage could thus be taken of the great local variations in weather: a crop that did disastrously in one region might entirely escape damage in another.[49] But even if Apollodorus owned properties in three demes, they were not necessarily very far apart; Plato's will shows that in his case the two estates he owned lay in demes that were both on the north side of Athens toward Cephisia, and one of his neighbors owned land on two sides of one of Plato's estates—two separate plots perhaps. Consolidation of property for convenience may have been as big a concern as diminishing risk by dispersing one's holdings.[50] Modern Greek experience suggests that fragmented holdings within a restricted area can be advantageous, because it allows maximum diversity of crops grown in the locations best suited to them—a few nut trees here, olive trees there, vines and grain somewhere else again. There is evidence for something of the sort in antiquity, in that small allotments of vineyard were made to new settlers at Black Corcyra, as part of their total land grant, the rest of which was elsewhere, and the leases of land belonging to Athena at Heraclea in southern Italy included sections of vineyard in one location and arable land in another. But if the dispersal of holdings went further than that, there is no evidence of it (that springs easily to mind, anyway). Perhaps it was a strong prejudice in favor of consolidated holdings which Theophrastus is arguing against, when he emphasizes the importance of locating plants according to what suits their nature best, instead of forcing them to grow in an alien environment.

*Plowing and Planting*

> Hither let all my feathered fellows come!
> All who dwell in the country plowlands
> rich in seed, the myriad tribes of barleycorn eaters
> and the races of seed gatherers
> that fly swiftly and utter soft notes,
> and all who in the furrows often
> gently twitter over the turned soil
> with joyful voices.
> (Aristoph. *Birds* 229–36)

> Hunger goes always with a work-shy man. . . . You
> should embrace work tasks in their due order, so
> that your granaries may be full of substance in its
> season.
> (WD 302–7)

There was a right way of farming which would achieve the desired results: so every good farmer understood. But as with all "right ways," there was some disagreement as to whose way was best. This continual debate is what lies at the heart of the experiences on which Theophrastus bases his analysis of plants; it is what made Greek agriculture at its best a dynamic activity that reached its full potential, not (what many scholars' perception has been) a static and inadequate response to a constant crisis of food shortage exacerbated by misuse of the land which was in any case unforgivingly poor.[51] The following discussion attempts a survey of agricultural crops and techniques together with other land use, bearing these propositions in mind: that the traditional practices of Greek farming already existed well within the Dark Age (to go no farther back) and that there was no major shift in emphasis from predominantly pastoral to arable interests; that no great changes took place during the historical period in either methods or the kind of crops grown, which does not point inevitably to the conclusion that Greek agriculture was a failure; and that decisions whether to stay with mixed farming or to specialize in one or two crops only, or to use the land in another way, might be taken at any period, depending on regional characteristics as much as on any other factor.[52] This does not mean that there were no additions to the traditional repertoire of crops but simply that the alterations that occurred were fitted into the age-old pattern of gradual accretion and gradual adaptation, as new elements entered into the farmer's calculations and as contacts with different cultures brought unfamiliar plants and variant methods to his attention.[53] At the same time, reference to the kind of work and the degree of effort required provides the context in which working landowners and laborers cooperated (or not, as the case might be), and suggests the discipline and organization required to keep the land under cultivation.[54]

Theophrastus argues repeatedly that the farmer's art consists in going along with nature, not in introducing conditions alien to the plant's natural tendencies and environment. Enhancement, not alteration, of the vegetable processes is the secret of good agriculture; thus innovation must as far as possible emerge from the familiar. Farming's great achievement had been the domestication of wild plants so that they gave more edible and abundant food; one of the farmer's constant worries was that plants would lose their domesticated nature and degenerate into their former wild state or worse.[55]

The first step in combating the wild tendencies of plants is to prepare the soil for planting. If superfluous stones have not already been removed, then the farmer must clear his fields, remembering that it is often beneficial to leave some stones in the ground to provide protection for the roots against heat and cold, and to drain the soil if required. A man who had learned his farming at Corinth removed all the stones, as he had done there, when he came to farm at Syracuse, "and ruined an estate of good repute . . . for the grain froze when the removal of stones left it without protection from the cold" (*CP* 3.20.5). Whatever the nature of the soil, it requires replenishment between crops; the standard practice as Hesiod, Xenophon, and Theophrastus see it is to let grainland lie fallow for a year and to keep it well turned over and free of other growth. Three plowings, in spring, summer, and autumn, with some supplementary digging, are usually recommended, but Theophrastus suggests that different soils require different treatments—poor, dry soil should be cultivated during the winter as well. Soils should also be mixed with their opposite, and so "every four or five years the Megarians spade deep, and turn up bottom soil as far down as the rain reaches, to renew the soil, since the nutritious part is constantly carried down by the water" (*CP* 3.20.3–4). Working the soil with a mattock is better than plowing alone, some think, because the plow "omits a great deal." So it is that the Thessalians use a tool more effective still, the *mischos,* which digs even deeper (*CP* 3.20.8). Some land is very heavy and requires drainage—by the digging of trenches and the mixing in of stones.

Together with tillage and drainage, the application of manure (*kopros*) is advised: "Everyone will say that there is nothing so good as manure in agriculture" (Xen. *Oecon.* 20.10). It is on this question in particular that Greek agriculture has been found especially inadequate; the difficulty has been perceived to be that there was too little land to spare for pasture, and hence there were not enough beasts to furnish sufficient manure for the arable.[56] Yet clearly farmers had been aware of the value of manure since the beginning of settled agriculture and the use of domestic animals, and were no less so in the Greek period.[57] When Odysseus first comes to the palace in Ithaca on his return, he finds his old dog Argos lying on the manure heap outside the palace door, the contents of which Odysseus's slaves will spread on the fields (*Od.* 17.296–99). *Kopros* may mean several things; here it is presumably stable manure from the stalls of mules and plow oxen, including a quantity of straw. The availability of this kind of manure is not denied by critics of the Greeks' fertilizing program. But was either quality or quantity adequate? Most farms had a stalled animal or two at least, an ox, mule, donkey, or even a pig; many farms had a *yoke* of draft animals and other beasts. In mourning the loss of his oxen to Boeotian raiders, Dercetes says, "Those oxen had always kept me in the manure to which I was used" (Aristoph. *Ach.* 1022–26). We are not told the source or nature of the manure that the lessee of a sacred estate on Amorgos was obliged to bring in before the end of his lease—150 baskets, each holding one *medimnos* and four *hemiekta exactly* (!)—and measure in the presence of the official in charge.[58] The alternatives are stable manure, "green manure" (compost), or dung. By "green manure" was usually meant the weeds plowed under in spring to prevent them from robbing the fallow of moisture and nourishment, and from competing the next season with the growing crop; but the practice of gathering up weeds and other excess vegetable matter for what we usually understand by compost is mentioned approvingly by Xenophon, although "some do not take the trouble to do this" (*Oecon.* 20.10–11). Dung, unmixed with stable straw, would have been difficult to collect as much of it would have been scattered wherever animals were grazing, but the pigsties, sheep and goat pens, and cattle feedlots (where these were in operation) might have proved good sources for other estates too, at a price. The regulations posted for the conduct of animals pasturing on sanctuary land at Tegea provide for the sale of *kopros,* and the *koprologoi* of Athens may also have made deals with local farmers.[59] The use of baskets for this (as for many other commodities) is reinforced by Xenophon's Socratic question, "Is a dung-basket beautiful, then? Yes, if it is well made for its purpose" (*Mem.* 3.8.6).

Chartodras's list includes human dung, and other references show that this too was commonly used on the land in gardens especially;[60] the *kopros* that the *koprologoi* had to take to dumps at least ten stades distant from the city (about one and a half kilometers) must have included household waste, which would then have been included in their transactions with landowners. But since it was regarded as too strong for many plants, they should have taken care to keep it separate from the rest. Whether this was ever a factor in the decision to reside on or near the land is not clear, but the rural residence would have been most conveniently placed for a useful way of disposing of household waste. It has been remarked that the land nearest the farmhouse is the most productive on any farm.[61]

The simplest way of fertilizing the land would have been to let animals graze it; but the strict practice of biennial fallow supposedly reduced the amount of pasture available on the very land that most needed animal droppings, and the practice of transhumance, which is also assumed to have been widespread, would have reduced their beneficial presence on the plowland in any case. It is now thought that the strict exclusion of grazing animals from the fallow has been exaggerated, together with the prevalence of long-range transhumance.[62] For one thing, Theophrastus himself refers casually to the grazing down of too-leafy young wheat and of persistent weeds in fallow land by sheep (*CP* 3.23.3, *HP* 8.11.9). The fact that some sacred leases forbade the pasturing of animals need not mean that the value of manure was underrated or that the owners were concerned to protect trees from damage, but rather that there was concern that the property not be damaged by *over*-fertilizing: hence the care with which the lessee of the Amorgan estate must measure the manure he brought in. So it is that Theophrastus remarks on the dangers of applying too much manure—fruit trees and cereals dry out if they are overfed (*CP* 3.9.1), wheat bears better than barley on unmanured land (*CP* 3.21.4), and vines are only manured once every three years (*CP* 3.9.5). That there was disagreement on the subject is perhaps reflected in his saying at one point that thin dry soil should be manured more lightly than richer soil (*CP* 3.9.2) and at another the exact opposite, according to what "they say" (*CP* 3.20.2). Yet the view that too much manure can be harmful seems to prevail; thus vegetables can take the most pungent kinds but only in dilute form (*CP* 3.9.2, *HP* 7.5.1).[63]

Greek farmers have also been condemned for failing to rotate their crops within a three-field system, which allows improvement of the land and at the same time makes for increased production.[64] Most pulses—beans, peas, vetches, and so on—attach nitrogen to the soil as they grow; they provide food in themselves; and if they are rotated with grain crops and fallow, only one-third of the land is idle at any one time, not half of it as in a biennial cycle. The Greeks knew and consumed beans (with some reservations) and were aware that they helped the land, so Theophrastus shows— in Macedon and Thessaly they were used as "green manure" (*HP* 8.7.2, 9.1). Farmers did not understand the process, but that was not necessary for it to be effective. Beans were not restricted to the vegetable plot but grown in the fields, or so we infer from the Homeric simile of beans being winnowed in the threshing floor (*Il.* 13.588–90). The connection between pulses and improved soil for cereals would have occurred to observant farmers wherever these two crops were cultivated. There are, moreover, some indications that bean crops were grown in the fallow, to be followed the next season by a winter grain crop, for Theophrastus says that a good reason for *not* planting beans is that they may delay the essential midsummer plowing if they are late—surely an indication that beans were often planted on fallowing land to be harvested quickly by midsummer if possible (*CP* 3.20.7). The alternation of bean crops with cereals is further suggested by lease regulations whereby tenants were allowed to plant pulses, one "as much as he wishes" in the arable, and another, one-quarter of the fallow land with pulses and one-half with wheat and barley, the last quarter to be left fallow.[65]

The land having been stirred up, rested, and replenished, it must be stirred up again by the autumn plowing, the most important of the three or four that it should receive. It is here that Hesiod's farmer starts his seasonal round: having built his little cart and made his plow (*WD* 424–36), he is to heed "the voice of the crane from on high in the clouds, making its annual clamor: it brings the signal for plowing" (*WD* 448–50).[66] The autumn plowing prepares the ground for the seed, so that, not surprisingly, a certain pattern of behavior was associated with it: the farmer sowed and plowed and reaped naked (*WD* 391–92).[67] Stripping for farm work in spring and summer (Pl. *Rep.* 372 a) would be only reasonable, but to do so in early winter suggests a preoccupation with ritual, not personal comfort.[68] Thus the point of the (few) vase paintings showing naked plowmen is to portray agricultural ritual, not merely "peasant" manners. As for the ceremonial inauguration of the autumn plowing, all Hesiod says is "Pray to Zeus and Demeter . . . ," but a very old ritual may underlie the Proerosia known at Athens from the fourth century on, a preplowing sacrifice and a ceremonial putting of the oxen to the plow at Eleusis.[69] Similar things must have been done in all Greek communities, despite the Athenians' view that the Proerosia could be performed in Attica "on behalf of all the Greeks" (Lycurgus fr. 87).

Plows remained much as they had been and were to be, except that during the Dark Age iron had come into common use, and was available to be attached to the blade: one of the prizes at Patroclus's funeral games consisted of "enough iron to last five years . . . no shepherd or plowman will need to visit the city for iron, for there will be enough at home" (*Il.* 23. 831–35).[70] Some plows always continued to consist entirely of wood, the share fire-hardened as is still done in some parts of the world.[71] There were certain variations in size and design, depending on regional re-quirements, but since digging was regarded as an essential supple-ment developments such as a mold board that would turn in the sod were not considered necessary. Mules were recognized as ef-fective draft animals, but oxen were generally regarded as the most suitable form of power.[72] They were reckoned to be ready for work at five years old, and would probably last for another ten years; yet Hesiod speaks of *nine*-year-old oxen for choice, perhaps because he had been unlucky in a yoke of younger oxen—he pre-fers beasts that will be unlikely to "quarrel in the furrow and break the plow and leave the job there undone" (*WD* 436–40).[73] Farm-ers therefore did not breed and train their own plow oxen, as a regular thing.[74] Admiration for the animals that helped to make agriculture a tolerable occupation is expressed in the comparison of the two Ajaxes defending the Greek ships at Troy to "two dark oxen straining at the plowshare in fallow land, each as hard as the other; with the sweat pouring out at the base of their horns, and separated only by the polished yoke, they press on down the fur-row until they are brought up by the ridge at the end of the field" (*Il.* 13.703–7).

The plowman's skill is one to which even Odysseus lays claim (*Od.* 18.371–75), but Hesiod sees the job as a laborer's (*WD* 441): the plowman should be steady, mature, and well enough fed that his attention will not be continually flitting off to other things. Ischomachus speaks in general terms of the beneficial exercise that farming can provide, but not of putting his own hand to the plow.

Owning a yoke of oxen was only feasible on farms of a certain size, so that there were many farmers who did not use oxen, and who did not have the resources to maintain even a pair of don-keys; they either hitched themselves to the plow (so Theophr. *CP* 4.12.13 suggests), or worked their land exclusively with mattocks and hoes.[75] But apart from the crippling labor involved, they were at no less an advantage in the sense that they were working their land more intensively, thus making it more productive in relation to its size than a slightly larger farm worked with oxen in the usual way, for they may very well have been able to get continuous crops.[76]

As the land is plowed, the sower sows the seed. He too, says Hesiod, should be steady and past his first youth (WD 445–46); he should avoid oversowing or, as Theophrastus has it, "sow less in poor soil, more in good" (HP 8.6.2); for too much seed in poor soil competes for the meager nourishment available, but may be plowed under when it has just sprouted so that it acts partly as compost (Xen. *Oecon.* 17.9–10). Should one sow all at once or, as Socrates suggests, little by little throughout the sowing season, ensuring that a spell of bad weather will not catch the growing crop all at the same stage of development (17.1–11)? The technique of sowing evenly was acquired only by practice, and each sower developed his own technique. But even so the unit of measure *kapbolaia* may be connected with a measured rate of sowing, even if like many other units of measure it doubtless differed from one user to the next.[77]

The main cereal crops were barley and wheat. Barley was more extensively cultivated because it is better suited than wheat to regions where the climate is Mediterranean and the soil comparatively poor.[78] The predominance of barley over wheat in traditional ritual contexts as well as in the regular diet indicates that it had always been the major crop, and it may well be that wheat had been introduced comparatively recently; although wheat came to be preferred for its flavor, its greater food value in proportion to its weight, and its cooking qualities, it never displaced barley as the staple cereal crop in large parts of the Greek world.[79] Theophrastus discusses its characteristics at greater length, to be sure, but perhaps because it may have been comparatively unfamiliar still in some areas, and did not do so well as barley in others. Barley was a particularly successful crop in Attica, so much so that one of the few named varieties was called *Achilleum,* after a farmer at Brauron in east Attica;[80] and still in the fourth century barley production continued to outstrip that of wheat. The records of firstfruits offered to the Two Goddesses at Eleusis in 329/8 suggest that ten times as much barley as wheat was produced in Attica, whereas in a group of other places including some Aegean islands the ratio was more like 2.5:1.[81]

Winter planting was the general rule, although some spring wheat and barley were grown too, taking about three months to mature. Theophrastus shows that farmers were concerned to improve yields by seed selection as well as by methods of cultivation, so that one could obtain varieties for planting even in "hollow and windless places" which would not succumb to "rust" (*CP* 3.22.1). The dream was, of course, to farm land that could produce good crops continuously (without too much exertion) and to get seed grain that would yield many more times than the known strains. Yet it was stories of fabulous crop lands which circulated, not of grain types—the Rhodian island of Chalcia contains a district so fertile that two crops of barley can be produced in succession, and the Melians can harvest a grain crop thirty or forty days after it has been sown (*HP* 8.2.8–9); such tales balanced the wry jokes so often made about the "fairness" of the land in rendering back only what it has been given in the way of grain.[82]

Millet was a less important crop, but it may not have been grown for fodder only, "food for barbarians" though it was said to be. Theophrastus does not mention its flavor or edibility, but simply that there is a quick-maturing summer variety requiring little water and which is less exhausting to the soil than one might expect (*HP* 8.1.1 et al.)—hence its suitability in Attica, as the inclusion of millet in the list of property confiscated from a Hermocopid suggests. A kind of millet was also known as a Thracian crop (Dem. 8.45); and somewhere in Greece one or another of the millets was cultivated in irrigated land (Xen. *Anab.* 2.4.13).[83] Fodder crops of other kinds were also cultivated; those that would manage in poorer soil might be planted in hillside orchards and olive groves. An important new fodder crop, alfalfa (Theophr. *HP* 8.7.7), may have been introduced with the Persian invasion. It was certainly well known by the later fifth century, when the horses of Aristophanes' *Knights* got ashore after rowing to Corinth and ate crabs there instead of alfalfa (*Knights* 601–6).[84] Perhaps Spartan horse breeders were as much responsible as anyone for its propagation (see chapter 2).

Another fodder plant, *kytisos,* was discovered within the Greek world on the island of Cythnos; highly regarded as feed for milk sheep in particular, it spread through the other islands and the mainland and was being cultivated at least as early as the fifth century.[85] Lupine and vetch, of the pulse family, may have been grown for human consumption as well as for fodder; lupine is essentially wild, and the seed must be planted as soon as it leaves the threshing floor, in unplowed land, but serious attempts were made to domesticate it (*CP* 3.1.5). Vetch, which animals dislike when it is still green (*HP* 8.7.3), is generally spoken of as a famine food, but Theophrastus groups it with edible pulses and speaks of the white variety having the sweetest flavor and of spring-sown vetch being more digestible than winter vetch (*HP* 8.5.1). If these crops were grown in what was technically fallow land, they too would have benefited it in much the same way as a bean crop.

> Outside the courtyard . . . with a hedge running down either side, lies (Alcinous's) large orchard, a day's plowing in extent, where trees hang their greenery on high, the pear and the pomegranate, the apple with its glossy burden, the sweet fig and the luxuriant olive. Their fruit never fails or runs short, winter and summer alike . . . pear after pear, apple after apple, cluster on cluster of grapes, and fig upon fig are always coming to perfection. (*Od.* 7.112–21)

Most orchards in the real world would have been considerably smaller (and less fruitful) than Alcinous's, but Delian Apollo's estate of Thaleion provides a parallel of sorts; it contained 147 cultivated, 87 grafted wild, and 200 pure wild olive trees; 143 fig trees; 101 apple trees; and 1,140 vines. The only source of olives in all of the Delian properties, it was probably located in that part of Myconos which in recent times has been found suitable for olives, and which may very well have been devoted to fruit trees ever since antiquity.[86]

Preparation of ground for a new plantation would have required considerable hard work; and even when an orchard had been established, the replacement of old trees with young ones and the tending of prospering and mature trees would continue to provide occupation. Usually the inheritor or purchaser of a property could expect at least some of the existing trees to produce a crop; he would also expect to find that in the nature of things some replacements were required. Keeping up the existing number of trees was essential to maintaining the value of the property which had been set up in accordance with traditional expectations of what an estate should yield, if so much was put down to cereals, so much to fruit, vines, and so on.[87] Of course the *dimensions* of an orchard or vineyard could be altered, but the *density* of trees could not, the limit of what the land would bear having been recognized long since. The spacing of trees varied according to species and terrain, from less than nine feet apart for pomegranates, myrtles, and bays to fifty feet or so for olive trees; on sloping ground they could be spaced closer together. Preferred methods of propagating were to graft, layer, or root from slips of the plant in earth; domesticated stock would be grafted onto a full grown specimen of the wild form so that the cultivated growth would mature quickly. Trees grown from seed did not do well— "This is why the Thasians graft buds onto their almonds when they are full-grown, since a soft [cultivated] almond tree when planted from seed turns into a hard [wild] one" (*CP* 1.9.1). Some believed that inverting its cuttings would improve the pomegranate, making it bushier so that it shaded its fruit more effectively; thus the fig too could be made a more manageable tree, less liable to shed its fruit (*HP* 2.6.12). Others thought that vine shoots were unaffected by being set upside down. Olives might be sprouted from pieces of the trunk chopped up; or an old tree could be cut down so as to sprout afresh, and so the deme officials of Aixon specified that olive trees be cut down to stumps to improve them.[88] The tenants could have expected a crop from the trees within ten or twelve years, but olives are not really mature until some time later.[89]

There is some disagreement about when the domesticated olive first came into the Greek world, or whether it had been known in the Bronze Age but had to be reintroduced thereafter.[90] If this latter were the case, then one would have to admit that agriculture must have experienced a quite radical shift, with what would have been a rapid spread of olive trees across the farming landscape during the seventh and sixth centuries. But Homer knows both wild and domesticated olive trees, and their absence from the *Works and Days* can be explained quite easily without assuming that they were in Hesiod's day still generally unknown, or rare at best.[91] Their introduction to southern Italy and Sicily may now be put back to the later seventh century; they would have been taken by the Greeks to the new settlements as plants with which they were quite familiar; only the indigenous peoples would have considered this a revolution of any kind.[92]

The provident farmer would have nursery beds of young olive trees waiting to be planted out where they were needed. The quality of soils must be judged as carefully as that for cereals, but it needed to be poor so as not to overnourish the young trees, and to be fairly stony to give protection, drainage, and purchase for the roots. But sometimes irrigation was considered necessary.[93] Their planting is discussed in detail by Ischomachus and Socrates: the hole should be considerably bigger than the cutting that is being set; the soil should be dry, and the cutting should be set slantwise in the earth so that as many as possible of the new shoots are in the earth. Olive shoots are planted in even deeper holes, the head of the plant coated with clay, and the rest of it that is above ground wrapped up; the whole plant is then further protected from extremes of weather by a lean-to of broken pottery (*Oecon.* 19.13–14; Theophr. *CP* 3.5.5). Myrtles are treated in the same way. As to their spacing, Solon ordained that all trees should be at least five feet away from the estate's boundary with the neighbors, and olives at least nine feet distant, because their roots spread further and may damage other trees by taking nourishment and moisture, "and giving off a powerful exhalation" (Plut. *Solon* 23.6). The fact that Solon legislated concerning olive planting does not necessarily mean that it was only in his time that olive cultivation had become widespread in Attica but rather that landowners had become careless of their neighbors' interests—something that was at the heart of the problem that Solon addressed by his reforms, after all.[94]

Once field crops and orchard trees had been planted, they required little attention until spring. Then the grain crops were examined to see if they were coming up too thick; in Thessaly the remedy was to let in sheep to graze the young plants down (*HP* 8.7.4). The fields must be cleared of weeds, accomplished by backbreaking work with the hoe or even hand weeding; insect pests hunted out, more handwork perhaps; and rain-washed earth redistributed about the roots of the crop, again with the hoe (Xen. *Oecon.* 17.12). Fruit trees were transplanted in autumn, and figs a little later; figs in particular benefited from spading and hoeing, while dust was applied as a fertilizer (or protection against capillary evaporation, prevention of which was the secret of dry farming). Encouragements to fruit well included tactics such as inserting a stone into the base of the trunk, although almonds were transfixed with an iron peg; or cutting the roots, the method for vines and figs; removing gum, from almond trees, pears, and sorbs "as they do in Arcadia"; or sprinkling ash about figs and gashing the stems; or lopping the branches of olives (Theophr. *HP* 2.7.6–7). Trees that did not have all these attentions paid to them would not fruit well, but they would last longer—hence Theophrastus's comment that the purposes of proper cultivation were defeated by landowners who only care that the tenant pays the rent and leaves behind as many trees as there were when he took up his tenancy, regardless of the neglect the trees may have suffered (*CP* 2.11.1–3).

Among the farmer's great worries were that the fruit blossoms would fall before they had set and the fruit drop before it was ripe. If rain fell on pomegranate blossoms, it reduced the chance of fruit forming; therefore a way was contrived of training the trees so that rain would not fall on the flowers (Theophr. *CP* 2.9.3–4).Efforts made to protect olive blossoms from wet sea mists took a less practical turn.[95] Figs were particularly prone to drop their fruit prematurely, and means were sought of aiding caprification so as to promote their ripening properly. One was to plant wild figs nearby with galls and gall wasps established in them, and another to attach galls from wild trees onto the cultivated figs; care must be taken too to defeat the gall wasps' mortal enemy, the *knips*. The importance of growing the fig successfully is evident from its place in the diet, and not surprisingly the vocabulary used to describe figs was a little more varied than for other fruit (*CP* 5.1.3, 6–11).

The keen interest that a landowner might take in the struggles of his fruit trees is exemplified in the anecdote handed down over two centuries to Theophrastus about an olive tree that had belonged to Thettalus, the younger son of Peisistratus; it had shed all its leaves and yet was able to produce fruit (*HP* 2.3.3). Why was this particular tree remembered? Because Thettalus himself had been struck by the phenomenon and told his friends, who were equally impressed (by the tree, or by the fact that it had belonged to a son of the tyrant, or both).

> In [Alcinous's orchard] there is a fruitful vineyard, in one part of which is a warm patch of level ground, where some of the grapes are drying in the sun, while others are gathered or trodden, and on the foremost rows hang unripe bunches that have just shed their blossoms or show the first faint tinge of purple. Vegetable beds of various kinds are neatly laid out beyond the farthest row. . . . The garden is served by two springs, one led in rills to all parts of the enclosure. (*Od.* 7.122–30)

Tending the vineyard required some more specialized skills than work in the olive grove or orchard. Like gardening and unlike the cultivation of other fruiting plants, it had developed a professional vocabulary in that the "vinedresser," *ampelourgos,* was the man who knew how to prune the vines.[96] Like figs, the various vines were defined by much more detailed nomenclature than other plants (*CP* 5.1.3). The vineyard, often enough a quite small section of the estate (three to four *plethra* being regarded as a realistic allotment for new settlers in the Illyrian settlement of Black Corcyra), was more intensively cultivated than any other part except the garden. In some regions landowners concentrated heavily on viticulture—Thasos, Chios, Cos, Rhodes, and Phleius, for example—and some very large holdings in vineyards must have existed, besides the Hermocopid Adeimantus's spreads of thirty and ten hectares in Thasos; for such owners the good years must have far outweighed the bad, unless they hedged their bets on vines with judicious stands of almond trees, which seem to have been something of a Thasian specialty (*CP* 1.9.1).[97]

The vineyard required thorough cultivation before being planted; the amount of manure to be applied depended on the variety of vine and its location, which could be anywhere from low-lying, well-watered areas to well-drained slopes. Old plants could be revitalized, but some varieties might require renewing at fairly frequent intervals, as the Amorgos lease suggests; here older vines were to be replaced, twenty plants at a time, in midwinter.[98] Vines were propagated not from seed but from roots, suckers and twigs by layering, during late autumn into winter (*HP* 2.5.4–5, *CP* 1.3.1, 3.11–12); regional variations were apparent, such as the intolerance of the vine of Aphytis for being pruned short (*CP* 3.15.5). New varieties evolved, such as to produce pipless grapes and bicolored grapes, as well as grapes with clearly distinct characteristics, which came out in the wines made from them (*CP* 5.3.1–2). That soil and situation could also affect the character of the wine, growers were well aware.[99] The possibility of grapes that would ripen at different times is already apparent in the *Odyssey*. Vines might be planted in holes as at Crimean Chersonesus, or in trenches as in Amorgos, the lessee having "dug the vines twice, first in February, and then in April *before the twentieth of the month*," as the lease insists.[100] When they grew up, they might be trained on trees (as perhaps is meant by the vines that grew in the orchard of Alcinous, not in the vineyard) or on wooden props, the value of which is apparent from the complaints in comedy about their theft, and from the plausible accusation that could be brought against political enemies, that they had cut vine props in sacred territory, as at Corcyra in 427 (Thuc. 3.70.4). Vine props were precious, not only because Greece was a comparatively timber-poor region, but because they were a trouble to cut and a vineyard could use a lot of them—one Attic lease provides for four thousand.[101]

Vines were pruned during the winter (*CP* 3.15); the importance of having this job done properly appears in the Athenian
deme lease whereby the lessees must permit the deme to call in
an *ampelourgos* during the last five years of the lease to make sure
that the vines are in good shape when it comes time to relet.[102]
Aristophanes' hero of the *Peace,* Trygaeus, is an *ampelourgos* and
*owner* of a vineyard, but the vinedresser may sometimes have been
a professional who went round treating other men's vines; this
would explain the presence of two *ampelourgoi* among the freedmen who dedicated silver bowls on the occasion of their manumission.[103] Old vines could, says Theophrastus, be regenerated
every ten years or so by the rather drastic procedure of cutting
away the roots on one side, and earthing the vine up, whereby it
would fruit well within three or four years; then the same thing
was repeated on the other side of the vine. (The intellectual problem then arose, Is this the same plant or not? See *HP* 4.13.3ff.)

Cultivation included removing weeds, draining the ground
when it was too wet, applying dust about the roots, and digging
about them to air them. High fruit yields were encouraged by
removing excess foliage and tendrils and by chopping the roots.
Women workers in the vineyards are heard of, tending the vines,
and there is no particular reason to suppose that they were not
employed fairly commonly (Dem. 57.45). The flowers might be
damaged by rain, or a *drying* wind, as at Methana, where extreme
measures were taken to ward it off: two men would tear a white
cock in half, and taking a piece each would run round the vines
in opposite directions, the two pieces of the cock being buried
where the men met (Paus. 2.34.3).[104]

A recommended method of drying out a too-wet vineyard was
to plant barley and beans in it, but on the whole the vineyard was
a separate place, contained within its walls where the vines were
protected from contact with other plants such as fig, olive, and
almond, which were "bad neighbors" (*CP* 3.10.6).

The garden too was separate from the rest of the estate, a place
where even more intense preparation, planting, and cultivation
went on to produce the vegetables, edible herbs, and other plants
useful to the household. The grant of land by the city of Zelea

included sections of scrubland and arable, a house and a *kepos*; here, as many other records suggest, the *kepos* was a separate entity with a particular role to play in the economy of the estate. Cultivating the garden was regarded as a specialized activity enough to give rise to the title "gardener," *kepouros,* who "gardened"; thus the lessee of an Athenian estate is bidden to "garden the garden" (*kepon kepourein*).[105] This estate also included a (separate) orchard. The lessee is instructed to treat the vegetable plot in much the same way as arable land, at the end of his tenancy leaving half of the plot fallow and planting the other half with cabbages. Irrigation plays an important part here, as in gardening generally: "He shall use the water flowing from the watercourse, impeding no one else from using it."[106] As in Alcinous's estate, so in Calypso's magical garden water is a prominent feature; springs of water are trained to go about among soft meadows of violets and parsley (*Od.* 5.63–73).[107] The prevalence of irrigation in gardens later is apparent from Aristophanes' reference to the swing beam used by gardeners at the garden well (fr. 679); Aristotle's comparison of a garden's watering system to the disposition of blood vessels in the human body (*PA* 668 a 14–18); and the early career of Zeno's successor as head of the Stoa: Cleanthes of Assos was forced in youth to earn his living and worked at night drawing water "in the garden," as the gardener who employed him could testify (Diog. Laert. 7.168–69).

Gardens no doubt varied in size but must not usually have been very extensive. One *kepos* we know of in Thessaly which measured over 5 *plethra* (5 *plethra,* 4 *pelethraiai,* ? *kapbolaiai,* 2 feet, to be exact), but this was probably larger than usual.[108] The garden was where much of the experimentation with plants went on (cf. Arabic gardens), such as attempts to domesticate wild plants; so Theophrastus comments on certain wild species that "some thought it worthwhile formerly to cultivate in gardens" (*HP* 7.7.2).[109] It was often situated close to the dwelling house, convenient to sources of fertilizer and attention, its water supply presumably being the household's source as well.

Vegetables were sown at three different seasons of the year: in late summer, from July onward, was the time for cabbage, radish, and turnip; from January onward, for leeks, celery, long onion, and orach; and from April onward, for cucumber, gourds, blite, basil, and purslane (Theophr. *HP* 7.1.2 and 7 passim). Secondary crops such as beet, rocket, monk's rhubarb, mustard, coriander, dill, cress, and lettuce might be sown at any of these periods. Seed was best planted, not scattered; water, manure—"they [gardeners] use fresh human dung as a liquid manure" (*HP* 7.5.1)—and applications of dust were recommended. The keeping qualities of seeds were of concern, and Theophrastus says that many kinds would remain good for use at least one or two years (*HP* 7.5.5). The care with which vegetables required to be tended, and presumably were so, comes over very clearly in Theophrastus's account of cucumber culture: in order to give them an early start, "if you plant the seed in winter in baskets, and then water it with warm water and carry the baskets out into the sun, and put them by the fire, then when the growing season comes round, plant them in the ground, baskets and all, they come out very early" (*CP* 5.6.6). If they have been planted by the well, they may be hung over its edge to keep cool, care being taken not to damage the cucumber vine itself (*CP* 5.6.5).

The ornamental garden as such was perhaps not known. Gardens were utilitarian, and *flower* gardens appear only incidentally, in that many of the useful and edible herbs had beautiful blossoms and scents.[110] But the charm of a well-stocked and well-worked garden, with such features as trellises made out of lettuce stalks (*HP* 7.4.5), could not have failed to impress all but the most practical cultivators intent on turnip production for consumption and profit only. Aristophanes' *Birds* "enjoy in the garden the white sesame and myrtle berries, and the poppy and bergamot mint" (159–60); their main interest, food and the destruction of pests, does not detract from the pleasure of gardens which Aristophanes conveys. The Homeric simile of the slain Gorgythion's helmeted head lolling like a garden poppy heavy with its seeds and the rain makes all the more terrible the appearance of his death by its comparison to so familiar and pretty a thing (*Il.* 8.306–7).

Field crops, trees, and garden plants were all prone to attack by pests and diseases. Aristophanes' *Bird* chorus declares, "I preserve the flourishing crops, slaying the brood of all tribes of animals which with all-devouring jaws feeds upon all that swells from a seed-pod on the ground and, sitting in the trees, upon their fruit; and I slay them that with most hostile injury ravage sweet-scented gardens, and all creeping and biting things perish in slaughter beneath my wings" (1062–71). Peisetairus also suggests that kestrels and owls will rid the vines of locusts, and the figs of their particular enemy, the *knips* (588–91). Birds themselves, flying insects, caterpillars, slugs, spiders, beetles, mice, and other herbivorous beasts could all ravage growing crops. Field mice were known to be capable of destroying an entire grain crop on a small farm; countermeasures might include fumigation and digging them out with the aid of pigs, a thing one would like to see done (Ar. *HA* 580 b 15–25). Plagues of insects obviously were not unknown, although only a few references to such calamities have entered Greek myth or the traditions about farming itself.[111] Both growing crops and stored foodstuffs could be attacked by chewing insects and grubs. That all grubs were produced from eggs laid by insects was not fully appreciated—Aristotle and Theophrastus still thought of some of them as engendered by the plant itself, the result of the plant's own moisture solidifying: hence grubs will occur in the roots of wheat during a drought. Fruit trees are all susceptible too, and stored grains will produce from their own fluidity animals peculiar to each variety (Theophr. *HP* 8.10.4, *CP* 3.22.3–5).

There were various means of discouraging insects, such as applying brimstone, strong-scented herbs, or olive oil (Ar. *HA* 534 b 17–25, Theophr. *CP* 6.5.3–4). Certain plants would act as repellants—roses are said to kill beetles—an excellent reason for growing them in the garden; and bitter vetch will deter flea spiders from radishes (Theophr. *CP* 2.18.1). Laborers may have picked pests off plants by hand, and set honey traps or other devices; fig tree tenders we are told went so far as to hang dead crabs in the trees to distract the *knips* from its attacks on the valuable gall wasps (*HP* 2.8.3).

"Rust" was another great bane, a form of mildew that could affect everything but was especially bad for cereals. It is apt to occur at the full moon when the moon's heat is greatest, and may also be caused by incorrect cultivation or adverse weather at one or another stage of the crop's development (*CP* 3.22.2). Prevention is the only cure offered. Again, no anecdotal evidence survives suggesting that rust was ever a devastating disaster, but this is perhaps because the ills of agriculture were so persistent and so general that they were taken for granted, like infant mortality and hunger; or it may be that in his discussion Theophrastus is only skimming the surface of what was a large and much-discussed subject.[112]

Not only crops but laborers and landowners too were vulnerable to attack from reptiles and insects. There are, however, few references to this problem outside Nicander's *Theriaca,* in which he speaks of the dangers lurking in farm buildings and country dwellings; he might also have added, in tall growing crops and weedy verges, in damp ditches, under stones, along rows of beans and vines, on sunny walls. The *Theriaca* includes numerous herbal and other remedies for snake and insect bites.

Another form of pest was the thieving passerby, along with light-fingered and no doubt hungry slaves and nibbling animals. The unwatched vineyard might be stripped (Aristoph. *Wasps* 449–50); and slaves were, almost proverbially, beaten for stealing figs.[113] Hence sources note the walls round vineyards and the fences and gates round gardens and orchards, such as Cimon had removed on his property so that the people could go in and take what they wanted at harvesttime (Plut. *Cimon.* 10.1).

Harvesting went on intermittently from midsummer into late autumn. First the winter grains and then the spring-sown grains were reaped. Ischomachus and Socrates debate whether the reaper should stand with his back to the wind or facing it, and the answer is to stand away from it so that the straw does not fly in one's face. Should he cut near the ear or close to the ground? If the stalk is short, he should cut low, so as to give more straw, but if it is long, he should leave some to be burned as stubble or put on the compost heap (Xen. *Oecon.* 18.1–2). Reaping is an activity that can very easily and beneficially be turned into a contest, for it was best if each reaper kept up with the next as they worked over a field (*Il.* 11.67–69, 18.550–60). So in Theocritus's idyll, the *Reapers,* one worker taunts another, "You can't cut a swathe straight as you used to once; you don't keep up with the next man but lag behind like a lame sheep." The rhythm of reaping could be maintained with the aid of music, and as it happens the reaper who is being teased has fallen for the farm girl "who played the flute for the reapers" (*Idyll* 10). The subject of one reaping song known of was Lityerses, a Phrygian who forced passing strangers to take part in reaping contests, then beheaded them at the end of the day and bound their bodies into the sheaves of barley or wheat; he was eventually killed by Heracles, but his praises continued to be sung as a champion of reapers (!) "to this day."[114]

The completion of reaping might be marked by a harvest supper, such as is portrayed on Achilles' shield, or celebration of the harvest might be left until all was threshed, winnowed, and ready to be stored. The grain was threshed on the threshing floor, under the hoofs of draft animals that wheeled round and round; so Achilles going into battle in his chariot is likened to "a pair of broad-browed cattle that a farmer has harnessed to trample the white barley . . . and his lowing bulls tread out the grain" (*Il.* 20.495–97). The floor must be well rolled as Hesiod says (*WD* 599), and the threshers must keep the grain evenly spread as the animals move round (Xen. *Oecon.* 18.5). Threshers also sang sad songs; one we know of concerned the death of Borimus, brother of prince Mariandynus, at harvesttime. Lugubrious themes probably kept the workers' minds on their work better than ribald or uplifting ones, and a slow rhythm would be more fitting for the sweeping and spreading actions they had to perform.[115]

The grain would be winnowed on the threshing floor when the wind was up—once more the winnowers would stand facing away from the wind, as Ischomachus and Socrates establish, so that the chaff blows away from the winnowed grain, which must be moved aside as it is cleaned. "So, Socrates, you seem to be capable of teaching the quickest way of cleaning grain."[116] Pulses were also winnowed on the threshing floor; at Philippi, "they" reckoned that winnowing beans in a cold wind made them tough (Theophr. *CP* 4.12.8)—or is this a workers' story told to gullible landowners and visiting scholars as an excuse for not doing an uncomfortable job? Aristophanes' reference to women singing as they winnow shows that this activity had its music too (fr. 339).

After the grain harvest had been completed, figs, almonds, and chickpeas would be gathered in August, grapes, pears, and apples in September and October, while olives very conveniently were not ready to be picked until after the autumn plowing. If fruit was harvested quickly and carelessly, the tree or vine might suffer damage, but olives could be knocked out of the trees which would even benefit from having a few twigs broken (Theophr. *CP* 5.4.2, *HP* 4.16.1). Transporting produce from the field to the threshing floor and storage place, or from orchard and garden to the house, was done mainly by the basket load (although Hesiod's little cart might have come in handy), or in sacks. The distances to be traveled within any one farm would generally be small—a fifth of a kilometer at most on a basic family farm, and perhaps one-half of a kilometer on a big 300-*plethra* farm; some sacred estates of course were bigger.

Storage was as important an aspect of the agricultural process as any other; the household must be able to keep reserves of food, grain, and vegetable seed unspoiled for at least a year if not considerably longer. Grain could be left in heaps out of doors for a little while, but should be stored in dry, airy, and unplastered chambers within the farmhouse or in a separate granary (Xen. *Oecon.* 9.3, Theophr. *HP* 8.11.1)—the farm tower, or not, as the case might be.[117] At Eleusis, where grain storage was a matter of some concern to the sanctuary, what with the barley produced on its own Rarian estate and the firstfruits from Athenian and any other farmers who could be prevailed on to send them, we hear of both a *tower* and *siroi*—pits or underground chambers requiring the sanctuary architect's supervision—being prepared for grain storage.[118] Underground "grain cisterns" would have served on any farm free from flooding, if they were properly covered. Large terra-cotta jars sunk into the ground would have achieved the same effect; thus we may understand some of the references to *pithoi* found in towers or listed among a farm's equipment. Jars and sacks also did for flour, and jars for all the fruits and vegetables that were dried, salted, or pickled. Drying would be completed on sunny patches of ground out of the way of farmyard traffic, on flat roofs, or in airy upper chambers. Many herbs would be cut and hung in bunches, and stored so. And of course the bulk of the olive and grape harvest was rendered into liquid form to be stored in jars. It is no wonder that the estate granted at Zelea included one hundred of these important vessels.[119] The cellar of Tellias of Acragas contained three hundred *pithoi*, each holding one hundred *amphores* of wine produced from his estates, which were probably on something the same scale as Adeimantus's Thasian vineyards (Diod. Sic. 13.83.3).

The essential requirement for the storage places was that they be dry and free of dust, weevils, and other pests. The danger from rodents is scarcely mentioned, curiously enough, apart from Aristotle's story of the prolific mouse in the millet jar: a mouse got in, and some time later there were 120 of them (*HA* 580 b 12–14). Theophrastus's *Superstitious Man* went to the interpreter to ask what to do if a mouse gnawed a hole in his barley-flour bag (*Char.* 16.6) and perhaps was told to get a ferret, for measures taken against mice may have included pets of this kind, and possibly cats too, although the *Superstitious Man* seems not to have derived much comfort from the cat that crossed his path (*Char.* 16.2).[120]

Persistent hard work was the way to succeed: so Hesiod advises the farmer, and so he should insist in turn that his laborers understand. They all rise at dawn, which by its coolness "will help you on your way and helps at yoking time" (*WD* 580–81). And Xenophon also points out the importance of steady hard work:

> It makes a great difference whether the farmer takes care that the men are working during the working hours, or is careless about it. For one man in ten by working all the time may easily make a difference, and another by knocking off before time; and if the men are allowed to be

slack all day, the decrease in the work done may easily amount to one half of the whole. . . . Suppose the vines are being hoed to clear the ground of weeds: if the hoeing is badly done so that the weeds grow ranker and more abundant, how can you call that anything but idleness? (*Oecon.* 20.16–20)

Related to this question of keeping the laborers hard at work is the matter of how many to employ. Putting hands to work without regard to the rate at which work could be done was like applying too much manure to land that does not need it—the profits from farming will simply be overwhelmed. Very little is said anywhere as to how many men it was reckoned to take to work a farm of given dimensions and prescribed features, but Xenophon's observations that "those who own land can tell how many yoke of oxen are enough for the farm, and how many laborers" shows that this was something the wise farmer did take into account (*Ways and Means* 4.5). Hesiod also implies that this is so when he advises getting a slave or two, or suggests that plowing requires three men.[121] An efficient farmer kept his eye on his laborers; if he was not working alongside them himself, he must go and see what they have done, or at least make them aware that he might very well do so at any time. Hesiod includes in his list of good and bad days for doing things *the thirtieth of the month* as the best for inspecting work and giving out rations (*WD* 766–67).

The rhythm of the agricultural year allowed some relaxation of discipline. When the harvest has been gathered in, says Hesiod, "then the laborers can rest their poor legs and unyoke the oxen" (*WD* 607–8). But probably not for very long; not only did tending the land impose a steady round of tasks to be done, the habit of disciplined work was best maintained so, and the slave laborer who was kept constantly busy had little time or energy to think of alternatives to his situation, like running away. The workday having begun at dawn ended at sunset, Homer's "unyoking time":

The plowman, whose two dun oxen have pulled the plowshare through the fallow all day long, yearns for his supper and welcomes the sunset that frees him to seek it and drag home his weary legs. (*Od.* 13.31–34)

## Livestock

> Let me give you some idea of Odysseus's wealth. On
> the mainland, twelve herds of cattle, as many flocks
> of sheep, as many droves of pigs, and as many scat-
> tered herds of goats, all tended by hired labor or his
> own herdsmen; while here in Ithaca eleven herds of
> goats graze up and down the coast with reliable men
> to look after them.
> (*Od.* 14.99–104)

As well occupied as the Greek farm would seem to have been, if
it was properly cultivated, with its crops, trees, and garden, there
was still room on many estates and in many landowners' calculations for livestock in addition to the draft animals—and if not on
the estate, then accommodation was found elsewhere. Livestock
constituted a valuable supplement—manure—to arable farming,
they provided additional food and other essential commodities,
and they were a form of insurance or savings deposit and a me-
dium of exchange in themselves, hives of bees no less in their way
than bulls, sheep, or goats. The property of the Hermocopid Panaetius included not only 104 *amphores* of Attic wine (presumably
produced on land he owned or rented as a metic) but also cattle,
sheep, and goats, and at least fifteen beehives.[122]

Bees, the smallest and altogether the least troublesome of livestock, could find suitable environments and were encouraged,
in most parts of the Greek world.[123] Although their domestication had been achieved long since, some household dependence
on wild bees' nests may have continued. A halfway stage seems
to be reflected in the *Odyssey*: the Nymphs' cave on Ithaca
contains some two-handled jars that the wild bees find congenial dwelling places (*Od.* 13.105–6).[124] The domesticating of
bees entailed a very small adjustment to their natural existence;
specially designed terra-cotta hives were quite commonly used,
and have been found at sites in Attica, for instance, on the
lower slopes of Mount Hymettus, which has always been re-
nowned for the fine flavor of its honey. Hives were also made
of wood and other perishable materials. They were usually set

about the countryside, and sometimes close to the house, as at Vari; more often they would be in the open, hence Solon's ruling that one man's hives should be set at least three hundred feet away from another's, so as to reduce quarrels or perhaps even litigation over strayed bees, or misappropriated hives (Plut. *Solon* 23.6).

Yet for all the popularity of beekeeping, and the fascination they undoubtedly had for some later writers in antiquity, the only detailed discussion of their characteristics surviving from the Greek period is Aristotle's, in his *History of Animals* (553 a 17ff., 623 b 6ff.). He is interested in the bee as part of the insect world, not in its economic aspects; like Theophrastus on plants he depends largely on those who worked with bees for his information: as to their generation, "some say that they *fetch* their young . . . ; [some] assert that they bring them from the flower of the olive . . . and it is stated as proof that, when the olive harvest is most numerous, the swarms are most numerous" (*HA* 553 a 17–22). He shows that beekeepers used smoke when they wanted to remove the honeycombs from the hive; that bees prefer thyme; that the place for their hive should be cool in summer and warm in winter; and that "men say they can muster them into a hive by rattling with stones or crockery" (*HA* 627 a 15–19)—but do the bees really hear the noise, and do they like it or fear it?

Bees took up very little space and required only occasional attention, the knack of which anyone could pick up. The rewards were very worthwhile, and the activity of the bees themselves appealing to any observant owner. Beehives would have been, and perhaps were, fitting additions to the gardens of the philosophers; they could often have constituted the focus of a garden specially planted to supply the bees with food, such as Aristotle recommends—a spread of "pear trees, beans, alfalfa, Syrian grass, yellow pulse, myrtles, poppies, creeping thyme, and almond trees" (*HA* 627 b 15ff.).

In the case of other livestock it can be argued that their profitability might often have been outweighed by the cost of maintaining them.[125] But if they were kept in small numbers, they could be found enough forage to live on without straining the household's resources unduly. Domestic birds such as geese, a feature of the palace farmyard in Ithaca (*Od.* 19.536–37), and poultry, introduced into the Greek world during the seventh century, could live more or less "off the country," giving a small benefit to the fields if they were allowed to pick about in the fallow, with just a little supplementary grain and household scraps. A few estates may have been devoted to larger flocks, for sale locally or even as far afield as from Boeotia to the market in Athens, for example; certainly Aristotle shows that owners of domestic birds took them seriously. He also suggests by his interest in the subject that pigeons were domesticated too (*HA* 544 a–b)—another possible source of good fertilizer, if so.[126] Exotic birds such as pheasants were known of as a rich man's amusement; Andocides' father Leogoras raised them for diversion (Aristoph. *Clouds* 109). Pyrilampus even kept and bred peacocks, the first of which may have been a diplomatic gift from Persia, and his son Demus inherited them; one pair was priced at one thousand drachmas, so that it is not surprising that the family also had a reputation for owning expensive horses, which may have been aided by the judicious sale of peacocks.[127]

The function of animal husbandry proper was partly to provide for the consumption of meat; but meat formed a comparatively small part of the diet, and beef and mutton were generally available on occasion only, when sacrificial victims were divided up, either after a private sacrifice or at one of the community's festivals.[128] Cattle, sheep, and goats were kept primarily for other purposes, cattle to provide draft power and milk in season, sheep for the wool and milk, and goats for their milk only; all provided hides in addition, and such extras as the basic ingredients of glues strong enough to be used in construction and shipbuilding. Nevertheless, some meat was consumed more as a matter of course; the butcher's shop was a familiar enough institution for Theophrastus's *Mean Man* to be portrayed surreptitiously adding a little bit extra to the scale when purchasing meat or running playfully away with a bit of stolen tripe (*Char.* 9.4). Most likely the meat he bought was pork, for one of the most commonly kept domestic animals may have been the pig, a highly thought of animal, as not only the character of Eumaeus himself but also the scale of the piggeries he built for Odysseus make clear (*Od.* 14.5–20).[129] Theophrastus's comments on the efficacy of pig manure suggest that it was readily available, as does his remark on the feeding of pigs—they could be fed tough, old beans, good for nothing else (*CP* 4.12.4). "Of all animals the most easily pleased in the matter of food," as Aristotle puts it, they love roots, (and of course could be pastured in woodlands); but when they are to be fattened up, pig breeders in Thrace give them barley, millet, figs, acorns, wild pears, and cucumbers (*HA* 595 a 15–29). This would have been just the sort of fare that almost any landowning household could supply from the garden, field, or accessible scrub to the family pig, with a little extra coming out of the stores if necessary.

References to pig dealers also suggest that pigs were often bought and sold at market, not simply bred and reared in small numbers on small farms. Pig breeders in Thrace could in one respect at least afford to keep pigs (and other livestock too) on a grand scale, even if the beasts were not so palatially accommodated as Odysseus's swine: there was land extensive enough for both pasture and fodder crops, as well as for all the cereal that the population could possibly want, and not only in Thrace, but in Macedon, Thessaly, Boeotia, Epirus, even Elis and Messenia, so that livestock of all kinds could be raised in comparatively large numbers without competing against other vital claims on the land. Some suggestion of Thessalian wealth in livestock comes from the cities' response to Jason's request for "moderate" contributions to the sacrifice at the Pythian festival: one thousand cattle and over ten thousand sheep, pigs, and goats came in—these were animals, one imagines, that were easily spared by the communities and owners concerned (Xen. *HG* 6.4.29).

In many parts of the Greek world choices had to be made as to how the land could be used, and limits set on the scale and type of livestock that should be kept. The Athenian Nausicydes, a barley-flour miller, took up pig and cattle breeding with such success that he became rich enough to perform liturgies; he must therefore have dealt in more than a mere styful of pigs and a yoke of oxen (Xen. *Mem.* 2.7.6).[130] He presumably owned land, perhaps fields that had grown some of the barley he ground—or now acquired property with which to provide accommodation, pasture, and fodder crops. The pigs he raised might have been sold to households in need of a pig to fatten, or for sacrifice; somehow or other, demand was enough to provide a worthwhile business, but he may well have been one of very few commercial breeders in all of Attica.

Pigs might be kept penned and given fodder much of the time, but most pig owners, even Nausicydes perhaps, would have wanted their animals to make use of woodlands and pasture when possible, for economy's sake. Taking animals to and from pasture must have occupied many man-hours and many people—the growing children of farming families, hired hands, slaves, some of them full-time herdsmen, others fitting a few weeks' herding in between other seasonal jobs.

The Archaic statue of the *moschophoros,* a man carrying a young calf across his shoulders, conveys a sense of great pride in the creature that is being brought as an offering, or displayed as an indication of the dedicator's wealth and of offerings to come. Who was the *moschophoros,* a cattle baron or a farmer whose plowing cow had recently calved?[131] Few estates in Attica maintained more than plow oxen in the way of cattle, for there was not enough good pasture to nourish dairy herds or beef cattle in any great numbers.[132] But this does not mean that fine cattle were not highly prized or that Attica as a whole supported few cattle altogether.[133] Even if only half the farms were big enough to merit the use of plow animals, this could mean that, allowing for those estates that supported more than a single yoke, there might have been 25,000 oxen and perhaps nearly as many mules and donkeys.[134] When the Athenians evacuated the countryside in 431, Thucydides says that they sent their sheep and cattle across to Euboea and other islands off the coast (2.14.1)—a formidable undertaking, for the number of sheep and goats would have been far greater.[135] But the Athenians did keep their cattle and other animals safe somewhere, for sure, retrieving them sometime before the peace of 421. They would have done the same thing in 412 when the Spartan occupation of Decelea began to make life in the country impossible once more, but for the fact that Euboea had now revolted from the Athenians and no longer offered a safe haven. And at this point in the war, Thucydides says, "all the sheep and farm animals were lost" (7.27.5).

How did Athenians usually maintain their animals? As suggested previously, they would have grazed their cattle as far as possible in woodlands and on wasteland within easy reach of the farm, on stubble land, and in the fallow before the weeds were plowed in. So it must have been in much of the Greek world, that plow animals were pastured up and down the back ways of the farm and the surrounding countryside; it was probably for this that Hesiod recommends getting "a slave woman who would follow the cattle" (*WD* 406). The value of scrub for livestock, long disregarded, is now recognized as quite considerable.[136] When cattle were stalled, forage was gathered from waysides, wilderness, field, and garden; some farms would have had land to spare for fodder crops; and there were a few good grazing areas available, marshy regions that dried out in summer enough to provide negotiable pasture.[137]

Some Athenians owned more than the plowing animals they needed to work the land: Nausicydes for one and Panaetius for another. Panaetius had two working oxen, two others, and four cows with their calves. Perhaps he and Nausicydes were rearers and trainers of plow oxen, which they sold when the animals were five years old and ready for work; the training of oxen and horses seems to have been in some sense a profession (Xen. *Mem.* 4.4–5).[138] Or their spare cattle were sold for sacrifices; elsewhere sacred herds were maintained specially for these purposes, but in Attica perhaps the supply of sacrificial victims was left to private enterprise.

An episode that has often been used to argue that Attica was indeed very poor even in draft cattle, let alone beef animals, may actually tell us more about the ox owners of Plataea. In the late 330s Eudemus of Plataea was honored by the Athenians for providing 1,000 yoke of oxen to transport stone for the construction of the stadium and the Panathenaic theater. This may mean neither that the Athenians had very few oxen altogether, nor that

Eudemus himself owned a (rather large) cattle ranch just over the Boeotian border. What beasts were they, then? The oxen were plow animals belonging to the larger part of the Plataean land-owning population, on whom Eudemus prevailed to share in a gesture of aid and friendship toward its old champions the Athenians, by sending practical assistance in the form of ox-power. The oxen came to work before the Panathenaea, which took place in July/August—as it happens, one of the slackest times in the agricultural year and just when the cart tracks would have been dry. Eudemus's generosity presumably lay in his subsidizing the whole undertaking, forage and all.[139]

Milk cattle in places like Attica consisted of no more than plowing cows that had happened to calve. Dairy cattle were raised in better pastured regions where scenes of "farmyard flies buzzing round full milk pails" (*Il.* 16.641ff.) and "droves of cows coming home full-fed from the pastures . . . welcomed by their frisking calves which burst out of their pens to gambol round their mothers and fill the air with the sound of their lowing" (*Od.* 10.410ff.) were familiar enough, in such places as Boeotia, Thessaly, Acarnania, Epirus. The cattle of Epirus were fabulous beasts—they "yield an amphora of milk a day, and the milker has to stand up" because the cows are so big, so Aristotle was led to believe (*HA* 522 b 15–19). The royal herd of Pyrrhic cattle alone numbered about 400 (*HA* 595 b 19–22). Not only in the vaster countryside of northwest Greece, but round about Delphi too, suitable pasture belonging to the sanctuary could be found for both cattle and horses; these animals brought in revenue, perhaps from the sale of calves and foals.[140] In Boeotia, the city of Orchomenus, situated as it was close to Lake Copais and the surrounding flatlands, could afford to offer grazing privileges to a rancher from Elatea in Phocis for 250 cattle and horses and 1,000 sheep and goats;[141] the marsh plants spoken of by Theophrastus as good feed for horses would have been found in abundance within such an area (*HP* 4.10.1–7).

Keeping horses was a luxury that in many places only a minority could afford, and in some places no one was allowed (see chapter 2). Thessaly was horse country par excellence; some individuals controlled hundreds, and Jason of Pherae could expect 8,000 cavalry altogether from the cities of Thessaly (Xen. *HG* 6.1.18–19). Sicilian Greeks considered training horses a slave's occupation, whereas Thessalians are said to have trained their horses themselves; pride in their horses is beautifully displayed on some of their coinage.[142] The *breeding* of horses was more or less restricted to regions with abundant pasture of the right kind; *keeping* one cavalry horse was probably as much as most horse owners in Attica could manage.

Even if the quality of pasture in many places did not permit the keeping of cattle and horses over and above the essential minimum, every community was rich in sheep and goats. Yet there were limits set on individual holdings: whereas Euboulos of Elatea could consider keeping 1,000 sheep and goats, Athenians seem to have owned considerably smaller flocks—Panaetius had 84 sheep and 67 goats, numbers closely matched by other well-to-do property owners and surpassed by none that we know of.[143] Ischomachus speaks approvingly of stock raising, and there is no doubt that Xenophon saw it as an integral part of the farming economy (*Oecon.* 20.23).[144] "Does Criton keep dogs to ward off wolves from his sheep?" asks Socrates (*Mem.* 2.9.2), making in the same conversation a picturesque comparison between Criton's poor but reliable friend Archedemus and the sheep dog near which other shepherds wish to station their flocks, for protection. The vow the Athenians made before Marathon, that they would sacrifice one goat for every one of the Persian enemy killed, also illustrates the dimensions of Attic goat keeping—since the Persian casualties were over 6,000, the Athenians ran out of goats in 490 and decided to fulfill their vow with an annual sacrifice of 500 animals instead (Xen. *Anab.* 3.2.12). These would have been goats that could be easily spared, *not* the core of the total goat stock of Attica.

Poorer landowners would have kept proportionately fewer animals; there is however no reason to suppose that poverty decreased their interest in as diversified use of their land as possible, or in the benefits that livestock could bestow on both land and household. Theirs too were presumably part of the migration of beasts to the offshore islands in 431.

Sheep and goats could be kept penned, without pasture, if they were few in number or if the farm had enough forage—straw, grasses, vegetable refuse, vine clippings, tree prunings, and so on, to maintain them so. The island of Ceos did not provide good grazing so that the farmers had to feed the few that they kept, and they made considerable use of *kytisos,* the fodder crop imported from Cythnos, together with fig leaves, olive leaves, bean pods and husks, and even thistles specially sown among the field crops.[145] Small flocks on many an Athenian farm could have been maintained in much the same way, and the fine-wooled sheep of places like Taras and Miletus were probably treated thus, for with their protective jackets over their precious fleeces they would have been all too likely to become snagged on low branches and other hazards if let to roam at will. The manure of penned and stalled animals would be easy to collect for use on the fields. But if grazing was easily accessible it could cost less to put them out to pasture. Thus one of the scenes on Achilles' shield suggests that the animals go out to pasture during the day and return to pens and byres in the evening (*Il.* 18.587–89). They would then have competed with pigs and draft animals also on the lookout for what they could pick up round about the farm, depending on the season of the year and the state of the crops. If there was scrubland nearby, they could be put on to that. Some estates included within their bounds just the kind of land suitable for grazing—Phaenippus's, for example, and various estates belonging to sanctuaries. Much of this kind of territory in Attica may have remained public, or in the control of the demes; so it is that one of the very rare pieces of evidence for pasture management comes in a record of lands managed by the deme of Piraeus.[146] In the case of publicly owned pasture, the grazier had to pay a fee, and probably to brand his beasts.[147]

Some herds may have been kept permanently on distant pastures, their owner (or manager) visiting them periodically to check the number of beasts and their condition and, if they were wool sheep, to oversee the sale or disposal of wool at shearing time. Regions such as the Megarian and Boeotian borderlands or the slopes of the mountains Parnes, Pentele, and Hymettus may have had more or less permanent "communities" of herdsmen and their charges moving about over them.[148]

In some instances animals may have shifted a fair distance between winter feeding about the farm or in the lowlands to summer pasture in the hills. Indeed long-range transhumance has been seen as a dominant feature of ancient herding, largely because of the episode in the Oedipus-story of the meeting between shepherds from Corinth and Thebes round about Mount Cithaerum. It is true that sheep and goats can feel the effects of extremes in climate, so that there is much to be said for avoiding summer heat and winter chill (as well as catching the best of the grazing) by moving between higher and lower elevations. But as Hodkinson now points out, the Greek landscape is generally such that it is not necessary to go far so as to achieve such a change; a shepherd on the upper slopes of a mountain need only be an hour or so away from farmland, even his own farm, and Hesiod at Ascra had but five kilometers or so to go between Mount Helicon where he herded flocks and met the Muses, and his father's farm in the valley below.[149] So the herdsmen of Locris and Phocis who came to blows in the pastures about Mount Parnassus may some of them have come not very far from their home farms on either side of the frontier.[150]

In other parts of Greece, longer journeys between winter grazing and summer pasture may have been necessary. Some of the herdsmen seeking refuge for their beasts from the summer heat of the Thessalian plain may have gone far into the hills, for example; and certain Aegean islands were the subject of fierce competition because they offered grazing.[151] But the large migrations of flocks typical of herding in medieval and modern Spain, France, Italy, Greece, or Turkey came about in political or commercial circumstances that did not exist in antiquity.[152]

The needs of sheep and goats varied somewhat as regards the kind of grazing they preferred, and they would have been pastured separately if they were kept in any numbers, sheep doing better on slightly less rugged terrain than goats. The herdsman's required knowledge was essentially the same as it must have been for long ages past, handed down through close observation and repeated lifetimes of experience from master herder to apprentice, from father to son. Herding was often enough a *profession* in that landowners who did not tend their own animals or depute their children to do so often hired or bought shepherds and goatherds who had already learned their job elsewhere, or trained a slave of their own to work full-time with the flocks. A good livestock owner would keep an eye on his beasts, and only a good shepherd retained his position. The lines of communication running through any country district would have brought news of wrong-doing or disaster in the pastures, for the neighborliness that involved knowing another man's business would include knowing his shepherd and sometimes even his sheep. Damaging though much local gossip could be, the exchange of this kind of information must on occasion have been very helpful.

Aristotle's discussion of the care that sheep and goats required suggests something of the rigors of the herdsman's life, as well as the attention to detail and quickness of reaction he must exercise. He should remember the ages of the females in particular, for if ewes are bred too young their lambs will be weak (*HA* 546 a 5); the ewes may continue to be bred until the age of eight, but some may do well for another three years even after that (545 b 31). Billy goats that are overweight must be thinned down to make them more capable sires (*HA* 546 a 1). When grazing in summer sheep need to be given salt regularly to help fatten them; but this means that they must have plenty of water—an additional reason for moving them to lusher pastures in the heat and drought of summer; milk ewes may be encouraged to give more milk in autumn by the addition of salted cucumbers to their feed (*HA* 596 a 13–22). To ensure that the sheep drink properly in the evening, they should be kept on the move during the day; and the herdsman must therefore make sure that their day ends near a water source, if not back at the farmyard (*HA* 596 a 23).[153] He may also look out for pasture that faces west, away from the full glare of the midday sun, and for autumn rain from the north rather than the south (*HA* 596 a 28–29). When walking the sheep on, he must not hurry or rush them; but he should always be aware of their foolishness—their tendency to wander off on their own, especially in stormy weather, to stop in their tracks if there is a snowstorm until the shepherd shoves them on again, and to scatter in a thunderstorm instead of gathering together (*HA* 610 b 22–28). Goats stand the cold less well—the north wind blows "through an ox's hide and through the hairy goat," as Hesiod says (*WD* 515–16); in bad weather "when a goatherd sees a cloud bearing down on him from across the sea . . . with the whirlwind in its wake, darkening in the distance till it looks as black as pitch, [he] shudders at the sight and drives the flock to a cave" (*Il.* 4.275–79). In winter the shepherd may distinguish the stronger from the more weakly sheep by the fact that the stronger ones do not shake the hoarfrost from their fleeces because they do not feel burdened by the weight of it (*HA* 596 a 32–b 1). Sheep are healthier than goats, but goats are stronger, although easily astonished if the beard of one of them is tweaked (*HA* 610 b 29).

Sheepshearing, like milking (and cheese making), would where feasible have been done on the farm, the sheep being brought in from pasture to be shorn at or just before the full moon, so Hesiod says (*WD* 775). Who sheared the sheep is not clear; shepherds must certainly have known how to doctor, slaughter, and skin their charges, but the shearer may have been another of the itinerant workers of country society. Sometimes the flocks may have been at far-distant pastures, so that all their care had to be dispensed at the sheepfold in the grazing ground; the owner might come himself with assistants at such times, and also to take over the wool and cheeses when they were ready to be disposed of.

The herdsman's life was not easy; out in all weathers, solitary much of the time because necessarily seeking out unfrequented stretches of country, he must keep watch not only for erring animals but also for wolves and unwanted human visitors. The herdsman's dependence on a good dog is made clear many times, to give warning of danger and no doubt to help in herding. There is no reference to this aspect of the sheep dog, but it would be surprising if shepherds in antiquity had not become aware that an intelligent dog could be trained for such work. Both man and dog would have slept with one eye open, the herdsman among his charges, especially in winter—goats, says Aristotle, will provide more warmth for the herdsman than sheep, because "their greater intolerance of the cold draws them more closely round him" (*HA* 610 b 33).

The principles of stock raising, of how to maintain quality by selective breeding, correct nutrition, and so on, must surely have been as much common knowledge as those of agriculture. Pastoral interests were so considerable a part of the economic traditions of Greek society that few men would have been without an opinion to express about the condition of a horse, a fattening pig, a wool sheep, a milk goat, or a plow ox in training; these, like the fields, the orchards, the vineyards, and the gardens were the instruments with which men built up their reserves against poverty and famine, and displayed their ability to control the natural world in some degree.

The traditional methods of utilizing the land were effective, and insofar as they suited the regions where they were employed, they were efficient too. The question remains, how well did the Greek farmers feed the population that the land was intended to support, directly by providing crops for consumption, and indirectly by making available produce for exchange? This is a subject that goes beyond the scope of this study, but the question was surely one which every landowner who thought at all about his economic situation must have asked, and every community that suffered a food shortage must have discussed.[154] What could be done to improve productivity? The answer, according to ancient concepts, was very little, beyond insisting on the fullest obedience to the best, traditional precepts of farming such as were laid down in the lease agreements for public and sacred lands, for example; there are various hints that the community may have intervened in the private farming of land to some extent too.[155]

Greek agriculture had its limitations, to be sure, but none, perhaps, that could have been overcome before the introduction of modern machinery, fertilizers, and methods of irrigation, just as stock raising could only go so far, by selective breeding, before the advent of modern pharmaceuticals and manufactured feeds. Discussion has tried to take account of the Greeks' methods and of the improvements that, it has been thought, the Greeks should have made, and to show that, for example, far from failing to adopt the system of rotation of crops and cultivation of pulses within the cycle of cereal growing, they were aware of the advantages of doing so but often enough chose not to use this method—for the same reasons, no doubt, that farmers in large parts of medieval Europe did not take to it later, either; it did not always suit.[156] Improvement of the plow, so that it would cut more deeply, or turn the sod better, was not thought generally necessary in an agricultural system that worked with shallow soil, on the whole, and depended more heavily than did medieval and modern farmers of northern Europe on digging.[157] They did not underestimate the value of manure nor were they so lacking in domestic animals as to be without the wherewithal to fertilize their crops. The land did not suffer from lack of investment, in that it was improved by the construction of necessary walls, drains, and irrigation systems, and by the stocking of farms according to the accepted understanding of what the land would and would not endure.[158] The quality of cereal and other plant stocks received continuous attention, again according to the traditional precepts of the farming community.[159] And if the Greeks' use of agricultural labor was what the modern view would characterize as inefficient and uneconomical, this is to judge their methods by criteria they would not have recognized; a brief consideration of the number of servants thought necessary to maintain a quite ordinary Victorian household should suggest that the employment of help is something that every age estimates according to its own preconceptions, of which the modern interpretation of economic rationalism may not be one.[160]

The Greeks' expectations were shaped by what they had come to realize the land could produce, under the type of treatment they had come to believe was best suited to it, and that was the traditional practices based on the accumulated experiences of many farming generations. Xenophon allows the possibility that "clever inventions" in farming have been made; he does not say what, but is mainly concerned to point out that it is not such things that make a farmer successful and prosperous (*Oecon.* 20.5). Ischomachus and his father have been in the habit of buying neglected and run-down properties to improve by bringing them back to full production in the traditional way, not to obtain farms that are already as productive as they can be according to the traditional system and then to enhance their productivity by applying new methods. It is not ignorance of new ways of doing things which causes a farmer to fail, but sloth. A man may know all about how to drain land, but it benefits him not at all if he refuses to get out and do what needs to be done—in the way that it has been done countless times before.

New discoveries there were, mainly concerning hitherto unknown plants, whose cultivation necessitated no major alteration of techniques and arrangements for either farmer or stockbreeder, but which helped to expand the repertoire of useful and beneficial crops available. Alfalfa, introduced by what means we do not know, became highly valued as a fodder crop, for horses in particular; *kytisos,* the herb native to the island of Cythnos and used there as an excellent feed for sheep, for some reason was not generally familiar even in the Aegean region until the Classical period, but then became popular especially in places that lacked suitable fodder of other kinds. In addition there were changes in the plant population which came about naturally, as one strain gave way to another, so that agriculture could not avoid taking them into account too. The strength of the farming tradition was that it did not block but freely admitted minor improvements of this kind.

There were agricultural disasters that no one could have prevented, the result of war, bad weather, insects, or diseases uncontrollable until very recent times (by methods which have brought their own problems). There were also landowners who failed to get the best out of their land because they were inept, inefficient, lazy, or careless, about whom no one except a creditor or an enraged relative, perhaps, could do anything either; Timarchus is a case in point (see chapter 2). But it would be unreasonable to condemn Greek farmers altogether on the grounds that some of them did not do very well by the traditional methods. Bad farmers have existed in every age; so too have obstinacy and narrow self-interest, and there may have been many a time when fear of taking

risks, sheer brute conservatism, or superstition impeded necessary undertakings by opposing the extension of arable cultivation
into hitherto uncultivated land, or the diversion of a watercourse
to provide a more sensible system of irrigation; or by delaying the
necessary destruction of trees or the shifting of a rocky landmark
when new boundaries or terrace walls were being planned. When
problems such as these affected the community's interest in the
land, they would have been solved by a communal decision that
brooked no challenge; often enough opposition to the opening of
new land for cultivation or the converting of conveniently located
pasture to fields may have had to be broken down, in order to
provide holdings for more citizen families.[161] But a landowner
faced with the unwillingness of his own laborers, herdsmen, or
bailiff, who countered every suggested adaptation of the received
way of doing things with the inherently hostile lead-in, "But we
always used to . . . ," must often have had difficulty in getting his
ideas implemented, and occasionally must have been defeated; in
this he would have experienced nothing peculiar to the Greek
world.

## The Troubled Countryside

Agriculture imposed its own discipline on the countryside; the
land was cleared, divided up, and drained where necessary, trees
cut down, watercourses put into use if not actually diverted, the
earth plowed, planted, and reaped, and order imposed on the
natural disorder of the landscape. Generally regarded as a divine
gift to mankind, agriculture could also have been considered a
kind of flying-in-the-face-of-nature, a disturbance of the natural
rhythms and waywardness of the countryside. The peaceful and
benign productivity of the agricultural cycle could in its turn be
disrupted by natural disasters on one hand—blights, insect infes-
tations, gales, floods, frost, or drought—and on the other by human intervention in the shape of war.

One of the root causes of many wars was competition for farmland lying between neighboring communities; and throughout
Greek history, among the pretexts for one war after another would

be a boundary dispute or a quarrel about grazing, if one or other were not itself the main reason for hostility.[162] The techniques of war generally included destruction of the enemy's crops and its agricultural infrastructure, and the looting of stores, farm animals, and laborers as far as seemed useful.[163] In the *Republic* Plato raises the question of ravaging in time of war: "What about devastating the lands and burning the houses of Greek enemies? . . . I do not think they ought to do either, but confine themselves to carrying off the year's harvests" (*Rep.* 470 a–b). This was the policy of Alyattes of Lydia against the Milesians in the early sixth century; he invaded the territory when the crops were ripe and plundered the land, but left the country houses undamaged, so that the Milesians would have somewhere to live and would therefore continue to cultivate the land, thus assuring the Lydians of something to take when they next invaded (Hdt. 1.17).

But there were varying degrees of destruction, from the incidental damage caused by the passing of a hoplite phalanx over grainfields or through young and still low-growing plantations to the systematic chopping down of vines and fruit trees, often enough simply for the sake of destroying them and diminishing the enemy's crops for the future, but sometimes so as to have wood for fuel or the construction of fortifications. If thorough devastation was the aim, special tactics and special forces were required. Heavy-armed hoplites whose success depended on holding the line could not afford to step out of rank to hack at trees or drive off cattle, so that light-armed skirmishers would be brought in for such purposes. Spartan tactics against the Athenians in the first part of the Peloponnesian War included a yearly invasion of Attica "just as the grain was ripening," as Thucydides mentions several times;[164] from 412 onward, the Spartans maintained a permanent base at Decelea, from which they carried out raids into the Athenian countryside until toward the end of the war, sometimes looting for supplies, and sometimes with specially assigned forces to attempt to destroy the farmland root and branch (Thuc. 7.27.3–5).[165]

The common assumption has been that Athenian agriculture was virtually stamped out for almost a generation, for when the sources say that the land was laid waste or the crops were burned, it is natural to suppose that the damage inflicted was total.[166] Hanson's reexamination of the subject shows that while pillaging of stores and seizure of men and animals would have been comparatively easy, the actual cutting down and destruction of crops and trees would have taken considerable time and energy. Green crops will not burn easily, and trees may survive the loss of leaves and even branches, unless fire is set about the base of each tree, for in a well-spaced orchard fire would not necessarily spread quickly. Chopping down even young fruit trees, let alone olive trees two or three centuries old, requires some application; and to destroy a mature vineyard might take something like eight men an hour per *plethron* of really hard work. The loss of the year's harvest would certainly be a hardship, if there were few reserve stores left, and even the threat of losing it could be enough to persuade a community to give in to the enemy, as when Brasidas addressed the people of Acanthus just as their grapes were ripening (Thuc. 4.88.1).[167] Even more serious would be the occupation of the land so as to prevent farmers from getting out to their fields in time to plow and sow. In the troubled times of the third century the land of Attica was "uncultivated and unsown because of war";[168] and the Spartans' pressure on the Thebans during the 370s was such that for two years the Thebans could bring in no crops from their land, so that they ran out of grain and had to send money and boats to get supplies in Thessaly (Xen. *HG* 5.4.56–57).

Some parts of Attica were certainly cut off from the farmers for a time during the Peloponnesian War, especially after 412. But there are signs even so that some farming did go on, and that by no means every olive tree, terrace wall, or grainfield was uprooted, flattened, or made into a cavalry horse's drill school. The olive trees on Hagnias's land, described as the glory of the estate around 360, must have been well established before Hagnias's death, in the 390s, which is to say at some point during or even before the Peloponnesian War, since olive trees take some time to mature; thus they would have survived some of the worst periods of devastation in Attica (Dem. 43.69). And the history of the sacred olive-tree estate suggests some resumption of farming before the war ended (Lysias 7).[169] Theophrastus shows that the repair of wounded and maimed trees was as much part of the farmer's traditional expertise as any other aspect of tree tending (*HP* 4.15.1–2). Everyone accepted the inevitability of the serious interruptions to the farming cycle that war caused, and equally the need to continue cultivating the land as long as the enemy was not actually barring the way; so, once the danger had passed, the work of recovery must begin, however thorough the destruction and however depressing to the landowners and farmers it must always have been. Just as their great-grandfathers had done after the Persian War—and thorough the destruction in Attica must have been then, after one sack carried out in triumphant expectation of quick victory, and the second in vindictive disappointment—Athenian landowners, rich and poor, started picking up the pieces as soon as it seemed safe to do so, rescuing what could be salvaged and casting about for laborers, seed grain, house doors, draft animals, tools, manure. Lessees of public and sacred estates were expected to carry on, paying the rent regularly and with "no deductions in either wartime or peacetime," as a Chian document says; whereas various Athenian leases provided that "if enemies ravage the estate [so that he cannot pay the full rent], the lessee is to hand over half of whatever he gets from what is left of the crops on the land to the lessors" or lose his lease.[170]

Work on the land went on even if it required military protection to get the necessary jobs done. The city of Istria honored Agathocles for raising a volunteer force to protect the land, the crops, and the flocks until the Thracian threat receded; and the Athenians honored their general Epichares for saving the fortress of Rhamnous during the war of the 260s.[171] He kept guard to enable the farmers to get in their crops safely from an area within a five-kilometer radius of the fortress, built grain silos, made efforts to protect the vineyards, put up defense towers, and provided guard dogs along with their rations.

Agriculture was disturbed even more frequently by natural disasters. Since cultivable plants and the techniques of farming were the gift of the gods, since anxiety for the food supply was one of the most deep-seated within all communities, and since they were predominantly agricultural in their economies, inevitably the concerns of agriculture and the rhythms of the farming year were central to the religious rituals by which the Greeks propitiated their gods: it was of prime importance that there should be good harvests, so that society could not only be maintained in the manner to which it had become accustomed, but would be assured of survival.[172] Yet the cycle of festivals and sacrifices performed in every Greek city was also intended to affirm its social and political solidarity, to identify the interests of each family with those of the community as a whole, to reduce any sense of insecurity, and to reconcile differences between one group and another. In some respects, then, it is possible to see that the primary or primitive preoccupation with the continued fertility of the land, as of the population, was overlaid and to some extent suppressed by more cerebral interests.[173] Thus the institution at Athens, for example, of the statewide offering of *aparchai* to the Two Goddesses at Eleusis (1/600 of barley and 1/1,200 of wheat from every crop harvested) may have seemed to the farmers concerned less a direct propitiation of the deities in the hope of good harvests to come, and a thank offering for harvests past, than a compulsory contribution to a cult that was directed more toward cosmic matters of life and death on one hand, and Athens's international standing on the other, rather than to the specific anxieties of the agriculturalist.[174] Was Eleusinian Demeter's association with grain such that her cult aided the growth of cereals first and foremost, or was it rather that the cereal association contributed to her cult? If, as one ancient source states, the central part of the Mysteries consisted of the revelation to the initiates of an ear of wheat, what if anything had this to do *directly* with the crops growing in the fields? Agricultural interests were present in religious practice, they shaped the religious calendar (of Athens certainly, and surely of other cities too); they formed a strand in the basic composition of cult but so intricately twisted in that they were an undercurrent, only, in the blend of cultural and political concerns that cult addressed.

Were there not less formal manifestations of the Olympian

gods which could be approached for the solution of specific agricultural difficulties, and lesser gods and heroes who were more immediately associated with the farmer's needs and with the natural features of the countryside which farmers confronted or worked round on their land?[175] The Zeus and Demeter to whom Hesiod recommended prayer before plowing were, surely, the rain-god and the grain-goddess. Drought was the threat to stave off which processions and sacrifices to Zeus the bringer of rain were held.[176] Ritual magic to deal with damaging winds included the strange performance reported from Methana for the protection of vines and probably Empedocles' maneuver with the bags of donkey skin (both noted earlier in this chapter). But to whom or what did the seers at Taras sacrifice, in the hopes of forestalling damage to olive trees in flower? To Apollo perhaps, in one of his various guises as the protector against specific dangers: we know of Apollo Smintheus, destroyer of crop-devouring mice; Apollo Erysibius, protector against "rust" or mildew on grain; Apollo Pornopius, slayer of locusts. Heracles, most helpful (and most forceful) of all the heroes, was also credited with the destruction of locusts, and of the vine pest *ips,* as well as with solving certain technical problems that cultivation of the land created.[177]

The forces that made the crops grow and farming prosper were recognized in the oath of the Athenian ephebes. Along with the Olympians Ares, Athena, and Zeus (concerned with war, the cultural existence of Athens, and the cosmic order), and local deities (Agraulos and others, all connected with the defense of the community and its households) are Thallo or Increase (as of a young, new-shooting tree), and Auxe or Growth, and "the boundaries of the country, the wheat (plants), the barley (plants), the vines, the olive trees, the figs."[178] The crops themselves are included among the beings that sustain and defend the community, although they are also among the objects of the ephebes' attention, and they are obviously regarded as autonomous in some way. Parallels to this thinking come in Herodotus's story of the statues of Damia and Auxesia which the Epidaurians set up after a drought had caused their crops to fail (5.82.1).[179] And the ephebic oath of Cretan Dreros includes the country's rivers and streams among the deities by which the ephebes swore, indicating the kind of recognition given to water, that most necessary element.[180] Greek rivers were commonly regarded as divine, as was the Strymon at Amphipolis, where the city dedicated confiscated property to the river and the god Apollo.[181]

Deities who did not receive the constant worship of their followers were liable to overthrow the established order in their anger, disrupting agriculture and, as a direct consequence, civilized life. Two myths that show most clearly the anxieties felt by Greek society on this score come, both of them, from Arcadia, the source of other particularly dire and strange themes.[182] Early in the fifth century the people of Phigalea suffered a terrible drought, because they had omitted to restore Demeter's statue after it was destroyed in a fire and had then neglected her cult. They consulted the Delphic oracle, which in its reply called them "acorn eaters," meaning that they were having to revert to the habits of life in the wild before Demeter gave them the blessings of cereal agriculture; her rage now threatened to upturn the civilized order so completely that they would have to take up nomadic herding without a settled city they could call home, and with habits to match, including that of cannibalism (Paus. 8.42.5–7). Arcadia presented other problems to the agriculturalist: not only was much of the land not very fertile, its proclivity to flood, especially round about Stymphalia, rendered it unhelpful even to herdsmen. Efforts were made to drain land so that it could be farmed, and thereby hangs the second myth.

Artemis was the goddess of the wild throughout the Greek world, her sanctuaries often located in marshes, her particular care the animals that lived in the wild, and her favorite pursuit, hunting, which if properly done made use of but did not wipe out the animal life with which she was so closely associated. But there were contradictions in her situation: she had also become the patron and protector of the Stymphalians, whose use of marshland had, incidentally, destroyed the terrain she really preferred and the habitat of creatures she cherished. When the Stymphalians neglected her worship, her anger caused the natural fissure by which the area was drained to be blocked up; and the ensuing flood was ended only after a hunter in pursuit of a deer fell into the fissure and vanished (Paus. 8.22.8–9). Artemis was thus appeased by the death (sacrifice?) of a hunter who had her original interests at heart, so that she then allowed her marshland to become cultivable once more. The myth creates contradictions in Artemis's nature perhaps in part to justify man's tampering with the natural order, as agriculturalists must, to gain ground in which to plant crops. One might also consider the sixth labor of Heracles, whereby he rid Stymphalia of the terrible birds that killed men and beasts with brazen talons and blighted the crops with their excrement—another version of the justification for draining marshes, which had the effect of driving away the water birds formerly accustomed to breed or flock there during migrations (Paus. 8.22.4).[183]

The realization that human settlement and agricultural activity disrupt the natural order of the territory in which they occur struck some Greeks quite forcefully, but preoccupation with the agricultural needs of society usually outweighed environmental and ecological concerns.[184] Yet the conflict of these interests is apparent in Odysseus's description of the island near the Cyclopes' country, which he readily points out would make an excellent farming settlement for them:

> Not very far from the harbor on their coast, and not so near either, there lies a luxuriant island, covered with woods, which is the home of innumerable goats. The goats are wild, for man has made no pathways that might frighten them off, nor do hunters visit the island with their hounds to rough it in the forests and to range the mountain tops. Used neither for grazing nor for plowing, it lies forever unsown and untilled; and this land where no man goes makes a happy pasture for the bleating goats. (*Od.* 9.116–24)

# Four

# Management of the Land

There were, broadly speaking, three alternative means of managing the land available to the landowner. He could either do so himself, as an *autourgos* "working on his own account"; he could employ an *epitropos*, or bailiff, who would deal directly with the other laborers and see that the estate produced its proper complement of crops and profits; or he could become a landlord and let the land to a tenant who would assume all the responsibility of farming the land while rendering a regular rent. The second and third alternatives did not necessarily rule out all participation or interest for the owner in the working of his estate, although these were the methods of choice if he wished to have as little to do with it as possible. It is not easy to decide to what category a landowner belongs: Hesiod's farmer is surely an *autourgos*, whereas Ischomachus employs a bailiff, at the same time retaining a lively supervisory interest in his land. But what about Ameinocles, who "possessed land" near Cape Sepias and who became rich after finding treasure washed up from the wreck of the Persian fleet in 480 (Hdt. 7.190.1–2), or Aphobus, Demosthenes' guardian and cousin, who was observed *farming his own land* (while supposedly living as a registered metic in Megara)

(Dem. 30.26–27)?[1] The Greek *georgeo* can mean either "I farm," in the general sense of directing work being done by others, or "I farm" literally, in the sense of personally cultivating the soil with mattock, plow, or hoe. Aphobus may have been glimpsed on one of his occasional visits as supervisory owner, to see how the bailiff was faring; or he may have acted, temporarily perhaps, as his own farm manager, overseeing and taking a hand in the work demanded by the season.

A simple way of deciding which is more likely would be to assume that wealth and status determined the landowner's mode of managing his property; thus the *autourgos* would generally be of modest social background and obliged by poverty to employ his own labor on the land, whereas more affluent and better-born landowners automatically hired or purchased bailiffs along with other laborers to manage their land for them, giving as much or as little of their personal attention to their estates as they chose. Those who rented their lands to tenants might then be considered the very great landowners who could best afford to remove themselves as far as possible from the concerns of stable, field, and vineyard. However, rigid distinctions of this nature do not fit the ancient situation, as far as we can determine it; landowners appear to have made their choice according to their personal tastes and whatever other preoccupations they had besides land. So that although the *autourgoi* certainly included all who worked on their land through necessity, there were also *autourgoi* who did *not* have to do so simply because they could not afford to maintain help beyond that of their own family; just as some tenancies may have involved small farms belonging to poor men who chose to live penurious but leisured lives away from the land, on a little bit of rent and whatever else they could pick up, rather than toil as *autourgoi* on the family plot.[2]

## The Autourgos

For Xenophon, the *autourgos* is synonymous with the poor farmer. In the *Cyropaedia,* Cyrus declares that those Persians who make the best bodyguards are *autourgoi* living poverty-stricken lives and struggling with a harsh land. One of them, Pheraulus, says of his own background:

> We were poor at home. My father supported us by hard work [*autos ergazomenos*] and economy; he managed to give me a boy's education, but when I grew older he took me off to the farm and put me to work. And there I supported him for the rest of his life, by digging and planting a very little plot of ground—a nice and honest little plot, in that it returned all the seed it received fairly and honestly but without much interest, though sometimes it made a twofold return. (*Cyrop.* 8.3.37–38)

Persian the context may be, but Xenophon's vocabulary and imagery come straight from the Greek experience; the disparagement of land and crops is of course a characteristic shared by all farmers, rich and poor, arising from an unwillingness to tempt fate by speaking of the possibility of good yields, and could perfectly well have been said by an Athenian—as it was by Menander's *Farmer*.[3] The *autourgos* is here presented as hardworking and poor, and in the *Oeconomicus* Xenophon equates hard work and *autourgia*— toil hardens men's bodies, both of the *autourgos* and the bailiff, who have to rise early to see to things (*Oecon.* 5.4).[4]

When Thucydides uses the word, however, he surely has a rather different meaning in mind. As he discusses the differences in resources between the Athenians and their allies on one side and the Spartans and their Peloponnesian allies on the other, Pericles says:

> The Peloponnesians are *autourgoi,* and they have no financial resources either as individuals or as states. . . . They have no experience of . . . any fighting that lasts a long time. . . . Such people cannot be constantly manning a fleet or sending out armies. . . . Moreover, *autourgoi* are more anxious in wartime about their money than their lives. . . . they may survive but their resources may not last out. (Thuc. 1.141.3–5)

He cannot mean that the Peloponnesians, including Spartans, Corinthians, Epidaurians, Elians, Arcadians, and Mantineans, were all of them poor men working their own small plots on their own; apart from the helots of Laconia and Messenia, there were agri-

cultural workers of one kind or another (free, hired, tied, enslaved) in all regions of the Peloponnese. It is unimaginable that
prosperous Corinthians, for example, rivals in their way of the
Athenians as to overseas interests, diversity of economic pursuits,
and so on, depended on their own and their families' labor for the
cultivation of their crops. The true meaning of *autourgos* to describe the Peloponnesians is revealed by the further remark that
the Spartans "showed great energy, but the allies were slow to
come together since they were concerned with getting their harvests in, and were tired of military service" (3.15.1–2). *Autourgos*
seems to have the pejorative sense of "peasant" in Thucydides'
depiction of the Peloponnesians, an impression heightened by his
having Pericles continue his speech by contrasting their concep-
tual and financial limitations with the resources of the brilliantly
active Athenians, whose horizons reach far above and beyond the
limits of their territory, and who are preoccupied with more than
the farmyard, furrowed field, or orchard of the mere farmer ob-
sessed by the state of the weather and his own crops. In which
case the term *autourgos* as Thucydides uses it has no particular
bearing on the scale of farming operations, but relates to the attitude of mind shared by landowners who may have differed from
one another in wealth and social position but who were yet bound
by common agricultural anxieties.[5]

The scorn implicit in Thucydides' use of the word is not intended by his contemporary Euripides, for whom the *autourgos* is
"a courageous man, rarely frequenting the city and the circuit of
the *agora,* an *autourgos* [farmer], one of those who alone preserve
the land"—that is to say, not that they necessarily farm on their
own, but that no other group in society preserves the land in the
way they do (*Orestes* 918–20). Likewise, the *autourgos* to whom
Electra is married is noble in descent (from the aristocracy of
Mycenae), as well as in behavior; he has nothing of the "peasant" about him except his poverty—he is an *autourgos* who happens to be poor, not a man who is poor and is therefore an *autourgos* (Eur. *Electra* 35–38). That there could be poorer and less
poor *autourgoi,* Menander's *Dyscolus* strongly suggests—the misanthrope "works his land himself, *alone,*" as an *autourgos* and on

his own. In order that he may be more inclined to talk, one of the other characters must get to work with his spade so as to resemble "an *autourgos with no resources*" (*Dyscolus* 326, 369–70).

Hesiod's farmer is surely an *autourgos*, although Hesiod does not use the word. He works on the land himself, but he does not work by himself; he has laborers whom he supervises and instructs, and whose labor he shares too to a considerable extent, like Aristophanes' *georgoi*, Trygaeus (*Peace*) and Chremylus (*Plutus*) and their fellows.[6] The Plataeans who were outside the city in the fields when the Thebans invaded at the beginning of the Peloponnesian War were many of them *autourgoi*, some no doubt working on their own, others in charge of and working alongside a hired or slave laborer or two—of sufficient status for the Thebans to have come hoping to capture and exchange some of them for prisoners taken from the Theban side (Thuc. 2.5.4). But what about Eratosthenes' killer, or his friends and neighbors who also spent time out of the city "in the country," presumably on their farms (Lysias 1)? Did they go to and fro to farm the land themselves, or only to supervise their laborers periodically and to bring back supplies? And when the assassin Apollodorus of Megara, and after him the "present owner" of the estate where the sacred olive tree might or might not have grown, are spoken of as "farming the land," are they also *autourgoi*, or simply "possessors and enjoyers" of the land they own (Lysias 7.4, 11)? The man accused of destroying the olive tree speaks of allegations against him that he supervised while his slaves wielded the tools with which the deed was done, which suggests at least that he was known to spend time on the estate, directing the work that was done there.[7] So the moderate oligarch Polystratus, a man of some political prominence during the rule of the Four Hundred, who is described as a "good farmer," might be considered an *autourgos* (Lysias 20.33); like the Persian Pheraulus he had been sent away to be educated, after which he returned to country life.[8]

The neighbors who witnessed the fight between the brothers Thoudippus and Euthycrates are described as *syngeorgountes*, which could mean "fellow-farmer-workers" or *autourgoi*, or, simply, "fellow-land-owners-surveying-their-estates" (Isaeus 9.18).

But is either Thoudippus (son-in-law of Cleon) or Euthycrates likely ever to have farmed land with his own hands? All that can be said is that the land that came to Euthycrates' son Astyphilus was very carefully tended by Astyphilus's stepfather on his behalf, to such effect that he doubled the estate's value; this sounds as if he took personal charge of farming it—as an *autourgos,* then, but no doubt with assistants (Isaeus 9.28).

Apollodorus, the son of the banker Pasion, may have chosen to consolidate his status as a properly set-up Athenian, not only by owning land and taking up residence on a portion of it but also by attending personally to its cultivation; the details that are included in the speech against his hostile neighbor Nicostratus, of the damage done to the fruit-tree grafts, tree vines, nursery beds of olive trees, and the rose bed, like his comment elsewhere on the drought that killed the vegetables and dried up the wells, are perhaps meant to heighten the impression he wishes to convey that he is a truly down-to-earth Athenian devoted to the land as well as to the city (see chapter 2). His neighbor Nicostratus spent most of his time in the country, for while Apollodorus was away on public service, Nicostratus had at one time overseen his farm for him (Dem. 53.4). Both men, and Nicostratus's brother too, who owned slaves for hire as harvesters (Dem. 53.20–21), may be considered *autourgoi* of a kind.

The *autourgos* may be as close as we get to the concept of citizen farmer or yeoman farmer in the Greek world. Xenophon's *autourgos* is poor, but he proves a good soldier. And for Aristotle, surprisingly enough, this is the kind of man he includes among those worthy of esteem: "Men honor those who are liberal and courageous and just. And such we consider those who do not live upon others; the sort of men who live by their exertions, and among them those who farm . . . with their own hands— *autourgoi*" (*Rhet.* 1381 a 24).[9]

## Landowner and Bailiff

Being a full-time *autourgos* had serious disadvantages, in Aristotle's opinion. The poor *autourgos* could not afford, and the more prosperous *autourgos* chose not, to manage his land in some other way that allowed time for the proper activity of a free man, studying philosophy and participating in politics. Why, then, would a man who could afford *not* to work his land choose to do so? Because the alternative, to employ a bailiff or *epitropos,* had disadvantages too, as Xenophon's extensive discussion of the topic strongly implies (*Oecon.* 12–15). Ischomachus is freed from the need to attend to every detail of the estate's working and is thus able to devote much of his time to business in town, by the fact that he has selected from among his field slaves a man with certain qualities that fitted him to be trained for the position of overseer or bailiff; he has gone to great lengths to teach the man all he knows so that he will treat the estate almost as well and in almost the same way as if he were the owner. But Ischomachus cannot now simply go off and forget about his property; he must maintain the bailiff's loyalty and concern through continuous personal influence—and Xenophon makes a great point of the fact that Ischomachus expects to visit his farm every day (*Oecon.* 11. 15–18).[10] He insists that the bailiff must be trained and encouraged to act as an extension of the master's authority and expertise and, at the same time, that the prudent owner should not feel that he can abrogate responsibility for his land and still expect it to be well managed (*Oecon.* 13–14).[11]

Here one is tempted to ask whether Xenophon's underlying preoccupation in the *Oeconomicus* with good government, and in particular the good ruler's command of his lieutenants, has not led him to overemphasize the need for the landowner to take such particular care in the choice of his bailiff, and the rigorousness of his supervision. Or is the parallel entirely apposite, in that an unchecked and ill-trained bailiff was as disastrous to the estate he was in charge of as an unwatched and unprepared official to the province whose interests he was supposed to be fostering? This built-in disadvantage of slave labor, that it required constant supervision to be made really effective, is perhaps what Glotz has in mind when he chooses to refer to "the great landowner, like the small farmer, working the land himself," with specific reference to Ischomachus.[12]

Xenophon's analysis of the proper relationship between land-owner and bailiff raises the question whether the use of bailiffs to manage estates was a comparatively new development of the Classical period, or an age-old feature of landowning, which just happens to be paid attention in his discussion because it fits his argument nicely.[13] A case might be made for the proposition that bailiff-run estates were a result of the new economic attitude, which some have supposed Ischomachus and his father to represent, with the alienation of land only then having become possible and the dispossession of small farmers after the Peloponnesian War opening up a whole new era of landowning on a different footing from before, and that Xenophon is thus advocating a revolutionary approach to land management to match—if there were anything to be said in support of this entire construct.[14] But there really is not. The employment of a bailiff, a reliable and trustworthy headman, fits right into the traditional way of farming, everywhere and in every age; it represents no great step forward in either the management or the scale of estates, during or after the fifth century or at any other time in the Greek period. All but the smallest and poorest of farms must usually have had a laborer on whom the owner could depend in times of illness or unavoidable absence—on military service, at a deme meeting, in court, attending the assembly, or fulfilling a religious obligation. For there were always things to be done which would not wait—harvests to be completed, animals to be fed, the land to be cultivated, crops to be planted.

Whether or not the formal concept of *epitropos* (overseer) existed in early Greece, the reality surely did—for what were Odysseus's swineherd Eumaeus and his cattleman Philoetius, if not faithful stewards of their absent master's estate?[15] The fact that we hear of no bailiff as such until during the fifth century signifies not that bailiffs were unknown (in name *and* function) before then, but simply that the evidence, poor enough even in the Classical period for details of domestic economy, has almost completely faded from the earlier record. So that the first bailiff we hear of, Pericles' man Euangelus, who took care of Pericles' estate, the disposal of its agricultural produce in the market, and the provisioning of his household, should be seen as one in a long succession of confidential servants who managed their owners' land to a greater or lesser extent. In any case, it is not Euangelus *as bailiff* which is a new phenomenon: Plutarch mentions him not because he manages Pericles' estate but because he manages it, on Pericles' instructions, in rather a special way—

> which seemed to Pericles the simplest and most exact method of dealing with [his inherited wealth], to ensure that his fortune should not be dissipated by neglect, nor yet cause him much trouble or loss of time when his mind was occupied with higher things. His practice was to dispose of each year's produce in a single sale, and then to buy in the market each item as it was needed for his daily life and his household. (Plut. *Per.* 16.3–5)[16]

This annoyed Pericles' family, but kept his income and expenses nicely balanced.

> He had one servant, Euangelus, who kept up this meticulous accounting, and who was either exceptionally gifted by nature or else was trained by Pericles, so that he excelled everyone else in the science of domestic economy.

If Pericles was unusual in his time for breaking with the concept of living on one's own stored and preserved crops as far as possible, he may indeed have set a fashion, so much so that this type of domestic economy could be called the "Athenian method" by the late fourth-century writer of the pseudo-Aristotelian treatise *Oeconomica*—"The Athenian buys immediately with the produce of his sales, and the smaller households keep no idle deposits in store" (1344 b 30ff.). Euangelus was unusual, not for his role as bailiff but rather for his ability to keep better accounts than most.[17]

The slave who could represent his owner's interests and who was a trusted ally is exemplified by Callarus, who belonged to Teisias and then to his son. Callarus was himself taken to court at one point by the neighbor Callicles in the matter of the wall and the watercourse, which suggests that Callarus was generally recognized as competent to act for his master—"Callicles knows that I value Callarus highly and wants to annoy me because of it"

(Dem 55.34). He is not called *epitropos* and was not one, strictly speaking, for his owner lived on the estate too; but he is surely the very kind of slave whom Ischomachus would have selected for this position. So far the personal record of one *epitropos* has turned up, on the farm of Timesius in southern Attica, a man who put his name and title to a sacred calendar inscribed on a rock face near the farmhouse—"An . . soros, *epitropos* of the farm."[18] The fact that he cared to leave a memorial of his services as bailiff suggests that for him it was a position well worth having. Deinias, whose grave has been found on the estate, may also have been a trusted servant or *epitropos;* this would account for a noncitizen's having a marked burial here.[19]

For Aristotle writing in the later fourth century, there was nothing remarkable about the existence of the position of *epitropos* or about the employment of slaves to fill it. "The use of slaves . . . consists in knowing how to direct slaves to do the tasks they ought to know how to do," that is, the slavish tasks of *farming under direction* (not as *autourgoi!*). "Hence those masters whose means are sufficient to exempt them from the trouble (of directing the slaves) employ an *epitropos* to take on this duty, while they devote themselves to statecraft or philosophy" (*Pol.* 1255 b 30–38). He has nothing to say about the possibility of free men taking up such jobs, although Xenophon hints that a very reasonable solution to a busy man's management problems would be to employ a trusted friend who happened to be in need of an income, and that some citizens who had fallen on hard times were pleased to accept employment of this kind.[20]

Aristotle has nothing to say either about the owner's training his own bailiff in the way he wants him to go, but he takes it for granted that the rich man will simply purchase a bailiff already practiced in the techniques of running a slave-worked estate. Nor does he care to consider the drawbacks that the employment of others so often entails, and which are implicit in Xenophon's discussion. One way round them would be to ensure the bailiff's devotion to the interests of the estate and its owner by treating him in some respects as though he were a tenant, not an employee. As the leading *resident* on the estate he would very likely tend to acquire a little sense of proprietorship, in any case, and he could be further encouraged to do a good job by being allowed to render a set return on the harvests to the owner, while retaining the surplus to maintain the labor force and to build up his own savings (the *apophora,* as allowed to semi-independent skilled slaves working in the crafts).[21] His treatment of the estate, meanwhile, and of the slaves under his command would be matters for discussion periodically, not daily, as in Ischomachus's system.[22]

## Landlord and Tenant

Letting land was a less troublesome alternative to the owner's managing it himself and a more reliable source of income, in fixed rent, than the vagaries of crop yields and bailiffs would permit. Some have indeed argued that dissatisfaction with slave bailiffs caused an increase in tenancy during and after the fourth century; this may be, although the evidence scarcely survives to support the argument.[23] What is clear is that tenancy had a long history in Greek land tenure, and always remained one of several alternatives available to a landowner. Whether it proved a better way in all respects of managing land depended on the individual landlord and tenant; a responsible owner still could not afford to leave his land entirely disregarded.

The tenancy of public and sacred lands was a familiar institution from early on in the existence of city and sanctuary;[24] private tenancy was no doubt an equally persistent characteristic of land management, but in quite what forms, or how widespread at any period, it is impossible to say. The history of tenancy before the later fifth century can scarcely be detected even at Athens; we really do not know what Isocrates means, for example, when he says of the "good old days" of Solon and Cleisthenes, that the rich dealt generously with the poor, including "handing over lands at moderate rentals" (*Areop.* 7.32). And if some Athenians, the "sixth-parters" of pre-Solonian Athens, were what amounted to tenants or sharecroppers, had they all come into this state through debt? If so, they were probably sharecropping what had been their own land, or some of them because they needed land to work, and tenancy was their only means of access to it, as long as there were landowners who wanted tenants, not laborers.[25] Even for the fifth and fourth centuries the evidence for private tenancy is not abundant, so the question is whether absence of reference means that this actually was an uncommon practice, or simply that the surviving record is very incomplete.[26] Consideration of the importance attached to owning land suggests that the first alternative is the likelier. Thus Zimmern argues that the enthusiasm for possessing one's own little bit of land meant that "tenancy in our sense of the word was practically unknown in Greece."[27]

Yet the few references to tenancy in the orators indicate that, for some private owners, letting their land was quite the accepted thing. The speaker of Lysias 7, *On the Sacred Olive Tree,* rented his land out five days after buying it, to a tenant who farmed it for two years, after which it was let to two other men in two successive years, and then to someone else for three years.[28] It has been suggested that the unsettled state of Athenian society and agriculture in the aftermath of the Peloponnesian War was the reason for this rapid shift in tenure, but the turnover of tenants and the eventual resumption of direct management by the owner may have been typical of private tenancy generally, if renting was regarded by many tenants simply as a temporary arrangement to be maintained during a period of difficulty.[29] From the landlord's point of view, an estate that had experienced a succession of tenants might well be in need of its proprietor's attention, if he cared to give it. A device in common enough use, tenancy obviously did not create the long-lasting relationships of landowner and tenantry typical of some land tenure in England; nor can a noticeable demand for land to rent be observed in the sources—there is little if anything to suggest that competition even for public and sacred leases was ever very keen.[30]

But without proof to the contrary, we should assume that landowners who wanted to let their land could usually find a tenant. However, a handful of examples is all that the sources yield: Lysias tells of an attempt to recover a debt by taking over the debtor's land, some of which the creditor proceeds to let, while another part of the property already has sitting tenants; the whole procedure as it happens is then nullified by the city's confiscation of the property because its former owner had been condemned for supporting the Thirty Tyrants (17.5–6). Included in the property of the Bouselids Stratocles and Theopompus was a farm at Thria valued at two and a half talents and let for a useful rent of twelve hundred drachmas a year (Isaeus 11.42).[31] And the institution of *misthosis oikou,* whereby orphans with property were supposedly assured a steady income during their minority from the leasing or investing of their inherited capital, must have put some land (and houses) onto the rental market.[32]

Those who took up tenancies would have been not only or even mainly poor and landless men, who could only have managed to farm a small property on their own, being without the resources to employ other labor. Men who were farming already and who needed extra income might rent another plot, which they could work by using the manpower they already had more *intensively*—especially if the rented land was nearby. It is conceivable that friends or relatives of a man in trouble of some kind might rent his land and produce an income for him (or help to conceal his real assets by pretending to acquire it outright). Tenancy might have interested metics, who were unable by law to own land, but who wished to invest capital gained from other sources in agriculture; perhaps Nicias of Olynthus was one such, and the *georgos* Manes whom he freed was his *epitropos.*[33] One of the tenants of the sacred olive-tree estate, Alcias, is described as a freedman, which is to say, a metic (Lysias 7.10); he may have been an *epitropos* who became a permanent or "professional" tenant farmer, moving from one farm to another as circumstances dictated.[34]

As for the landlords, the decision to let their land depended not on wealth or status so much as on personal tastes and preoccupations, and on their views of bailiffs and their effectiveness. Owners of widely dispersed or very large holdings would perhaps have found it simpler to let part of their land rather than try to keep control of it all themselves, or worry about a large number of employees. But whatever their thoughts on the matter, no opinion of tenancy is preserved, other than Theophrastus's remark on its drawbacks (quoted at the end of the chapter). We know virtually no landlords and absolutely no tenants by name or cir-cumstance other than Alcias, and the three other tenants of the sacred olive-tree estate.[35] There is no hint either of disdain, the one for the other, or of a landlord or a tenant considering his own status enhanced by association with the other, as in Sir Walter Elliot's eager reference to his tenant Admiral Croft, "the Croft who rents Kellynch."[36] When successful adventurers like Aristophanes wanted to settle down on an estate, they bought one; they did not search out an aristocratic family seat for rent (Lysias 19.29, 42).

The terms of private tenancies presumably varied from one tenancy to another, depending on the personal circumstances of either party. As to their duration, the only tenancies of which we know any details were short, two or three years (Lysias 7.9–10); judging by the terms of public leases, the date for entering on a tenancy and for paying the rent probably differed according to individual circumstances.[37] Rents may by the Classical period have been fixed and in cash, but it is possible that sharecropping remained a feature of tenancy, when and where this seemed the more satisfactory arrangement, the advantage over a fixed rent going in a good year to the landlord and in a bad year to the tenant; some rents may have continued to be paid in kind, as they were in some sacred tenancies, of the Eleusinian Raria and the estates of Athena at Heraclea in southern Italy, for example (barley in these instances).[38] The tenant might have been required to find guarantors against nonpayment of the rent, as in public tenancies, but often enough the landlord might have been satisfied to accept the pledge of personal property—a slave or an ox, a house or a half-dozen goats—which the tenant gave up if his farming failed. Some sort of formal agreement prescribing the terms would prob-ably have been drawn up (see Theophrastus's reference to Thasian tenancies in the subsequent quotation), although the possibility of a purely spoken agreement sealed by a handshake cannot be ruled out. It may well have included work regulations like those in sacred land and leases; the form taken by the one kind would have influenced the other. Often enough tenants would be left to their own devices on the assumption that economic pressure would force them to do well enough to be able to pay the rent.

In such cases, the only check would be to count up the number of barns, doors, window frames, and fruit trees on the property, make sure that there were, for example, as many fruit trees standing at the end of the tenancy as there had been at the beginning, and inquire no further. For as Theophrastus states it, fruit trees that have been encouraged by industrious and correct cultivation to bear large crops do not last as long as trees that have received little attention and have therefore produced low yields:

> So when the Thasians let out their orchards for cultivation, they are concerned about no year of the lease but the last, and even welcome bad husbandry, but for the last year they stipulate [write into the contract] that the lessor shall recover the very [same] trees that he is renting out. (*CP* 2.11.3)

The tenant was thus spared the trouble of farming properly and the expense of replacing old trees with new ones, which would perhaps not have matured before he had to give up the tenancy, so that he would have lost the chance of even a minimal crop from part of the orchard.[39] The landlord for his part received back an estate containing its proper complement of mature (if discouraged) trees, which he could rent out to another tenant as fully productive.

Tenancy obviously had drawbacks, in that the land could be seriously mistreated, when both landlord and tenant sought only the short-term advantage; for in the long run the landlord lost. Ischomachus quotes the story of the Persian king's questioning a horse trainer about the quickest way to improve a horse: "The master's eye" is the reply (Xen. *Oecon.* 12.20). The story is applied to the training of slaves as bailiffs, but it could just as aptly have referred to the proper management of the land.

# Five

## The Laborers on the Land

> And now, like reapers who start from opposite sides
> of a rich man's field and bring the wheat and barley
> tumbling down in armfuls till their swathes unite,
> the Trojans and Achaeans fell upon each other.
> (*Il.* 11.67–70)

t was axiomatic that the owner of land employed others to help him cultivate his fields and tend his orchards and flocks. Hesiod's recommendation, that the farmer should acquire a hired worker and a slave or two as well as a yoke of oxen and a dog, surely stemmed from perceptions as old as the technique of agriculture itself: that, practically speaking, cooperative effort of some kind was needed to get an adequate return from the land, and that, ideologically speaking, farming should be done *with assistance,* if not *by somebody else.*[1] For some landowners extra labor was an unaffordable luxury, so that the distinction which it is natural to assert between owner and worker was by no means clear-cut. If some *autourgoi* directed as well as worked alongside their laborers, others worked their land on their own or with only the help of family members, because this was the way things had to be; many of them clearly proved the age-old perception wrong, that farming sufficient to provide a living for the owner and his family could only be carried on with additional labor, by subsisting adequately on small, and therefore manageable, farms.[2] Menander's misanthrope who is presented as working his farm without assistance, "having no fellow worker, or house slave, or local hired man, or neighbor, just himself alone" (328–31) may have been less rare than the comic situation tries to suggest. Even so, all but the most committed *autourgos* would have felt the need of some help, particularly for harvesting; there must always have been some seasonal work to offer, even on farms where full-time labor was employed. At the same time some farmers, in particular the poor, may have provided one another mutual assistance in times of crisis, but this arrangement is not really apparent in the sources. Hesiod's view of life in the farming community does not include more than the possibility of lending tools and draft animals, and he otherwise emphasizes the inadvisability of becoming in any way dependent on one's neighbors (*WD* 364–67).[3] Mastery of a man's economic situation was seen to rely on both ownership of land and control of the means (other than his own strength) of making it properly productive: in principle landowners commonly employed agricultural laborers.[4]

The main source of agricultural labor everywhere in the early period, and in some places for the larger part of Greek antiquity, was the surrounding or outlying population—the *pelatai,* "neighbors" or "those dependent on or working for others," the propertyless who could only support themselves by working as laborers.[5] At Athens these were the *thetes,* poor relations and distant connections of the central landowning power group; in the societies of Sparta, Thessaly, or Crete, they were the subject groups, fellow Greeks, but in formal terms quite separate from the landowners and power holders (although there may have been some common ancestors among them too); elsewhere, at Miletus or Syracuse, Heraclea Pontica or Olbia, they were the local non-Greek populations. The *pelatai* formed the equivalent (or as near as we can come to one) of the cottager or farm-laboring population of the medieval or early modern European rural community. As such, their circumstances were in certain respects similar to those of a peasantry, and it is these people who can with some justice be called the *peasants* of Greek society, if any social group is to be so classified. There are also parallels to be drawn with the depressed tenantry that existed in Scotland and Ireland under English rule for a period.[6]

If the *pelatai* proved inadequate or unsuitable in some way, which became the case at Athens, the alternative was to obtain slaves to make up the required labor force. Slave labor had always played some part in agriculture, but it is clear that slaves came to be employed in greater numbers from the sixth century on—in certain places, however, not generally throughout the Greek world; for although some slave labor may have existed even in Sparta, as in other communities where there was also a dependent or tied population, there is no question of their predominating over other types of labor as they surely did at Athens.[7] Wherever chattel slavery did so, we can assume that it was the result of a social and political transformation as profound in its way as the changes brought about by Solon in the early sixth century; but, as so often, it is only the Athenian situation that can be discussed in any detail, or with some hope of understanding what actually happened.

When Epaminondas and the Theban army were threatening to attack Mantinea in 362, the Mantineans informed their Athenian allies that "all our cattle and laborers, and our children and our older men from among the free population are outside the city walls" (Xen. *HG* 7.5.14–15). As Epaminondas had pointed out to his own troops, it was harvesttime, and everybody except for the fighting men was helping to gather in the crops; if war had not threatened, the younger men would have been in the fields too. Were the Mantineans' laborers partly noncitizen hirelings, mainly slaves, or members of an indigenous but subjugated section of the population similar to Spartan helots or Thessalian *penestai*?[8] All that their statement makes clear is that the laborers were a necessary supplement to the labor of the landowners and their families, not a replacement of it. The standing of the agricultural laborers in the scheme of things is also defined: they and the plow animals are classed together, the cattle being given precedence—as the goats are over the goatherd in the valuation of Euctemon's property (Isaeus 6.33).

But this was not necessarily the whole story of the relation between landowner and laborer. The ideological barriers between them could have been broken down to some extent by some of the realities of farming. Such seems to be the situation suggested by the strange story of the laborer and the slave employed by Euthyphro and his father as they were farming on the island of Naxos (Pl. *Euthyphro* 4 c).[9] A hired man (*pelates*) of Euthyphro's got drunk, quarreled with a slave belonging to Euthyphro's father and killed him. Euthyphro's father tied up the laborer hand and foot and threw him into a ditch while he sent to Athens to consult the religious authorities about the blood pollution attendant on his slave's death. Meanwhile the laborer died of cold and hunger, and Euthyphro felt obliged to prosecute his father for the man's murder. Each employer felt in some way morally responsible for his employees, regarding them as something more than subhuman tools, to be discarded when no longer useful.[10]

Not only did many landowners work alongside their laborers, sharing the toil and the achievement of a good crop well tended, there were aspects of working on the land which might have brought some personal satisfaction to the laborer, if he were not irrevocably alienated by his situation and too embittered to take pleasure in anything to do with his employment; they could even have provided him with a certain autonomy within the bounds of his overall subordination as an employee. The position of bailiff raised a man above his fellow workers and demanded of him that he exercise some initiative, often allowing him the opportunity to make some profit for himself, and to look forward to greater independence as a freedman. The herdsman who tended animals at a distance from the farm was necessarily a man of many skills and considerable competence (or he did not get the job in the first place), answering to no one while he was off in the grazing grounds, and being responsible for the well-being of an important part of the farm's substance. There were many other occupations that called for a practiced hand, such as tending ailing cattle, shearing sheep, making cheese, building terrace and boundary walls, extending irrigation ditches, making wine, pressing olive oil; many estates would have their own resident experts in some if not all of the required skills, including often enough the owner himself. The laborer who demonstrated a particular bent for dry-stone walling or mud-brick construction, for bee handling or supervising farrowing pigs would gain a recognized importance in the farm's little hierarchy, and the corresponding respect of his owner. There would also have been room for professional practitioners of such skills, for no landowner or bailiff could acquire himself every kind of expertise required in farming, nor could he rely entirely on his laborers to supply them; experienced retainers only lived so long, after all. The vinedresser is the only professional of this kind who can be identified with any certainty, but the silence of the sources once again does not mean that other itinerant farming experts were not known and looked for in the Greek countryside. Such workers would have been to all intents and purposes their own masters, and have commanded the respect of those who needed their services.

## Hired Free Labor

If a landowner required additional labor for the regular routine of the farm, the obvious solution as we might see it would have been to hire men from among the free poor, the *thetes* or *pelatai* as they may be called for convenience. They made up a reserve of labor close at hand and close in another sense, in that they were a part of the native population and of its social structure, so much so that in Attica they would have been more or less distantly related to men who actually owned the land. Some *thetes* might once have owned land themselves, which they had lost through debt or some other misfortune, or now had the use of a little plot, but one so small that they must hire out in order to supplement its tiny yield. In fact, free hired laborers who were free in the Classical Greek sense of being fully recognized citizens—that is, after Solon's legislation had taken effect—were not a major element in agriculture; it thus happens that the clearest perception of the hired laborer's lot is gained from Homer and Hesiod, not from the later literature, although there are enough condescending comments to show that hired workers were common enough in the Classical period too.[11]

One of the scenes on Achilles' shield shows hired reapers at work on the king's land (*Il.* 18.550–60); and Odysseus remarks that "a man who could do without sleep could earn himself double wages, one for herding cattle and the other for herding sheep" (*Od.* 10.84–85). Hired herdsmen were probably always in some demand; thus when Poseidon and Apollo appear in the *Iliad* as hirelings serving Laomedon, ruler of Troy, for one year, their wages to be paid at the end of their time, Poseidon builds the walls of Troy and Apollo herds cattle on Mount Ida.[12] But Laomedon does not keep his side of the agreement; he refuses to pay them, and drives them off, threatening to sell them into slavery and lop off their ears (*Il.* 21.441–57). Other episodes suggest that the hired laborer ought to be able to expect a fair deal; Eurymachus offers Odysseus (in his disguise as a beggar) employment building field walls and planting trees on one of his hill farms, in return for a "proper wage, . . . regular food . . . and clothing and shoes" (*Od.* 18.357–61).

For Hesiod, hired labor is one of the essential elements of the farming establishment; he recommends making arrangements to hire workers by the year, in the slack season between harvest and the winter plowing—"When the harvest is gathered in, get for yourself a hired worker with no household of his own" (*WD* 602–3).[13] West's translation reveals a quite different situation from the one usually envisaged by those who would understand the passage, "Get rid of your hired worker when the harvest is over."[14] The homeless hireling is not turned away like an unwanted stray but is guaranteed a place in his employer's establishment, and may expect to be kept on another year if he proves satisfactory; and in seeking out a poor and unattached hireling, the employer hopes to get loyal service. Therefore the terms between farmer and laborer must be properly sealed and observed— "Let the agreed wage for a man of goodwill be assured" (*WD* 370).

Hired labor remained a factor in Greek agriculture, as it did in the economy as a whole—there was always carting, digging, fetching, and carrying to be done—but not a very well-documented one. The *thetes* of Attica, their name suggesting their fundamental economic role as serving men or hired laborers, emerge from obscurity in the early sixth century only because their rights to citizen status were established by the reforms of Solon; one result was that their ties with full-time agricultural labor began to weaken. What had previously made these ties so strong? The *thetes* and groups like them in other communities would always have been the "poor relations": they can be considered *free* hired workers only in the sense that they were part of the *Athenian* population, but as Solon's reforms showed, neither their Athenian birth nor that of better-connected citizen landowners who had pledged their persons for debt had been a guarantee against enslavement at home or sale into slavery abroad. The debt bondsman, who certainly figured in pre-Solonian Athens, also formed part of the laboring class; in theory his labor was only required for a certain time or until he had worked off his debt, but often enough he would have been trapped in servitude as long as he could work, and even if he did shake off his debt he might have found it impossible to regain his former way of life, so that hired work and the status of *thetes* were the only options available to him. After Solon's reforms, of course, debt bondage became illegal in Athens; the practice survived elsewhere and could have gone on informally within Attica too, imposed by threats that friendless men or those of weak character or feeble understanding were unable to resist.[15]

To what extent was the thetic status one that men sank into, rather than being born *thetes*? If there was a rural laboring class, was it a stable country population in that it perpetuated itself from one generation to the next, or did at least the poorest laborers within it constitute a demographic dead end, too poor for the most part to establish households of their own?[16] Many laborers probably died young or childless. But there must also have been poor families that survived on the fringes of economic viability and social respectability, with a cabbage patch here and a few vines there, taking whatever laboring jobs they could manage and wherever they could find them. Truly migrant workers moving over great distances were probably rare; it is not clear how far Odysseus in his guise as a beggar is presumed to have come, when he is offered work in Ithaca and Telemachus pretends to employ him, saying "I keep no man idle who has eaten my bread, however far he has tramped" (*Od.* 19.27–28). Most *thetes* would have depended on their more prosperous neighbors for work, as their neighbors depended on them for their labor. The sourness of this relationship contributed to or was a concomitant of the crisis that developed by the end of the seventh century from the tensions caused by indebtedness on one side and the desire for closer control of agricultural labor, compounded with greed for agricultural income, on the other.

What then became of the *thetes* of Attica after 594? Why did there not continue to be numerous hired workers of free (citizen) status working on the land for men more prosperous than they, throughout the Classical period? The answer, briefly, is that Solon's reforms converted them into Thetes, politically defined as the fourth of the census classes into which Solon divided the citizen body of Athens, a group that now included all of citizen descent; the thetic property qualification ranged from comparatively little to nothing.[17] The Thetes now had guaranteed minimum privileges of citizenship, an important aspect of which was that they could look to the courts of the city for protection of their property *and persons;* if they had not been able to do so earlier, they could now expect to inherit within the limits of the *anchisteia,* if the possibility arose. The availability for and interest in laboring jobs gradually diminished on the Thetes' part, especially as more attractive alternatives turned up, such as the chance to own and inherit land securely, to take up a craft, or even to live a comparatively leisured life, supported by a small patch of land, a little part-time work, and the odd windfall of pay for public service as a juryman or rower in the fleet (these last only under the radical democracy). We can imagine that the employers had their reasons for losing interest in free hired labor too, such as the Thetes' growing unwillingness to be coerced, and the likelihood that they or someone on their behalf might bring lawsuits for assault or failure to pay wages, if landowners and free laborers had words. The lack of evidence for full-time free hired laborers in the Classical period, notably at Athens, may then be seen not merely as the accident of survival but as a reflection of the real situation.[18]

Nevertheless, there would always have been a few free laborers on the land in the later period too, men driven there by misfortune or an incapacity to earn a living in any other way. One sphere of farming in which citizens may have participated as full-time employees is that of farm managers or bailiffs. Some have doubted that this was actually so, preferring to see Xenophon's reference in the *Oeconomicus* to this possibility as part of an entirely hypothetical case (1.3–4).[19] The best support for the idea that citizens became bailiffs is provided by Socrates' conversation with Eutherus, in which Eutherus as it happens expressly *refuses* to contemplate such a fate (Xen. *Mem.* 2.8.1–4).[20]

Eutherus's situation was, that after Athens's defeat in 404 he lost his land abroad (either a cleruchy somewhere, or an estate appropriated in the same way as Adeimantus's in Thasos, for instance); because his father had left him no property in Attica he was destitute and forced to "work for his living with his hands," as a hired laborer, for he could not borrow, having no land to offer as security (2.8.1). Socrates suggests that he could find a more comfortable position, with security for his old age—whether he means the savings from Eutherus's pay, or continued employment as a manager after his physical strength had begun to fail, is not clear—as bailiff to a wealthy landowner, "helping to get in his crops and looking after his property" (2.8.3). The proposal is unwelcome: "I do not wish to enslave myself," says Eutherus, "I am not willing to lay myself open to any man's censure" (2.8.4). His thinking accords exactly with the generally held view that "the condition of the free man is that he does not hire for the benefit of another" (Ar. *Rhet.* 1367 a 3). But can this mean that citizens never took up such employment? Was the bailiff's post now so widely recognized as a slave's job that no free man could possibly associate himself with it? Principles would quickly have yielded to need, in the case of other men, if not of Eutherus.

His objections to being a bailiff and his preference for a laboring job are linked to the concern for personal autonomy. The great advantages of a merely laboring occupation over that of a professional one are that the laborer has less responsibility for the outcome of the work as a whole and stands at a greater remove from his employer. Casual or menial work may be squalid and less well paid, but it affords greater freedom than skilled and professional occupations. For while the skilled professional may operate on a higher plane, the laborer need never feel deeply committed to a specific craft or calling; his work is merely a means to an end, that is, the sustenance of a free man, whereas the professional must surrender personal autonomy to the work in hand, himself the means to an end, which is the proper exercise of his expertise.

The concept that *employment* was demeaning had deep roots in the aristocratic or heroic sense of self: there could be no real equality in the relationship between employer and employee, between the man who wanted things done and the man who had agreed to do them. The wage contract was never seen as achieving this kind of equivalence.[21]

How far the persistence of this attitude goes to explain why, by the fifth century in Athens, Chios, and other places chattel slavery had replaced to a very large extent the agricultural laborers who had been indigenous and connected with the free citizenry (the *thetes*), it is impossible to say.[22] But it probably played a part in making the Thetes less willing to work for hire and the land-owners more chary of hiring them even if they were available.

Seasonal work, on the other hand, does feature in the sources, enough to show that it drew citizen hirelings into agriculture at all periods. Harvesting above all required extra helpers for a short time and in some numbers, and citizens' participation in hired harvest work was common enough for Aristophanes to make an insulting comparison between the Athenian jurymen of the democracy scampering after their pay for court attendance and "olive pickers going at the beck and call of the man who has your wages" (*Wasps* 712). Xenophon, discussing the tyrant Hieron, speaks of despots "hiring their guards like harvesters" (*Hier.* 6.10); and Demosthenes calls his political rival Aeschines "not the friend but the hireling of Philip—unless a harvester or other hired man is to be called a friend" (Dem. 18.51). Labor-intensive jobs of other kinds could also absorb extra labor; in times of hardship citizen women were to be found in the fields tending vines, as Euxitheus says of the period after the Peloponnesian War (Dem. 57.45).

Armies on campaign too are known to have provided temporary labor at harvesttime: when the Spartan forces were cut off in

Chios, "they supported themselves during the summer from the seasonal produce, and could get money by hiring out their labor in the island" (Xen. *HG* 2.1.1). Iphicrates' rowers hired out as farm workers when they were stationed at Corcyra, probably to help with the grain or the grape harvest (Xen. *HG* 6.2.37). These instances illustrate the farmer's difficulty in obtaining enough extra help at critical times of year, for the presence of military and naval personnel at loose ends was not to be looked for regularly. Nor was it necessarily very beneficial, for many such hirelings must have helped themselves; and the Spartans were driven by the lack of supplies during the following winter to attack the city of Chios itself.

Wherever there was a metic population, it may also have been a source of free hired labor—in a small way, only, for most metics operated in the industrial and commercial sector of the economy; but there may have been some who fell on hard enough times to seek farm work. And there were freedmen metics, a few of whom appear in the sources as "farmer," "gardener," "vinetender"; they were probably chattel-slave farm laborers who had earned their freedom and naturally remained in the occupation they had been trained for, now that they were free. Some of them may have hired out as skilled professional agriculturalists (if they did not become tenants themselves).[23]

There is some suggestion of pride in one's work, in the dedicatory record of these freedmen, for they stated their profession alongside their name—very few other men in the Greek world identified themselves by their occupation.[24] Any future employer could be assured of their competence and reliability by the fact of their having been freed; and perhaps the purpose of such dedicatory inscriptions was partly to make this clear. But the general perception of the hired laborer was that he led a wretched life. Achilles can think of no more miserable and degraded existence when he says, "I had rather be alive and the hired hand of a poor [landless] man, than reign as king over all the kingdom of the dead" (*Od.* 11.489–91). For Plato, some men are by nature fit only to be hired laborers—"those who have no great powers of mind to contribute, but whose physical strength makes them suitable for manual labor. They market their strength and call the return they get for it wages" (*Rep.* 371 d–e). Plato's bias is all too apparent; there is no reason to suppose that all hired laborers were "dumb oxes" with muscle. But certainly a man who had to depend on laboring for his living could not expect to do so well, once his strength began to fail.[25] And if he had no children, or had been cut off from his family by quarrels or poverty, or had outlived them, his end might be depressing indeed—lonely, detached, uncared for. Such is the situation suggested by the Athenian deme decree concerning corpses:

> If nobody takes up for burial those who die in the demes, the demarch is to give notice to the relatives to take them up and bury them and purify the deme, on the day of decease in each case. As regards slaves, he shall give notice to the master, and *as regards free men* [hired laborers?], *to those in possession of the property* [their employers?]. If the relations do not take up [the body and bury it], let the demarch contract for [this] . . . at the lowest possible price. (Dem. 43.57–8)

So it was that the administrators of the Eleusinian sanctuary paid someone to remove a corpse from, and purify, the Raria. This was the barley-producing estate belonging to Eleusis; the corpse might have been that of a farm worker, a free hireling employed temporarily perhaps by the tenant of the Raria, who simply dropped in his or her tracks, unrecognized and unclaimed.[26]

## Dependent Labor

The landowner who employed laborers wanted to ensure that they were on hand when required. Hiring men by the year was one way of doing so (if there were hirelings available on suitable terms), but seasonal work obviously could not be pinned down in the same way; and an innate disadvantage of free labor was that it frequently disappeared just when it was most needed. Economic pressures on the free poor were not enough to guarantee without fail their regular attendance at harvesttime. But how much more convenient for the landowner to be able to coerce his workers at all times of the farming year. He might control, as an individual, the members of his own family; as a powerful neighbor, those in debt to or otherwise dependent on him; or as a member of the landowning group dominating its territory, the dependent population within it. Land that had value was often conceived of as *land with labor attached to it*—so the Locrian *woikiatai* "went with" the land when it was confiscated.[27]

There are several different approaches involved here to the matter of subjugating others in order to force them into agricultural labor. One is the age-old practice of putting prisoners of war to work on the land, and often enough on land they had just lost to their conquerors; another, to impose what amounted to a restrictive *tenancy* on the dwellers roundabout (the *pelatai*, who thus became dependent laborers as well as being "neighbors"); and another, to subjugate troublesome and uncooperative fringe groups, by compelling them to work on the land of their subduers—all of which elements can be seen in the relations between Spartans and helots, Thessalians and *penestai*, Heracleots and Mariandynoi, and so on. Other communities that did *not* customarily employ dependent labor could also think along these lines if occasion warranted: when in 427 the Athenians had put down the revolt of their allies in Lesbos, they appropriated some of the land and allotted most of it to 2,700 Athenian *klerouchoi*. These lot holders did not come to Lesbos to work the land themselves; instead, the Lesbians were obliged to work the estates, surrendering a set "rent" of two hundred drachmas a year to the *klerouchoi,* who became to all intents and purposes their landlords (Thuc. 3.50.2). The arrangement only lasted until the end of the Peloponnesian War, but for about a generation many Lesbians were no more than the dependent tenants or even laborers of the Athenian democracy. This is perhaps to take the argument rather to the outer limits of what is usually considered to be the dimensions of dependent labor, but it illustrates some of the motives and means by which dependent labor came into being and was exploited.

The best-known subjugated laboring population is of course Sparta's—the helots.[28] According to tradition, the first helots were part of the indigenous inhabitants of Laconia conquered by the invading Dorians during the early Dark Age; they thus became the hereditary labor force on the estates held by the conquerors' descendants, the Spartan citizens.[29] Whether the Laconian helots were pre-Dorians subjugated all at once by Dorians in a single episode of conquest, it is not the object of this study to attempt to inquire, except to suggest that the traditions may have been colored somewhat by the later and well-attested conquest of Messenia during the seventh century. The Messenian Wars resulted in the doubling of Sparta's territory and, presumably, of the helot population too. No other Greek state conquered its neighbor and subjugated a Greek people in quite so wholesale a manner—and no other Greek society came to be so sharply divided between a small landowning elite, single-mindedly military in its way of life, and a huge surrounding population entirely under its control.[30]

There must have been some marked differences between Laconian and Messenian helots. For one thing the Messenians of the Classical period retained a sharper impression of their loss of freedom, together with a sense of national identity and of the cultural differences between themselves and the Spartans of Laconia, as the traditions noted by Pausanias suggest.[31] It is not surprising that the most serious helot revolt occurred in Messenia (during the 460s, at the same time as a severe earthquake centered in Laconia); nor was it sheer coincidence that had brought about the drastic reforms in Sparta after the end of the Messenian Wars, whereby the Spartan state was converted into a military camp.[32] But the Spartans had reason to fear the Laconian helots too. What illustrates very vividly the Spartans' constant anxiety about the reliability of the helots and the potential threat they presented to the Spartans' own security is the *krypteia,* whereby the state declared an open season for helot hunting during which the killing of a helot brought no pollution on the community or guilt upon the killer.

> The magistrates sent out into the country those who appeared the most resourceful of the [Spartan] youth, equipped only with daggers and the minimum of provisions. In the daytime they dispersed into obscure places, where they hid and lay low. By night they came down into the highways and dispatched any helot they caught. Often too

they went into the fields and did away with the sturdiest and most powerful helots. (Plut. *Lyc.* 28.2–3).

The *krypteia* would perhaps have offered more sport to the young Spartans who took part in it when Messenian helots beyond the Taygetus mountains were the quarry, but there is no reason to suppose that Laconian helots were in any degree exempt.[33]

How did other communities with dependent populations working the land keep them in check? We do not hear of anything to equal the Spartans' methods of dealing with them, but there are certainly signs of discontent and periodic unrest elsewhere. As long as the workers remained quiet, and continued to provide the agricultural quotas expected from each estate, they might perhaps be left untroubled, the fruits of their labors functioning, from their point of view, as "protection money." Outbreaks of unrest would perhaps have been met with a swift punitive raid on the settlement or dwelling place of the offenders; or an example might occasionally be made, whether or not offense had been given. The Spartan system of discipline seems to have been the most thorough by far of all, but there is no means of discovering if the productivity of their estates was higher than elsewhere as a result.

Another difference between the Messenian and Laconian helots lay, simply, in the Messenians' being at a greater distance from the central settlements of Sparta itself. This might have affected their relations with the owners of the estates on which they worked in that they were in less close touch and less closely supervised than the helots in Laconia. But the extent of the Spartans' personal interest in their land is entirely unknown, likewise the degree of contact between any Spartan and any Messenian.[34] It is conceivable that the Messenians resembled, much more closely than did the Laconian helots, the tenants of absentee landlords, left much to their own devices as long as they paid the rent and made no trouble—the big difference between their position and that of a true tenant being that in order to give up their tenancy they must run away and evade capture, and that, if they did, refugee status was the best they could usually hope for.[35]

Generally speaking, all helots were subject to these conditions:

only the Spartan state had the right to dispose of helots—by executing or selling them, or promoting them into the ranks of the army, police, or civil service (insofar as Sparta can be said to have had one); only the state could give them their freedom. For their part the helots were bound to stay with the estate to which they had been assigned and to render a fixed quota of the crops they grew.[36] The poverty of the evidence is such, however, that it is by no means certain that helots' assigned *residence on a given estate* was also *hereditary,* not only their *tied status;* if it was, this would have allowed for the possibility of a sense of attachment developing between helots and the families that owned the land. Nor is there any indication whether the helots who served in Spartan households or accompanied Spartans as attendants when the army went to war were selected by the Spartans from their own estates, or whether the government had the final word in this aspect of the helot's existence too. Even though helots were expected to mourn at their master's funeral, there need have been no true attachment between them (Tyrtaeus fr. 7); their presence was enough to show who was in control of whom.

The land the Spartans owned seems to have consisted partly of "ancestral" portions controlled by the state and held by all qualified citizen families, and partly of private land to be disposed of as the owner saw fit. Presumably helots were stationed on both kinds of land, the point of their existence being to spare Spartans the indignity and preoccupation of working the land themselves.[37] Whatever the precise working of the system, the main point is that we have no indication how big any of the landholdings were, how many helots would have been needed to work them properly, how many helots were deemed *by the Spartans* necessary to work them, or how many helots there actually were at any period on any estate or on the land as a whole.[38] There are various hints that the helots vastly outnumbered the Spartans even before the citizen population became so disastrously small in the fourth century, implying that helot families prospered and increased. But if the number of helots increased beyond a certain point on a given estate, what steps were taken to make sure the estate could still provide its quota and maintain the helots living on it? Might the *krypteia* have had other purposes than simply to impose discipline by instilling fear? One might also see the readiness with which the Spartans drafted helots into the army and posted off contingents to distant campaigns as a means of reducing not only the security threat posed by large numbers of helots but the economic pressure on the food supply. It is possible that the helots themselves tried to make sure that their families were not forcibly *reduced,* by cultivating the land as well as they could, perhaps to the extent of farming even more intensively than was usual practice. Certainly, whatever successes were achieved in Laconian and Messenian agriculture, they were the helots' doing. Perhaps this was the reason for King Cleomenes' remark, that Homer was the poet of the Spartans, and Hesiod of the helots: for Homer had given the necessary directions for warfare, and Hesiod for agriculture (Plut. *Mor.* 223 a).

The system of quotas meant that whatever was produced in excess was the helots' to keep—an added incentive to make the land as productive as possible.[39] How they may have disposed of surpluses beyond what they needed for maintenance, we do not know. Perhaps they provided their own work clothes and tools; but the state may have preferred that equipment be supplied to them, in order that they not acquire too many mattocks, sickles, and other potentially dangerous weapons in time of unrest.[40] No great helot fortunes are heard of, but some helots may have been by no means wretchedly poor, and no less comfortable than their austerity-ridden masters.[41]

If helots were allotted to a certain estate on a long-term basis, they may either have lived in scattered dwellings about the estate, in a settlement or hamlet, or in villages populated by helots belonging to several different estates. Spartan security would have been equally well or ill served by any of these arrangements—if they were scattered, the helots could less easily mass for an attack on visiting owners; if they were gathered together in larger groups, disciplinary action would have been easier to arrange, and informers (supposing that the Spartans employed them, which is all too likely) would have found their task of spying on their fellows easier to accomplish. Strabo merely remarks that the Spartans had "assigned to them certain settlements to live in" (8.5.4), and Livy, that they "had been farm or fort dwellers from earliest times" (34.27.9)—which might have meant a farmyard full of huts or merely a single dwelling on a rise with a fox-proof fence round it.

Relations between Spartan landowners and their helots were inevitably affected by the underlying fear and hostility between the Spartan state and helots as a whole. If they had occasion to meet in connection with the running of the estate (or the breeding and training of horses—see chapter 2), they may have broken some of the barriers between them, if only in the context of stable or wheat field; but the ingrained sense of superiority that the Spartan must have over those who were his closest assistants and at the same time his nearest enemies would have stifled any real friendship. To the helot the Spartan's behavior must have seemed capricious in the extreme, vacillating between kindly familiarity and disdainful cruelty; for a man who had been bound to the soil might find himself summoned to the army, while those who were led garlanded as to a festival and freedom one day were mysteriously done away with the next (Thuc. 4.80.3–4).[42]

The lives of dependent farming populations elsewhere were not, as far as we can tell, so very dissimilar. The name *penestai* suggests an ethnic or local origin for the Thessalians' tied laborers; it is probable that a subjugated people in Thessaly existed from the time of invasion and conquest when the Thessalians were deciding who would own the fertile plains and valleys of the region.[43] In both Sparta and Thessaly there were limits set on the landowners' freedom to dispose of their tied laborers; at Sparta only the state had the right to sell, kill, or free them, whereas the Thessalian tradition had it that the *penestai* made an agreement with their masters, that they would work their land on condition that the Thessalians never allowed them to be sent away from their place of occupation or to be executed. In return for their masters' "protection," the *penestai* handed over an agreed portion of the harvests from the estates, keeping any surplus for their own consumption; and so it was that "many *penestai* are better off than their own masters" (Archemachus fr. 1).[44]

How, or in what numbers, *penestai* were assigned to the Thessalians' estates; whether they lived scattered through the farmland or in settlements from which they went out to the land; how big the estates were; and how much produce the *penestai* were supposed to hand over—the evidence does not reveal. Clearly some Thessalians were very rich indeed: Menon of Pharsalus provided out of his own wealth for the Athenian campaign at Eion in 476 a cavalry force of three hundred men raised from among his own *penestai*, and twelve talents of silver (Dem. 23.199). The *penestai* made up a good part of the Thessalians' fighting force—perhaps always in contingents led by the owner of their estate (or his son). But the real nature of their relations with the Thessalians is hard to assess: like the Spartans' helots, they were considered reliable enough to take along on campaign, and yet they revolted quite frequently, seizing the opportunities (so says Aristotle) given by the Thessalians' constant preoccupation with war against their neighbors (*Pol.* 1269 b 6–7).

What was it that made the *penestai* dissatisfied with their (reasonably secure) lives working and profiting from some of the best farmland and cattle-raising country in the Greek world? What resentments did they harbor, deep enough to attract the interest of an anarchist like Critias of Athens? About 406, when he was between oligarchic revolutions, Critias spent some time in Thessaly, "with Prometheus, arming the *penestai* against their masters," in what is said to have been an attempt to establish a democracy. The revolution failed, but the effects of his experiments may be guessed at from the comment of his enemy Theramenes, that he hoped that "none of the things he did there will ever happen at Athens" (Xen. *HG* 2.3.36–37).[45]

Why would tied laborers have wished to break out of their way of life, however comfortable?—because it has been forced upon them. Menon's three hundred cavalrymen may have been sorely tempted to ride off into the hills; possibly part of the reason why his descendant Menon, who knew Socrates in Athens, took mercenary service with Cyrus among the Ten Thousand was that his bad temper turned his *penestai* against him and contributed to his exile.[46] And yet there were surely many seasons in which the cultivation of the land went on uninterrupted by rebellion, and many laborers who passed hardworking, docile lives. Mere inertia could have held them in their place, or the sense that change could only be for the worse—an outlaw's life, scrambling for the pickings of brigandage, and the meager fruits of hill farming and herding, in exchange for a prosperous life in the lowlands. For many, dependency was a price worth paying for security of tenure, however restricted it was, and however few rights or means of redress against the insults of their masters the *penestai* ever possessed. Those who talked of killing or driving out the owners and seizing the estates for themselves were probably suppressed often enough by methods like those the Spartans used against the helots: unexpected disciplinary visitations upon their settlements, or traps laid with the help of informers. Many *penestai* might have been encouraged to go along with the regime by the frequent divisions within Thessalian society between one aristocratic clan and another, which allowed them to change allegiances to their own profit.[47] It is conceivable that in some instances the *penestai* developed a real sense of loyalty and obligation to families that dealt fairly with them from one generation to the next; and that incidentally, here and there in all the various tied populations were to be found the *peasants* of the Greek world, men genuinely under obligation and rendering labor services in return.

So it may have been among the *klarotai* of the Cretan cities, the "lot men," assigned to work the estates of the citizen owners. They were native to Crete, having been subjugated in the course of war.[48] They were the *perioikoi* who provided "tribute" or quotas for the maintenance of Cretan citizen life (Ar. *Pol.* 1272 a 17–18). In their case we have no idea how much they were supposed to surrender, from how big an estate, or with how large a labor force. But the law code of Gortyn shows that the *klarotai* had some clearly defined rights: their marriages were recognized, not only between themselves but with free persons; and they had certain property rights in that they could claim ownership of goods in their possession, cattle and dwellings, even houses in the city if they were resident in them. Other references to the rights of *klarotai* are difficult to interpret; it may be that they had claims of some kind on the heirs to the estate, perhaps touching their continued residence or employment.[49]

According to Aristotle, whereas helots and *penestai* revolted against their masters, "nothing of the kind has occurred in Crete" (*Pol.* 1269 b 3). He attributes this not to any fair treatment that the *klarotai* may have received but to the Cretans' being careful not to draw the *klarotai* of their enemies over to their cause in the numerous wars between cities. Nevertheless, the impression is that dependent laborers in Crete had somewhat better expectations than elsewhere, expectations that were guaranteed by the law and were not merely subject to the whim of the landowners.

Elsewhere some groups of farm workers had distinctive names based on appearances—such as the Konipodes (Dusty Footed) of Epidaurus, the Katonakophoroi (Sheepskin Wearers) and Korynephoroi (Staff Bearers) of Sicyon, and the Gymnetes (Stripped Men) of Argos. They may not all have been *dependent* farm laborers; but the Korynephoroi and the Gymnetes are both included among those described as "between free men and slaves" (Pollux 3.83).[50] The Gymnetes of Argos were, some would say, "bare of weapons," as distinct from the landowners who could afford and had the right to carry arms; others would suggest that they were "stripped for work," as Hesiod recommends for plowing (*WD* 391–93). Whichever the case, they may be identified with the "slaves" who were brought into the citizen body to manage the city after a disastrous Argive defeat at the hands of the Spartans. They were therefore not chattel slaves, but indigenous, and closely enough linked to the Argive people for the Argives to admit them to the citizen body. But once the Argive youth had grown up, the "slaves" were thrown out again; they withdrew a few miles to Tiryns, where they settled peacefully enough until an Arcadian troublemaker urged them to rise up against the Argives (Hdt. 6.83).[51]

The new settlement of Heraclea in Trachis founded in 426 was provided with a dependent laboring population, not surprisingly, as it was a Spartan venture. A contemporary comic poet speaks of seeing "the beautiful city of Heraclea" when he traveled to the *splenopedon* of the Kylikranoi; he also calls it "prostituted and heloticized."[52] Who were the Kylikranoi? A local people who had been forced into dependent labor and whose sphere of operations could be called a *splenopedon,* presumably on the analogy of *oino-pedon,* or vineyard, but whose meaning is unknown: perhaps "boneyard" or something desolate and equally unpleasant. The myth connected with the creation of Heraclea had it that long ago Heracles had suppressed the brigandage of the Kylikranoi, which was an obvious rationalization of or justification for their being subjugated: they deserved it. Consequently, when the settlement began to fail in the early fourth century, the Kylikranoi themselves it was, presumably, who countered with a different myth, which said that, on the contrary, they had accompanied Heracles to Trachis from Asia Minor to help him pacify the region. It needs little imagination to picture the bitterness of relations between landowners and laborers in this brief episode of Spartan-inspired land management.[53]

Other peoples in central Greece, the Dryopes and the Kerkopes, were associated both with brigandage and with the Kylikranoi, and with Heracles; the impression is of an extensive network of rural hill peoples lying partly or wholly outside the sphere of the city-states, until such times as their unruliness became too intolerable, or the city-states' need of more labor became too pressing for these outsiders to continue unincorporated.[54]

In all these instances the dependent worker was indigenous and Greek, if not necessarily cultured or amenable. The Mariandynoi who worked land for the citizens of Heraclea Pontica were indigenous, but not Greek.[55] In their case, as with the other tied populations poised between the Greek world and the barbarian, the peculiar strains for the landowning community of subjugating a closely related group—one's own kind, as it were—did not exist. To a large extent, too, these tied populations worked land assigned to them as *tied tenants,* rather than their being assigned to individual citizen estates, so that there was a greater distance between landowners and dependent population. The traditions concerning Mariandynian subjection to the Greeks include a theme that, if it was historically based, and not just a propagandist's invention, suggests another reason why relations between Greek landowners and non-Greek dependent laborers might have been less strained: it was said that the Mariandynoi had agreed to serve the citizens of Heraclea forever, so long as the Heracleans provided them with what they needed and did not sell them away from their country (Posidonius-Athen. 6.263 d).

What would they have needed, which the Greek city on the coast could provide? Posidonius says simply that, realizing that they were too stupid to manage their own affairs, the Mariandynoi willingly submitted to the superior political organization of a Greek city-state. The Greek prejudice against barbarians is here combined with the disdain of employers for dependent labor. The situation of the Mariandynoi may have been very difficult, in that their nation as a whole had come under Persian rule, but that the coastal Mariandynoi chose (or were forced) to exchange Persian domination for that of the Greek settlement; perhaps it was only thus that they broke a cycle of vendetta or other internal strife, preserving at the same time a claim of sorts to their ancient lands, which were now "allowed" to work partly for the benefit of their new protectors.[56]

The attitude of the Mariandynoi may always have been that they would use Heraclea as a means to regaining their independence, or rebuilding "Greater Mariandynia," and that service on Heraclean land as tied tenants, or in the city's fleet, was a price that had to be paid, for as long as it had to be.[57] When Clearchus took advantage of a revolution in the 360s to make himself tyrant, the "slaves" whom he liberated were most likely Mariandynoi, glad to support a change of government, even his tyranny. It comes as little surprise that Clearchus was of the same school as Critias; the precise impact of his policies on the system of land tenure under which Mariandynoi had cultivated land controlled by Heraclea, or on their subsequent status, is unclear, however.

The Heraclean settlement of Chersonesus, on the southwestern tip of the Crimea, also had its indigenous population of dependent laborers, the Tauroi.[58] They too may have seen the advantages of making a pact with the Greek settlers, to the effect that they would work the land in return for protection against raiders. The fact of their subjugation, and of their giving up the ownership of land in the area, is well illustrated by the superimposition of a Greek farmstead over a Tauric burial; a Hellenistic inscription refers to them as *perioikoi,* which in this period seems no longer to have meant merely "dweller roundabout," who might or might not be a dependent, but more specifically "dweller in the territory of a Greek city without citizen rights who has been reduced to the status of a tied laborer."[59] It is not clear what their relation was to the Greek owners of the large farms west of Chersonesus itself, whether they worked the land there as laborers or as tenants of a kind; elsewhere in the territory, specifically in the Pedion, which was probably a grain-growing plain, they may have worked as tied tenants on similar terms to those in effect at Heraclea (whatever they may have been).[60]

The Tauroi were culturally distinct from the other indigenous peoples of southern Russia, namely the Scythians, and they may have had many opportunities to be grateful for the protection of the Greek city against Scythian and other raiders, all of whom would have gladly taken away agricultural stores as well as captive farm labor. Herodotus depicts a concentration of farming communities within what is now the Ukraine, some half Greek and half Scythian, and others wholly Scythian, including those who "grew grain not for their own consumption but for export" (4.17.2). Other rural populations like those attached to the Greek cities of Olbia and Istria further west along the Black Sea coast certainly experienced destructive raids. At Istria, troops were raised against Thracians, who ravaged the land just at harvesttime, from among the citizens and "barbarians" who had taken refuge in the city; the "barbarians" were, presumably, dependent laborers or tied tenants. At Olbia the raids of the Gauls and their allies caused serious dislocation in the countryside, "in that all the slaves and Half-Greeks who live in the plain along the river bank were lost . . . , no less than 1500 who fought on our side in the city during the previous war."[61] The "slaves" may have been chattel slaves or dependent laborers from the local population, while the "Half-Greeks" were perhaps tenants (tied?) of grainland leased to them on restrictive terms but with the supposed advantages of the Greek city's protection.

The dependent populations all had a part to play in the defense of the community that controlled them, and in the challenges to established authority which came about. The Killyrioi (or Kallikyrioi) of Syracuse, the enslaved or tied local Sicel population, sided with the *demos* against the Gamoroi, the ruling and landed aristocracy, in the early fifth century; but the revolution failed, and the Gamoroi returned with Gelon, who became tyrant. The Killyrioi were presumably punished and terrorized into resuming their former role. About three generations later, the tyrant Dionysius provided himself with an enlarged citizen body by shifting people from elsewhere and emancipating the "slaves"—after which the Killyrioi are heard of no more.[62] Precisely what the liberation of agricultural populations meant for the tenure and cultivation of the land they had previously been working is not clear, at Syracuse or wherever this action occurred: Did Sicel laborers become free, citizen tenants, or even owners, or did they merge into a laboring proletariat, free in principle but tied by the need to hire out so as to survive?

Rural populations were open to political manipulation; they could also turn altogether against their Greek masters. The Pedieis of Priene, "plainsmen" or perhaps plain-cultivators, and *paroikoi,* "fringe-dwellers," had guaranteed use and limited enjoyment of a recognized section of farmland; a grant of the right to purchase land in Priene made to a priestly eunuch of Ephesus specifies that "he may *not* acquire property where the Pedieis have possession."[63] They lived in villages, some of which at any rate lay toward the border with Magnesia-on-the-Maeander, with forces from which they joined up, probably during the war between Lysimachus of Thrace and Demetrius Poliorcetes (287), to slaughter many citizens of Priene and seize their land.[64] Had the Pedieis long fostered ethnic resentments, or did they merely take the opportunity for pillage and revenge when it offered? Whichever the case, the episode serves as yet another reminder of the constant unease in the relationship between landowners and dependent laborers; if the tied population were also Greek, it was culturally close enough to cause persistent fret in the mind of the established group over the question of who was, and who should be, included in the citizen and landowning group.[65] If it was non-Greek, its members were perceived as alien and incalculable. Horror stories of atrocities committed by the "natives" are few and far between, but perhaps few were needed to make the point, however unjustified much of the time, that the rural dependents could not be relied on. The tale of how the Gergithes turned on their masters at Miletus would have had immediate, and obviously did have long-lasting, currency among Greek landowners. The Gergithes, originating from or perhaps always centered upon Gerga, a Carian settlement on the inland side of Milesian territory, are said to have revolted at some point in the Archaic period, and to have set the plow oxen to trample the children of the rich to death on the threshing floors, perhaps during some harvest festival at which the landowners and their families customarily came together in the country to celebrate with their laborers (or tenants) their common interest in the successful cultivation of the land (Plut. *Mor.* 298 c–d).[66]

The troubles at Priene were resolved in a general settlement made by Lysimachus, which shows that not all the Pedieis had rebelled; only those who did were punished. The settlement seems to mark the end of their connection with Priene, for Lysimachus designated their villages as *royal* domain, and the Pedieis disappeared from the records of Priene.[67] What was their situation thereafter? In a sense, Lysimachus might be said to have emancipated them, so that as *laoi*—"people" (the term by which the rural population subject to the Asiatic rulers were known)—they remained *tied,* but with the right to transmit their holdings to their children without question.[68] They still paid over a proportion of their crops, but to royal representatives, or to the agents of remote owners who had been granted the land by the king; as taxpayers, they were at a greater distance from their masters, and so were freer in some respects to order their lives without the interference and uncertainties to which the dependent populations of the city-states must so often have been subjected.

## Chattel Slaves on the Land

The landowner accused of destroying a sacred olive tree on his property says that not even the neighbors who dislike him have alleged
that he "supervised, while the slaves cut it down" (Lysias 7.19).
In this vignette of rural activity is contained the farming ideal, of
being able to utilize others' labor on one's land and to direct their
efforts unquestioned. How more fully could this ideal be realized
than with field slaves? There had always been chattel slaves: warfare and piracy ensured the supply of human labor for sale, and
this availability itself may sometimes have encouraged the acquisition of slaves beyond the limits of any actual need of labor.
Slaves were employed in every sphere of activity, from plowing to
nursing the master's children, and from supervising his sheep and
goats to accompanying his wife to market. In many slave-owning
households the slave's duties were doubtless clearly defined, but
in others where perhaps no more than two or three were kept, the
same slave might fill several roles, at least to the extent that a
house servant also worked on the farm. One of the difficulties in
assessing the importance of slavery as opposed to other forms of
labor lies in the fact that the Greek terms are not used precisely
enough (from our perspective, at least) to show clearly whether
the "laborer" is a slave (and not a free man or a dependent), or the
"slave" a farm laborer exclusively and not a domestic. But there is
no doubt that employing slaves was as characteristic of Greek agriculture as hiring laborers or allowing dependent rural populations the use of the land.[69]

In the Homeric world slaves are to be found indoors and out,
along with hirelings and dependents; it is slaves who spread manure on the fields from the heap where Odysseus's old hound
Argos lies dying (*Od.* 17.297–99), and the swineherd Eumaeus
himself tells the tale of how he was kidnapped and sold into slavery by Phoenician traders (*Od.* 15.415–84).

"First, a household, a woman and a plowing ox—a chattel
woman . . . who could follow the herds"—so Hesiod advises the
novice landowner (*WD* 405–6). The extent to which slaves, as
distinct from other forms of labor, were used on the land varied

considerably, however, especially from the sixth century onward. In Attica as in Chios and numerous other places, chattel slavery became the most important form of labor, *not* because the *pelatai* or *thetes,* the "nearby dependents," were reduced to slavery but because they were emancipated. Similarly, with the absorption of Killyrioi and Mariandynoi into the free population of Syracuse and Heraclea during the fourth century, the proportion of chattel slaves in these cities presumably increased. Dependent labor had existed in Attica in the persons of the pre-Solonian *thetes,* the sixth-part sharecroppers, and others caught in the trap of indebtedness to more prosperous and powerful relatives or neighbors. With the transformation of *thetes* into Thetes and the abolition of debt bondage, hired citizen labor became less easy to coerce, partly because Thetes had rights under the law and might invoke them, if abused, cheated of their wages, or detained against their will by the landowners who had hired them.[70]

For the land owners, the obvious answer to a growing shortage of coercible and readily available labor was to bring in more chattel slaves. And so it appears that after the early sixth century chattel slaves became more numerous in Attica, so that by the Classical period full-time citizen hired labor played a very small role in agriculture. The link between the advance toward democracy and the increasing importance of chattel slavery can be seen not only in Athens's political and economic character, but also in what was happening at Chios in the same period.[71] Political adjustments promoting the power of the *demos* may have prompted a similar emancipation of laborers and debtors, so that by the later fifth century Thucydides could say that "there are more slaves in Chios than anywhere else in Greece, except Sparta" (8.40.2). Large numbers of them worked on the land.[72]

The advantages of slave labor for the landowner were manifold. On the lowest consideration, slave laborers could be beaten into compliance and productivity, fed cheaply, and worked long hours, with no objections raised by relatives or "patrons," no invoking of the law by inimical neighbors or informers; slaves had no rights, no claims, and no connections in the place where they had been brought to work. A more constructive appraisal of its advantages would be that the slaves were constantly on hand, instead of being somewhere else at a critical moment (see earlier comments on the flightiness of free labor). Whether slave labor tended to be more compliant, because a slave had nothing but the environment and the occupation in which he had been thrust—and nothing to lose except his pride by doing what he was told—is a moot point; sheer resentment of his status may have made many a slave recalcitrant and uncooperative. Since chattel slaves were usually non-Greek, the relationship between master and slave, difficult as it may have been in many respects, with often enough a language barrier to overcome, must at least have lacked much of the uneasiness that the subjugation of other Greeks entailed—as in the case of helots. Growing doubts there may have been about the justification for enslavement, that some men (or nations) were slavish by nature, but there is no sign that anyone denied himself the use of slave labor on this account.[73] If he could not afford slaves, that was another matter; but the initial expense, especially for a young or untrained slave, could be borne by all but the poorest or most parsimonious of landowners.[74]

What then does Aristotle mean when, after quoting Hesiod—"Get first a house, a woman, and an ox to draw the plow" (*WD* 405)—he remarks that "the ox is the poor man's slave" (*Pol.* 1252 b 12–14)? He takes "woman" here to mean *wife,* not *slave,* and so he is suggesting that even those landowners whose farms were just big enough to make the use of ox-power economically feasible—that is, the owners of plots of fifty to sixty *plethra* and up (see chapter 2)—did not employ slave labor. But the argument can also be put that whereas ox-power would have been an extravagance and an impracticability in a small and intensively cultivated plot, a prolonged illness, the death of a useful family member, or a lack of children to put to work might have made it necessary to bring in labor to help cultivate the plot. An ox need have been little cheaper at the outset than a slave, who would have proved more useful throughout the year. It is possible, in any case, that oxen were shared among farmers to some extent (see chapter 3). Aristotle's comment is presumably an amplification of the quotation from Hesiod, which is intended to make Hesiod's recommendation fit Aristotle's own argument, that the household consists of an association between the master of the house and his wife and slaves; but they seem not to mesh very closely together, either with one another or with agricultural realities.[75]

The disadvantages of slave labor are less immediately obvious. One problem was how to ensure that they were not kidnapped for use or resale elsewhere; another, how to prevent them from running away. But this was a most desperate course of action for slaves to take, however terrible the conditions from which they were trying to escape, for at best they could only expect to exchange one master for another, and at worst they were sent back to their owner to be punished severely.[76] In principle, all slave owners would have agreed that all slaves were unreliable and should be watched closely, especially when they were using sharp or heavy tools. A slave who proved unbiddable, or incapable of following instructions, was a financial loss, in that he was not earning his keep and could not be sold with very high recommendations for a very good price. And a slave who fell ill or died was, more or less, a dead loss.

Were there economic advantages in buying farm slaves rather than hiring free labor? Most farms, however small, needed someone permanently about the place, whether it was a hired man or a slave; both had to be maintained the year round, and both would probably have received much the same maintenance, equipment, and rewards according to their experience and deserts. Judging from the evidence for slave and free labor in other occupations, slaves seem not to have undercut free labor; the economic advantage lay, then, in their availability.[77]

The slave population was made up of a variety of people mainly from north, east, and south of the Aegean, as the mixture of ethnic names in the Athenian sources suggests. But there is nothing to indicate that slaves from any one nation or region were preferred over others for farm work; no particular physical characteristics or methods of cultivation were the monopoly of any particular culture, in any case, and the most desired attribute in the slave field hand would probably have been dexterity and endurance.

Slave employers doubtless took care to buy slaves of different ethnic backgrounds, so that Greek would be the common language in the establishment, and there would be no opportunity for slaves from the same area to build up any solidarity based on national feeling, against their master. Thus, in Aristophanes' *Peace,* the chorus has the (presumably Syrian) slave Syra go and fetch the (Phrygian) slave Manes in from the vineyard (1146).[78] Whether ethnic names were applied precisely or at random to chattel slaves, it is not altogether clear; they probably tended to indicate a slave's actual place of origin, as far as would make sense to the slave marketeer and the purchaser. But many slaves had purely Greek names; thus their original identity was lost forever.

Plato represents the slave owners' view of their slaves as one of ambivalence and apprehension. On one hand, he says, "Let us consider a wealthy private slave owner with a large number of slaves. . . . They don't live in fear of their slaves . . . because the individual owner has the support of society as a whole." But on the other hand, "imagine that some god were to [transport] just one man who owned fifty or more slaves . . . with his [family . . . and] slaves to a desert place where there would be no other free men to help him—wouldn't he be very much afraid that he and his wife and children would be done away with by the slaves? His only salvation would be to curry favor with them, and give then their freedom" (*Rep.* 578 d–579 a)—which in the circumstances would be rather superfluous![79] The solidarity of slave owners in the face of their slaves was important to the maintenance of the property owning status quo. In a network of small estates such as existed in Attica, neighboring landowners would usually know one another's laborers by sight, and each look out for the other's interests; property rights were respected in that runaway slaves were not generally guaranteed a warm welcome even by the enemy in time of war.[80] But this did not prevent slaves from chancing their luck; three ran away off the farm of Nicostratus, the neighbor of Apollodorus. They were successful so far, in that Nicostratus did not catch up with them but was himself captured at sea and put up for sale in the island of Aegina, whence he had to be ransomed (Dem. 53.6).

Runaway slaves who were returned to their owners would be severely punished and perhaps marked for life by a brand as incorrigibles. Successful escape as the result of a large-scale slave revolt seems to have been almost unknown, for slave revolts in themselves were extremely infrequent in the Greek world. Only shock waves caused by the great rebellions in Roman Sicily in the late second century stirred up trouble in Attica and Delos, among other places; earlier, the disasters that befell Athens with the Spartan occupation of Decelea from 412 onward included less a slave rebellion than a withdrawal of slaves, among whom were certainly farm workers as well as skilled craftsmen and miners.[81] Most of the runaways were probably included among the slaves whom the Thebans bought cheap—no return to their homeland for them (*Hell. Oxy.* 17.4). The Athenians might have been able to do something to redress this loss of slave labor—if they had wished to do so, with all the difficulties of farming that the Spartan occupation created, for the Athenians' own fortress on the island of Chios during this same period encouraged the slaves there to desert from their overbearing masters to the Athenians in large numbers, but we are not told what the Athenians did with them. It seems that the Chian slaves were predominantly farm workers—"because of their knowledge of the country it was they who did the most harm" to the Chian cause; Thucydides adds that "because of their great numbers they were punished particularly severely when they did wrong" (8.40.2).[82] It is in Chios that the only other slave rebellion we know of occurred: in the early third century, runaway slaves gathered in the mountains under the leadership of Drimacus. He led a tight-knit organization that remained in communication with the city while guaranteeing its own members protection if they needed it. This was not a liberation movement as such, but what has been called a "counterstate" like the pirate states in Cilicia and Crete later in the Hellenistic period.[83] Drimacus became a hero after his death, for both slaves and slave owners, curiously enough.

No such event and no such leader of slaves appear anywhere in the Athenian traditions. Slaves were better treated in Attica, so Thucydides' comment on Chios implies, but whether this was simply because there were fewer of them in Attica than in Chios or for some other reason, it is hard to say—or indeed how much better their treatment actually was. If farms in Attica were on the whole smaller than Chian estates, there might have been fewer *bailiff*-run operations and more owner participation, but this in itself would not necessarily ensure kinder treatment of the slaves: Was cruelty likely to be greater in a larger group managed by a professional "boss" or in a small, close-knit organization immediately under the owner's eye?

Xenophon thought that "one ought not to punish even a slave in anger; for masters who have lost their tempers often do more harm to themselves than they inflict" (*HG* 5.3.7).[84] The implication is that this was a common occurrence; certainly farming could be a fretting business, even (or sometimes especially) when the crops did well, for "those who reap a harvest past their hopes are merciless to their slaves" (Aesch. *Ag.* 1044–45). The indolence of slaves in the field was proverbial; Herodotus says of the Athenians under the tyrants that "while held down they were willfully uncooperative, like slaves laboring for their master" (5.78). But there were great differences in the treatment of slaves: "Some men use their resources badly, and others use them well and with profit. . . . In some households nearly all the slaves are bound, and yet they continually try to run away, whereas in others they are not restrained and willingly stay at their posts and work" (Xen. *Oecon.* 3.4). Chain gangs were known on Roman estates, and the tone of the few references to their use in the Greek world suggests that fettered workers were not uncommon there either. Aeschines speaks of Greek captives working chained in Philip II's vineyard (2.156); the mother of the hero in Menander's *Dyscolus* dreams that Pan puts chains round her son's ankles, gives him a leather jacket and a hoe, and tells him to "get into that next field there and start digging" (410–19); and the chorus of farmers in Aristophanes' *Plutus* suggests to the disrespectful slave Carion that his shins "are shouting 'Ow! ow!' in longing for gyves and fetters" (275–76). Chains may have been used as temporary punishment as much as for permanent control, of course.

Crimes such as theft were punished with a beating. So Philocleon reminds a slave of the time "I caught you stealing grapes, and tied you to the olive and flogged you" (Aristoph. *Wasps* 449–50). Plato prescribes that the slave who takes fruit without permission is to receive as many stripes as there were grapes in the bunch or figs on the tree; he may have been improving a little on an existing Athenian law (*Laws* 845 a).[85] That slaves were often tempted to "borrow" the occasional piece of fruit is suggested by the evidence for slaves' food—a man who "dined daily . . . on spiced cheese cake and salt tuna . . . would be ready to dig among mountain rock and stone—and peck at the fodder on which slaves are fed, a little bit of figs and barley bread" (Phoenix fr. 8 Loeb). Others speak disparagingly of barley products as food for slaves, and Trygaeus proposes converting a war trumpet into a pair of scales for weighing out figs for the slaves in the field, which also suggests that owners kept close watch on the amount of food their slaves consumed (Aristoph. *Peace* 1248–49). Sour wine and salt fish were provided for agricultural workers at Panticapaeum in the Crimea, to be supplemented presumably by bread from the grain the farmer grew himself (Dem. 35.32).[86]

Wretched as this fare sounds, the slaves' diet was probably little worse than that of many a citizen, landowner or not, who lived frugally, with little or no meat other than the occasional allotment from a sacrifice. And for all the disdainful remarks about barley, it remained a staple for free men as well as slaves throughout Greek antiquity.[87]

So with slaves' clothing: the leather tunic, the felt or leather hat, the rough shoes, the shaggy fleece jacket that the master provided for his plowmen and herdsmen were no different than the garments worn by any working farmer, except that they might have been patched and pieced even longer, like "the smocks and tunics of yesteryear" that Philocleon buys his slaves, with caps and foot coverings in winter (Aristoph. *Wasps* 442–47).[88] When Odysseus comes upon his father Laertes at work in his orchard, he finds him indistinguishable from the most lowly laborer, in "filthy, patched, and disreputable tunic, a pair of stitched leather gaiters round his shins to protect them from scratches, and gloves to save his hands from the brambles, and by way of emphasizing his wretchedness, a goatskin hat on his head" (*Od.* 24.226–31). Hesiod's farmer is no less uncouth in appearance as he scuds along in a winter rainstorm wearing oxskin boots, long tunic and wrap under a kidskin jacket, with an ear-covering felt hat (*WD* 541–46). Whether the Old Oligarch is thinking of country people too, or only of the city's inhabitants, is unclear, when he remarks that slaves cannot be distinguished from citizens by their appearance (1.10); this would have been even more true in the country when farmers and their laborers were working in the fields stripped, as both Hesiod and Plato recommend.[89]

The Old Oligarch resented the lack of differentiation in dress between free men and slaves; he would certainly have disapproved of the familiarity between some masters and their slaves such as Theophrastus depicts in his characterization of the boor. The boorish man distrusts his friends and relatives, and instead discusses all his business with his slaves; when he comes back from the Assembly he tells his farm laborers everything that was said there (*Char.* 4.2–3).[90] Closeness of contact would have existed not only in the context of work on the land, but also in the patterns of residence. When the landowner actually lived on the land himself, field slaves and cattle would very often occupy outlying chambers in the farmhouse, living in like the domestic slaves. But on some estates they inhabited simple cabins apart, along with the draft animals, pigs, and so on; this was probably the case on the estate of the Dema house in Attica, which must have been a landowner's residence, being so far out in the country, but which included no farm buildings—they presumably stood somewhere nearby but quite separate.[91] During the summer months some field hands may have camped out in temporary shelters close to whichever task was requiring to be done; thus Hesiod's farmer advises his laborers to look ahead and build winter huts for themselves, "for it will not always be summer" (*WD* 502–3).[92]

But neither physical proximity nor separation of abode necessarily accounted for sympathy or dislike between landowner and slave—personalities and attitudes of mind on either side were the determining factors. Sometimes all question of master–slave relations would have been ruled out by the fact that some farmhouses were no more than barracks for slaves working under a bailiff, while the owner lived elsewhere and visited only occasionally if at all. This may have been the case with, for example, the dwellings on the large farms known at Crimean Chersonesus, likewise on various sacred estates. The lessees of the Delian estates almost certainly did not reside in the farmhouses that went with each estate but left them for the farm laborers. Several of the farm complexes included both upper-story living quarters and *andronia;* if the latter were the men's sleeping quarters, then presumably the former were reserved for the female slaves (employed as cooks, herders, or vinetenders). Most but not all the estates included *thalamoi*—chambers for married couples—*not* for the lessee and his wife, more likely for a married bailiff.[93]

When the owner took a hand in working the land, he inevitably came into direct contact with his laborers, and often enough a kind of friendliness would have developed through sharing good experiences and bad, and cooperating in tasks that for the moment leveled all differences between them. Sometimes the contact might have grown into genuine friendship and respect, the earliest and best-known portrayal of which appears in the *Odyssey.* The relationship between Odysseus and the swineherd Eumaeus has no doubt been heightened beyond the bounds of reality; just as Odysseus is no ordinary man but a hero, so Eumaeus is no mere pig keeper but the true friend of a hero. Nevertheless, this is not all pure fantasy; the trust and confidence between master and slave which Homer depicts are rooted in the experience of the real world. One of the very few farm slaves known to us by name in the Classical period is Callarus, who belonged to Callicles' neighbor in the hill country north of Eleusis.[94] Callicles had brought suit against Callarus on the grounds that he had built the wall that Callicles alleged caused flooding on his land, "because," says Callarus's owner, "he knows I value Callarus highly, and he wants to annoy me on this account" (Dem.55.32, 34). Callarus's owner was resident on his farm, but Callarus was the trusted servant, and must have been known to be legally competent to act for his owner if necessary, otherwise Callicles would hardly have taken him to court.[95]

In the first instance, however, the acquisition of a good bailiff, like the proper treatment of field slaves as a whole, was primarily a business matter: proper management would produce good results for the estate. So slaves should as far as possible be encouraged by fair treatment and material rewards—for the sake of profit, not because the slaves' quality of life would or should be bettered.[96] The Ischomachean view of farm management was that "nobody can be a good farmer unless he makes his laborers both eager and obedient. . . . A good farmer must therefore give frequent encouragement to his workers no less than a general to his troops—and slaves are no less in need of good expectations than free men" (*Oecon.* 5.15–16).[97] The slave selected to be bailiff must be loyal; he may be made so by rewards such as better clothing and more varied food, perhaps, and by some share in the master's good fortune (*Oecon.* 12.6). The slave bailiff was then to be allowed to earn a certain income over and above what it cost to maintain him, in much the same way as skilled slave craftsmen might if they work independent of their masters, handing over part of their earnings and returning a portion as their *apophora,* or freedom money.[98] Men with very obvious bad habits are not fit to be trained as bailiffs, unless their love of money can lead them to understand that diligence can be profitable. And so on.

The bailiff must also be able to deal firmly with the slaves working under him so as to make them effective; just as with breaking in horses or training puppies, he should reward his trainees with something that they like and punish them for failure to learn what they are being taught. Free men can be taught by word of mouth, but "for slaves, the same method as for training wild animals is required—give them the food they like, and praise those who are ambitious" (*Oecon.* 13.7–10). Aristotle, on the other hand, feels that reason should not be withheld from slaves but that the master must produce the kind of goodness in the slave which will enable him to fulfill his function adequately (*Pol.* 1260 b 2–6).[99]

For many slaves, it was their relations with the bailiff which really made the difference between a tolerable and a miserable life. Some bailiffs could be got round with a bit of flattery (Xen. *Oecon.* 13.12), whereas others were doubtless utter martinets—partly because their masters expected it, but also because, having endured in the ranks themselves, they would see no reason why other slaves in their turn should not suffer as they had. The opportunities for unlicensed abuse, both physical (of the workers) and material (of the land) which lay open to the bailiffs of estates whose owners hardly ever visited must have been boundless. But if the bailiff was to get a good return from the estate with some benefit to himself, his concern to run an efficient and therefore not too oppressive operation would have been of the same order as the good landowner's, however outrageously he fixed the books and cheated his master.

As suggested earlier, the farm slave's life might in some instances have been affected by the kind of work he did, developing a particular knack for one task or another, although the majority would have had to turn to a wide range of agricultural tasks; for even a large farm could not afford more than the most basic division of labor, between field work and herding. Occasionally a specialist in vine tending or tree propagation might have been able to confine himself to his specialization, if he was lent or hired out where his expertise was in demand. If a slave was trustworthy enough to be made herdsman, he could be sure of staying largely apart from the agricultural work of the farm, with the animals he tended; the advantages of such employment could often have outweighed the exposure to the elements, the sparse diet, and the other privations of the herdsman's life, for he was well out of the way, much of the time, of his master or the bailiff and to some extent then independent. Even in far distant hill pastures there would have been other shepherds to provide at times a certain professional solidarity—when they were not quarreling over strayed animals—while herdsmen in areas where (limited) transhumance was carried on would even have gained a recognized place in the country community, as they went to and fro among the pastures round about and above the farms and settlements of the inhabited countryside.[100] The small-scale and purely local herding of a handful of sheep or goats would of course have been left to any slave available—one who was young, inexperienced, or otherwise ill-suited to harder or more complicated tasks.

Were slaves on the farm, even bailiffs, permitted a family life? There are no overt references to the breeding of slaves, and when slave children or infants are (rarely) mentioned they could as well be the master's own illegitimate offspring, as have been born of slave parents, or have come into the household with other chattel slaves from the market. If married bailiffs managed some of the Delian estates, then it is not clear whether they were still enslaved or had gained their freedom and, by that means, the privilege of married life. When Eumaeus speaks of what a slave could expect from a good master—the grant of a house, a piece of land, and a woman—perhaps this should be seen as the Homeric equivalent of manumission in a society where "freedom" was a concept that had not yet come into full flower, and where the ties between slave and master could be both looser and more enduring than in a Classical democracy.[101]

Plato sees the promise of manumission as the stranded slave owner's only hope of escaping the vengeance of his slaves. Freedom was the dearest wish of the enslaved, but comparatively few farm slaves may have gained it, specifically the headmen or bailiffs, Pericles' man Euangelus, Callarus, and their like. The *georgoi* listed among the newly manumitted men and women who dedicated silver bowls, like those who were included among the metics granted privileges for helping the Athenian democrats in the crisis of 404/3, are more likely to have been *epitropoi* than mere laborers; for one thing the owner would want to retain the promise of manumission as an incentive to a good worker to do even better, and for another, if he manumitted more than one or two laborers as well, he would not only diminish the value of the privilege, but it would have little meaning for workers with only lowly or minimal skills, who could find little or no alternative to working for their former owner on much the same terms—so the owner would argue, not wishing to lose control of all his laborers in any case, or to leave his heirs an estate with no labor attached to it.

Manumission did not in any case mean that the freedman was immediately and automatically released from all formal connections with his master. Far from it—in many cases there were various obligations to be borne, embodied in the *paramone,* "remaining with" the former owner for a certain period and performing certain duties. This may have been less of a burden to many farming freedmen than might be supposed, for it could have ensured continued employment in familiar surroundings, and have proved the basis of long-lasting connections between an estate and free laborers of slave descent. The freedman herdsman Tibius who appears in Menander's *Eros* has a son, Gorgias, who also keeps sheep for the household on which the comedy centers; and perhaps Deinias, whose memorial has been found on land belonging to Timesius in the mining district of Attica, and who may have been a freedman bailiff, had reason to consider himself *and his family* permanently attached to this farm—for the memorial states that his children and their descendants are to occupy the same burial place.[102]

But until slaves gained their freedom, they could be disposed of in accordance with the owner's best business interests. A herd of goats would sell better if its slave herdsman were included in the deal (Isaeus 6.33), and so the men who stole some sheep took the shepherd as well (Dem. 47.52). Land that was put up for sale might also have sold better if the slave labor that had worked it for the previous owner was available for the new owner, to ensure some continuity of practice, with workers who knew something about the locality and the nature of the land. Often enough, though, purchasers of new estates might have found it more satisfactory to bring in their own slaves, so that bailiffs and vineyard overseers like Pistus and Aristomachus, trusted though they may have been by their Hermocopid owners, were seemingly sold away from the land where they had been working.[103]

The owners' object in employing slaves was that their labor problems should be solved by the simplest means available. But slaves were human, and not automatons, and capable of being lazy, resentful, and potentially threatening. The owner of the estate that was missing a sacred olive tree says that if he had cut it down, he would have had to run the risk of being seen in the act, and of being blackmailed by his own slaves—they could turn state's evidence or become the tools of their master's personal enemies (Lysias 7.16). Slave owners might have liked on occasion to pretend that relations with their slaves were not hostile, and that a kindly familiarity on their part was met with grateful respect from the slaves; and indeed the temptation is to make much of the ritual celebrating in which masters and slaves joined at harvesttime, or when the new wine was sampled, and to see in such activities a generally meaningful bond of sympathy between them. Some slaves may genuinely have rejoiced at their masters' good fortune, and grieved for their losses in a bad year; but more often than not the slaves' participation in festivals such as the country Dionysia would have been unwilling or passive at best. Furthermore, by seeming to sanction total freedom of behavior for the duration of a holiday, as happened at various festivals, the owners were simply reinforcing the total control they actually possessed over their slaves. For many landowners, untroubled by what their slaves' inner thoughts might be, it was in a way no more than letting the plow animals out to grass every once in a while, or decking them up for a triumphal carting of crops to the barn or to market.[104]

There was a persistent uneasiness underlying what seemed on the surface the simple and straightforward matter of putting slaves to work on the land. It is partly for this reason that utopian dreams of getting food from the land without labor, one's own *or anyone else's,* existed at all periods. The Golden Age had been one of effortless fruitfulness; the Cyclopes lived uncivilized and untroubled by labor problems of any kind; and it was surely in search of the same freedom from the difficulty of dealing with employees that Constantine IX of Byzantium made "ingenious inventions that enabled him to dispense with farm workers" (Psellus *Chronogr.* 6.176).[105]

# Six

# The Farmers and the Rest of Society

I n Aristophanes' *Plutus* the slave Carion asks the sycophant if he is a farmer, to which the sycophant replies, "Do you take me for a fool?" (903). This would have seemed as bad a joke to the villagers of Locris or Achaea, to the Mantineans, or to the people of Aphytis as it must to large numbers of Athenians. Much of the citizen population everywhere had an interest of one kind or another in farming. Work on the land was arduous, and owning it often enough fraught with anxiety, while to be both farmer and owner, or *autourgos,* was to endure both the toils and the worries of agriculture. The preoccupations and experiences of dealing with the land affected even Pericles, who had to decide what to do with his own estate, should it be left undisturbed in recognition of his guest friendship with King Archidamus, when the Spartans invaded Attica. At the same time the Greek community, in the way of human society generally, was continually subdividing itself into numerous informal but for the moment clearly differentiated groups, which coalesced and dissolved as personalities came and went—differentiations based on wealth and birth, sources of wealth and gradations of breeding, place of origin and place of residence, political alignment, cult affiliation, social alliances, physical characteristics, standards of dress, manners, where a man sat in the theater, perhaps, or even where he went for haircuts, shoe repairs, and the latest gossip, or which seer he patronized.[1] And because a natural consequence of such subdividings is for one segment of society to regard another segment as in some way apart and different from itself, so that its own sense of superiority is enhanced, not surprisingly the "farmers" and "country people" too were often seen as a group distinct from "us," and typified as "garlic-chewing," "thyme-smelling," "dusty-footed," "rustic," or "boorish." At Sparta, of course, the distinction between the farmers and those who had no contact with the land (theoretically) was perfectly straightforward, and long and consistently maintained, between helots and Spartan citizens. Elsewhere, even in places where either chattel slavery or dependent labor played a large part in agriculture, the differentiation between "the farmers" and the rest was less clear-cut, because some citizens labored on their own land (if not on someone else's), and others managed their estates personally.

Nevertheless these characterizations of the farming populations persisted. It has often been argued that they reflect a real ideological split between town and country which was much more than a matter of difference in tastes, as to what a man ate, or whether he chose to live in the country and work his own farm or not, and more serious than a passing irritation with landed affairs; and that this division can be seen fully expressed in the debate about Athenian policy before and during the Peloponnesian War.[2] The farmers' attitude is characterized thus: they wanted peace, not war, for war meant the disruption of agriculture; they were the most affected by Pericles' plan to evacuate the countryside and abandon it to the Spartans' raiding; they represented the conservative elements of the Athenian citizen body in that they were among those who had never really approved or seen the point of Athenian domination over the allies. The townsmen despised them in turn, and voted for war regardless.

Leaving aside such questions as the size of the resident population of Athens itself, and what percentage of it had really no contact with the countryside and its concerns, the heart of the problem is, how such a division of opinion would have operated in the political debate. The supposition has been that the assembly was usually attended and manipulated by those who were based in the city and who had other interests than farming and landed property, and that those who lived by farming and (by implication) in the country had no interest in the advantages of empire—in taking up land grants overseas, and no time or energy either to go off rowing in the allied fleet for pay—and that they therefore attended assembly meetings infrequently, and were outvoted when they did come.

Aristophanes has been assumed to be the spokesman in his comedies for the rural point of view, against that of the city-dwelling warmongers, the demagogues and their cronies. When someone complains that men are drafted for a campaign without warning, the comment is, "They do all that to us country folk, not so much to the townspeople" (*Peace* 1179–86). "They" are the politicians, another favorite target of those—this time the farmers—casting about for someone to blame or despise; the country people here reverse the process of defining and picking on a group different from themselves, too, by setting themselves up as the typified and victimized section of society. Is Aristophanes in this, as in many other passages used to make the argument, actually depicting a real political divide between *the farmers* and the majority within the democracy, or is he simply putting likely remarks into the mouths of the characters he happens to be representing? Always his main interest is the Athenian people as a whole and the working of the democracy. When he speaks of the "laboring folk" coming in from the fields, not understanding that the demagogues are misleading them (*Peace* 632–35), he is not distinguishing the stupid country people from the canny town dwellers who are taken in by nobody, for he means that all Athenians who voted in support of the demagogues' proposals were being duped. His farmers represent not a distinct group within the Athenian population, in numerical or physical terms, but the agricultural aspect of Athenian society as a whole. Demus himself, the personification of the Athenian citizen body, is "rustic in his bad temper, a bean chewer, quick to be inhibited" (*Knights* 40–41). The country folk who are easily cheated—by Paphlagon (Cleon) who cuts leather hides so that they look thicker than they really are—stand for the whole electorate, which supported Cleon's policies so readily in the face of more cautious politicians (*Knights* 316–17). So Dicaeopolis says, "I know the ways of the country folk—that they're tremendously pleased if some fraud of an orator spouts eulogies on them and the city, true or false; that's how they can be bought and sold, and never be aware of it" (*Acharnians* 370–75).[3]

A case can be made for Aristophanes' representing the real interests of a separate peace-party, which included the farming country residents of Attica, but the evidence of the comedies far more easily supports the argument that there was no great opposition of countrymen to townspeople, and that the points of view expressed in the plays emerged from the mix of opinions running through society as a whole, and from Aristophanes' own awareness of them. Opposition to the war with Sparta, as to the evacuation of 431, led to some violent swings of opinion, not just within a minority group of farmers; Pericles' deposition from the board of ten generals was a *popular* decision, after all. As for the advantages of empire, many a farming family may have been glad to find an alternative to splitting an inheritance by having a younger son take up a cleruchy somewhere, just as some farmers and farm laborers may have been pleased to put in a few weeks' rowing, between the grain harvests and the demands of the vineyard and the olive grove during the autumn.

The interdependence of town and country, in Athens no less than in smaller communities, was close; those who lived completely out of touch with local landed concerns could probably be counted on the fingers of one hand, for there was scarcely anyone who did not at least obtain agricultural supplies in the Athenian market for consumption. Aristophanes certainly reflects lively prejudices felt against groups that are defined by one or another social or economic characteristic: the countrymen who come into the city for an assembly meeting trot nervously up so as to be in time, "covered in dust, happy with a bit of garlic, all vinegar-and-pickle-faced"—dirty, smelly, and therefore easily recognizable (*Eccles.* 289–92). But what, one might ask, did most Athenians eat, even in the heart of the city? And who could walk very far anywhere in summer, even within the back lanes of Athens, without getting dusty? What is being picked on here is slight but detectable differences of habit and taste, perhaps—no more— and not very deep differences, just enough in which to base a mild and unreasoning antipathy.

So for some sections of society the man who talks on terms of familiarity with his farmhands, the *agroikos* who claims that thyme smells as sweet as scent, who wears shoes too big for him, and feeds his plow animals at the breakfast table (so to speak?), who talks of his dog as the "guardian of land and house," is a *rustic boor,* the sort of man who is unimpressed by almost everything until he happens to see some animal in the street, who worries about every little loan of farm equipment to neighbors— a man who lives and talks in rural clichés (Theophr. *Char.* 4). We know what Theophrastus means, and why this character is to be despised; it is easy too to see the injustice of the criticisms, but then justice is not the object. Impatience with the *boring man* may be aroused by his idle comments on the state of the weather and the crops (*Char.* 3.4); the *rude man* causes offense by boasting of his own garden while dining out on someone else's vegetables (*Char.* 20.9). No social differentiation is being made here, between poor cultivators and rich men who can afford to eschew all contact with the land; the typifier and the typified are more likely than not to have been of the same social and economic status, both concerned with the land to some extent, and hence, the one all the more sensitive to the other's grating ways.

Scorn for the poor and lowborn is frequently expressed by the wellborn, and in a way this has to do with the distinction between those who live in or are of the city and those who are outside it, politically or physically. Theognis who lost his land by the reforms of the Megarian tyrant Theagenes complains of "a tribe of lawless men who grazed outside the city walls like deer, and wore the skins of goats. These men are nobles now" (55–59). The Goatskin Wearers of Megara may have been a recognized group, of land laborers and herdsmen, rather like the Katonakophoroi (Sheepskin Wearers) of Sicyon, or the Gymnetes (Stripped Men) of Argos, the Killyrioi (Donkey Men) of Syracuse, the Konipodes (Dusty Footed) of Epidaurus: such epithets must often have come into use, regardless of precise legal significance as to the free or subordinate status of those so described, to refer to anyone who did not belong to the ingroup, who was on the edges of society in one sense or another. This was surely the attitude maintained toward the Ellopieis, a people connected to the city of Histiaea in northern Euboea, and perhaps at some period a dependent population providing labor on the land; their name, regional in origin, was also understood to mean "fisherman," "scaly," or "dumb as a fish."[4] Jokes about ethnic origins and characteristics must be as old as human speech itself; their point would be enhanced if they could also be linked to an ignoble occupation such as laboring on another man's land. Solon's retention of the epithet *thes* (hired laborer, serving man) for his fourth category, the poorest Athenian citizens, can be seen as a very sure way of marking their incorporation into the citizen body—an intentional reverse use of the hitherto demeaning group definition. In the same way, perhaps, Cleisthenes of Sicyon employed derogatory-sounding names for three of his four new tribes (Pig Men, Swine Men, Ass Men), not merely to suppress the Dorian or Argive connection of the old names but to promote or integrate social groups formerly depressed—men relegated to the ranks of the Katonakophoroi unjustly, or even the Katonakophoroi themselves.[5]

The ambivalences of the Greeks' attitude to farming, farmers, laborers, and country dwellers are expressed, rather than explained, in the first of Plutarch's *Greek Questions*:

> Who were the Konipodes and the *artynoi* in Epidaurus? There were 180 men who held political power, out of whom were chosen the *artynoi*—directors. Most of the *demos* worked in the fields. They were

called Dusty Footed since, presumably, they were recognized by their dusty feet whenever they came into town. (*Mor.* 291 E)

It looks as if Plutarch means that the *artynoi* had their lands worked for them by the Konipodes who were a subordinated rural population, coming to town only occasionally with produce for their masters, perhaps; but there may be no close connection between the two. He may simply have included two items concerning Epidaurus which he happened to have before him in a single paragraph for simplicity's sake, not meaning to imply that the Konipodes were the Epidaurian equivalent of the Sicyonian Katonakophoroi, and therefore a farm-laboring group identified here by a different aspect of its members' appearance. In this case the *demos* would consist of the rest of the citizen (or citizen-related) population, part of which worked their own farms and part labored for hire. The dustiness of their feet would indicate the need of town-dwelling farmers to come and go between house and farm, and of country residents to walk into the city on business occasionally; it might also have distinguished them from the ruling oligarchs who could no doubt afford to ride out to their estates, as Ischomachus is supposed to have done.

All such economic and political distinctions could be set aside by quite other considerations; Theocritus's *Idyll* 7, set in the island of Cos, may suggest how. Friends walking through the countryside to a harvest festival being held by "the best of an old family" meet a "good man" who is unmistakably a goatherd, from the "coarse-haired, shaggy goatskin the color of rust, smelling of milky rennet" hanging from his shoulders, the threadbare smock tied with string about his waist, and the olive-wood crook in his right hand. He hails them as an equal, and they recognize him as "the best at making music among herdsmen and harvesters." The poet, who has also been a shepherd and has learned his craft from the Nymphs in the mountains, is eager to compete with him. The poetic skill that they share overrides any sense of separation between them, and poetry itself, one of the most civilizing arts, is seen as a consequence of time spent in the wilds of the countryside. The herdsman then goes on his way, and the poet and his

friend arrive at the harvest festival, the peak of the farmer's year.
The concluding wish of the poet is that

> I may set
> the winnowing fan in another year's heaped grain while
> the laughing goddess clutches her poppies and
> sheaves.[6]

# Appendix

# A Lease for Land Belonging to the Deme of Aixone in South Attica, 345/4

On these terms the demesmen of Aixone leased out the Phelleis [stony place] to Autocles son of Auteas and Auteas son of Autocles for forty years, at a rent of 152 drachmas a year, on condition that they use [?cultivate] the fruit trees, and the other way [?meaning the arable side of the estate] as they wish. They are to pay the rent in the month of Hecatombaion [July/August]; if they do not pay there will be securing [of the rent] for the Aixoneis out of the crops from the estate and out of all the other property of him who has not paid. It shall not be permitted to the demesmen of Aixone to sell or lease the land to anyone else until the forty years have gone by. If the enemy hinders or destroys anything, the deme is to have one-half of the produce from the estate. When the forty years have passed, the lessees are to hand over half of the estate fallow, as many trees as there are on the estate, but the demesmen of Aixone are to supply an *ampelourgos* [vinedresser] during the last five years.

The start of the lease for the grain crop begins in the archonship of Euboulus [345/4], and for the fruit trees in the next archonship after that. Having engraved the lease on stone *stelai* the treasurers of the demarchship of Demosthenes are to set one up in the sanctuary of Hebe, and the other in the ?meeting hall, and three-foot-high boundary markers on the estate, two on each side.

If any *eisphora* [special tax] is imposed on the property by the city the demesmen of Aixone are to make the contribution, but if the lessees pay it, it is to be reckoned into the rent.

It is not permitted to remove soil from diggings to any place except within the estate.

If anyone speaks or votes against these agreements before the forty years have gone by, he is to be liable for trial for damages, with reference to the lessees.

Eteocles son of Scaon, of Aixone, spoke: since the lessees of the Phelleis, Autocles and Auteas, agree to the cutting down of the olives for the [?benefit of] the demesmen of Aixone, men are to be chosen who with the demarch and the treasurers and the lessee will sell the olives to the highest bidder. Reckoning the interest on the money which is raised at 1 drachma [per mina per month—12 percent], they are to reduce the rent by half the amount, and so inscribe it on the *stelai*. The demesmen of Aixone are to take the interest of the money [raised from] the value of the olives. The purchaser of the olives is to cut them down when Anthias [the previous tenant] brings in the harvest of the archonship of Archias [346/5], before the ploughing [in autumn]. And [the olive cutter] is to leave the olive stumps not less than one palm high in their potsherd-bordered enclosures, so that the olives may become as fine and as big as possible in these forty years.

These men were chosen to sell the olives: Eteocles, Nauson, Hagnotheus.[1]

# Notes

*Introduction*

1. Cf. Zimmern (1911) 230: "The landed tradition is the strongest and most persistent force in the inherited social economy of Greece."

2. Dionysius of Halicarnassus, *Argument to Lysias 34*. For the questions raised by this statement, see Finley (1952) 56–58.

3. See de Ste. Croix (1972) 218–20, 254–55.

4. Cf. the passage quoted at the end of chapter 3. On the question of the connections between farming the land and the creation of civilized society, see Vidal-Naquet (1986) 15–38, esp. 21–24.

5. But Borgeaud (1988, 160–62) discusses the possible link between the official introduction of Pan's worship at Athens in the early fifth century and the development of a citizen-farmer ideal, with the growing political power then of the smaller farmers of Attica.

6. Xenophon quotes Prodicus at length elsewhere (*Mem.* 2.1.21 ff.). Cf. Cole (1967) 7 n. 18.

7. On what Hesiod's aims were *not,* see West (1978) v and Osborne (1987) 17. Whereas Starr (1961, 356) tends to reject the view that they were partly to encourage a new kind of land use, Snodgrass first endorses it (1971, 378) but later modifies his view of the matter (1987, 197ff.).

8. Osborne (1987) 18–21 perhaps overemphasizes the distance that the Attenians put between themselves and the working countryside.

9. Greek tastes seem to have differed in this respect from Roman, so Leach (1988) suggests in her discussion of Roman landscape painting.

But perhaps the (now almost entirely lost) panel and wall paintings of the Greeks took more account of the landscape than we realize.

10. See Fairclough (1930) for a collection of poetic references to the pleasures of the natural scene.

11. See, e.g., Starr (1982) 422; cf. Snodgrass (1980) 36 and (1987) 207, where he suggests that the numerous bronze figurines of oxen dedicated at Olympia c. 900–700 are beef cattle, not plow animals, not only because they were found together with sheep and goat figurines, thus reflecting herdsmen's concerns, but because they look more like beef cattle. It may be, rather, that the stylization of Geometric art did not distinguish one from the other. Style, not agricultural innovation, may also be the explanation for the presence in rich Athenian burials, c. 800 on, of the terra-cotta model granaries mentioned by Snodgrass (1980) 36; they represent agricultural wealth, no doubt, in some sense, but need be no more indicative of an interest in a *newly introduced* technique of arable farming than, say, the manufacture of teapots in the shape of thatched cottages is of a new line in domestic dwellings. On the granaries, see Smithson (1968) 92–97. For comment, see Coldstream (1977) 313–14.

12. Lloyd-Jones (1971) 159.

13. R. S. Surtees, *Handley Cross, or Mr Jorrocks' Hunt* London, (1854) 403.

## Chapter 1 Ownership of the Land

1. MacDowell (1978) 133; cf. Finley (1952) 54 on the lack of a word for "real property" as well.

2. Xen *Oecon.* 3.10—a child slave may be a *georgos;* 5.16—an owner farmer is a *georgos.* Cf. Finley (1952) 258 n. 98 for this and other ambivalent usages.

3. The *kleros* was *allotted,* or it was the share of an inheritance that a man *drew by lot;* see Murray (1980) 41. *Kleros* sometimes seems to have the sense of a specific amount of land, as in the Zelea inscription (quoted in the Introduction), which mentions a *kleros* and a *half kleros* as if they are standards of measure.

4. The Classical city-state had its roots far back in the Dark Age; the rights of community and family were interdependent, and there was no stage before the existence of a community in which property rights existed only within the kinship group, the *genos,* or some other family-based unit. See Bourriot (1976) for extensive argument to this effect.

5. On the organization of overseas settlements, Graham (1982). On Thera and Cyrene, Hdt. 4.150–59.

6. For the continued drawing of *kleroi* by lot, see *SIG*³ 141.8–9, at Black Corcyra, c. 300.

7. The allotment of house plots is also included in the settlement at Black Corcyra. See Martin (1973) for comment on the question of cemetery spaces, and the need for more discussion of cemeteries in relation to the settlement as a whole.

8. Sparta in the mid-tenth century: Cartledge (1979) 93. Corinth: Salmon (1984) 39.

9. See Demand (1990) for a useful survey of such occasions.

10. The areas given here are approximate only; the boundaries of mainland states shifted frequently, and although islands are susceptible to exact measurement, the area of land which would have been considered useful in antiquity is not. On the synoecism of Athens, see Andrewes (1982) 360–63, and on synoecism in general, Demand (1990).

11. See my comments in the Introduction.

12. See his Seventh, or Euboean, Discourse. On the probable state of relations between Trachis and its hinterland, or the Thessalians and their immediate neighbors, see the section on dependent labor in chapter 5.

13. See the section on livestock in chapter 3 for further comment.

14. For an example of land management by the demes, see the Appendix. On the public control of grazing in Attica, see the deme records, *IG* II² 1196 (Aixons) and 2498 (Piraeus). Cf. Guiraud (1893) 65.

15. On public and sacred land, see Andreyev (1974) and Walbank (1983).

16. On Athenian leases in general, see Walbank (1983), and Jameson (1982). On Delian leases, Kent (1948). On Heraclea, Uguzzoni and Ghinatti (1968).

17. See Kent (1948) 320–38, and Vial (1984) 287–316 for Delian lessees. For Hyperides, see *IG* II² 1672.253.

18. On Athenian demes, see Whitehead (1986) 43–44, 152–58; Osborne (1985) 54–59.

19. See the Appendix, for an example of a lease. Osborne (1987, 37, 42–43) translates the lease from Amorgos and gives a useful tabulation of clauses from leases in various parts of the Greek world.

20. Perpetual leases might be seen as resembling inalienable ancestral allotments, in that the lessee and his descendants had full possession of the property, except that they could not alienate it; their possession was further limited by having to pay rent. On the other hand, the rent they paid was usually lower than in a short-term lease. The advantage to the landowner lay, presumably, in being assured of a regular and perpetual income.

21. The land known as the *orgas* ("well watered," "fertile," "meadowland") belonging to the Eleusinian sanctuary on or near the Megarian border was regarded rather differently. Although it had been cultivated at various times, in 352 it was designated as sacred and not to be culti-

vated, by the Delphic oracle. Yet there were building projects in the sanctuary itself which would have benefited from additional rental income. See Sokolowski (1969) no. 32 = *IG* II² 204; de Ste. Croix (1972) 254–56.

22. See the section on farming in its setting in chapter 3 for quotation, and Uguzzoni and Ghinatti (1968). Cf. the boundary markers on the estate belonging to the deme of Aixone (Appendix).

23. Ar. *Ath. Pol.* 60.2; Lysias 7 *On the Sacred Olive Tree.* Dem. 43.71 cites the law prohibiting the uprooting of more than two *privately* owned olive trees a year, on pain of fine.

24. Cf. Dunbabin (1948) 331—32; Thomson (1949) 320–21.

25. This is one of the implications of sacrifice—see Jameson (1988). On sacrifice in general, see Burkert (1983).

26. On taxes and liturgical services, see Jones (1957); Finley (1983) 32–33, 36–40; Littman (1988) with bibliography. Taxes at Teos c. 300 affected landed interests; see Austin (1981) no. 99.

27. See Vial (1984) 287–316, 336–37.

28. Cf. Asheri (1966).

29. Schwyzer, *DGE* 567.

30. Quoted at the beginning of this section.

31. Meiggs–Lewis no. 13.9–14; cf. Buck (1955) no. 59, p. 257, for a translation.

32. Forrest (1968) 143–47.

33. In 411 the people of Samos rose up, executed about two hundred of the ruling class, exiled another four hundred, "and took their land and houses for themselves" (Thuc. 8.21).

34. For Black Corcyra, see *SIG*³ 141.9–10: 1.5 *plethra* only! For Pharsalus, see Schwyzer, *DGE* 567.4: "ancestral for all time."

35. On the alienation of land, see Finley (1975). Fine (1951, 195) provides the classic statement of the view that land could not be and was not bought and sold at Athens before the late fifth century.

36. This is not expressed in the sources; what a man owned *now* and what *he* had inherited were the facts that counted. At Tenos in the third century land was bought and sold freely, but it was still important to record that a purchase had consisted of land that the seller had inherited, as well as land that he himself had purchased (from his brother, as it happened)—*IG* XII 5, 872.50–55. Cf. Osborne (1987) 72.

37. See Finley (1952) 13–15. Private land sales were no doubt posted temporarily, but no permanent archive of land sales existed to be adjusted as properties changed hands. Public sales were recorded in permanent form, but so as to emphasize the seriousness of the events that had prompted them, not mainly for the sake of maintaining an accurate land registry.

38. So the Apollonians compensated the wrongfully blinded shepherd Euenius with estates and a town house obtained by forced sale from their owners (Hdt. 9.94).

39. Cf. Osborne (1987) 75–92, for a review of uses of the land other than agricultural.

40. On the Hermocopids, see Pritchett (1953) and (1956) for texts and discussion of the sales lists. For Mylasa, see *SIG*³ 167. For Amphipolis, *SIG*³ 194.11–16.

41. For Halicarnassus, see *SIG*³ 46; for Ceos, Tod no. 162.36–39.

42. Cf. Alexander's decree concerning exiles at Tegea—Tod no. 202.9–16; for Mytilene, see Tod no. 201.

43. Schwyzer, *DGE* 424.

44. So at Iasus, Pyron's property went to at least four new owners; see *SIG*³ 169.32–41.

45. For much of what follows, see Lacey (1968); Schaps (1979); Fox (1985); Sallares (1991) 193–221; Davies (1971), for specific individuals; and the Attic orators.

46. This is no doubt an unanswerable question, but its answer lies in the nature of Greek society's origins, and in the reasons for the variations in practice from one community to another.

47. West (1978) for commentary; see West (1988) for translation. The usual translation—e.g., that of Wender (1973)—is "If you have two (sons) you will need to have more wealth and live longer."

48. On population figures and variations, see Sallares (1991). The hypothesis that there was a sharp increase in population during the later Dark Age is supported by, e.g., Murray (1980) 65, and Snodgrass (1980) 19–25, but disputed by Morris (1987) 156–67.

49. At Athens a concentration of land in fewer hands may well have come about as the natural consequence of a decline in the citizen population by the later fourth century. See Strauss (1987) 70–81.

50. On the exposure of children, see Lacey (1968) 164–67; Cantarella (1987) 43–44; Garland (1990) 84–93, and on population policy, 100–102. Sallares (1991, 151–54) argues that exposure of children was not established practice at Athens. On conditions in Arcadia, cf. Borgeaud (1988) chap. 1. We do not know, however, what Arcadian inheritance law may have done to drive out younger sons.

51. Nevertheless Apollodorus inherited an apartment house under his father's will "as being the elder" of two sons (Dem. 36.34).

52. See West (1978) 33–40, on Perses.

53. See chapter 2, nn. 105 and 108, for other examples of violent confrontations concerning land.

54. What this passage cannot refer to is the division of *common* property; but see Thomson (1949) 318.

55. For Diogeiton and Diodotus, see Lysias 32.4; for Menecles, Isaeus 2.28.

56. Isaeus 11 *On the Estate of Hagnias;* Dem. 43 *Against Macartatus.* See also Davies (1971) no. 2921: Bouselus; and MacDowell (1978) 103–8.

57. What links did Inferiors (*hypomeiones*) retain with the Spartiate families? See Cartledge (1987) 169–70 for the difficulty of answering such questions, given the nature of the evidence.

58. Cf. Gernet's comment, in the Budé edition of Dem. 42.

59. See MacDowell (1978) 100–101. On written and spoken agreements and public notice, see Finley (1952) 18–23. For a different view of the importance of wills, see Asheri (1963) 6–10.

60. *Epinomia* here is probably better understood as "inheritance right," not "right of pasturage." See the discussion in Meiggs–Lewis.

61. Introduction to Dem. 43, Budé edition.

62. This lawsuit was the moving force in Dickens's *Bleak House.*

63. See Schaps (1979) for much of what follows and see Cantarella (1987) 47–48 for disagreement. Cf. Sallares (1991) 217 on the evident anxiety to check the fragmentation of family holdings and their subsequent absorption into other families' estates.

64. Aeschin. 1.95 refers to a man "still having some means left *from what he had got* through marriage to an *epikleros.*"

65. In third-century Thespiae women leased public and sacred property in their own right; see Feyel (1936) 405.

66. Cf. Cartledge (1979) 308–9 on reasons for restricting the number of children. See also Hodkinson (1986) on the problems of inheritance at Sparta.

67. Lysias 7.4 shows that the olive-tree property was sold twice, between 407 and 404.

68. These considerations may help to explain why, when there were so many words for sellers of other things, none is known for "broker" or "seller" of land—so Finley (1952) 270 n. 46. Land was never on sale enough to become simply a market commodity.

69. On Solon and the crisis of the early sixth century, see Austin and Vidal-Naquet (1977) 58–60, with references. On the *thetes,* see the section on hired free labor in chapter 5; cf. also Gallant (1982).

70. Oxylus, an early or legendary king of Elis, is credited with a law that "prohibits a man from raising a loan on more than a certain proportion of his land" (Ar. *Pol.* 1319 a 12). The story suggests that problems like those that afflicted Athens were experienced elsewhere.

71. Solon was not a radical reformer, as he said himself; he claimed to have redressed the balance within society, not to have imposed an entirely new order on it.

72. On Pasion, see Davies (1971) no. 11672.

73. Isocrates 15.287 mentions gambling as one of the vices of youth. Cf. Flacelière (1965) 183–84.

74. The source, perhaps, of some of the properties sold off by public bodies in the late fourth century at Athens; see Lewis (1973).

75. Lewis (1973). Cf. Osborne (1985) 56–58; he questions the possibility of arranged sales without causing questions to be asked. But if there was little competition for extra land, as is likely in the late fourth century, there need have been no difficulty.

76. On cleruchies, see Gauthier (1973).

77. On Adeimantus, see Pritchett (1953), "Attic Stelai" 6.55–56; and see Salviat (1984) 150—perhaps forty hectares in all. On Oeonias, see "Attic Stelai" 7, col. 2, 78; 9, col. 1, 314—over eighty-one talents' worth.

78. Pečirka (1966) 145–47. Cf. Whitehead (1977) 64 n. 43, 70–71, and 96: *enktesis* was a rarity for the ordinary metic.

79. Xen. *Anab.* 5.3.6–13.

80. On pasturing rights, cf. the section on livestock in chapter 3.

81. For a concise account of Xenophon's life, see Grote (1888) vol. 7, 343–46. See also Anderson (1974).

*Chapter 2  Landowners in Society*

1. A much discussed subject. To begin with, see Pečirka (1973), (1970); with Dufkova (1970). On a specific settlement pattern, see Hodkinson and Hodkinson (1981). Cf. Osborne (1985) 37–41, and (1987) 53–74.

2. This is a point made in many discussions—e.g., Pritchett (1956) 275–76: some Hermocopids owned land in widely separated parts of Attica; but as he suggests, elsewhere large concentrated holdings were perhaps more common.

3. Higgs (1972), chap. 3, with particular reference to conditions in the Fertile Crescent; cf. Chisholm (1968), especially chap. 4.

4. Traill (1975). Cf. Eliot (1962).

5. Osborne (1985) 192–95 on the remains of nucleated settlements which can be associated with demes. Cf. Whitehead (1986) 9 and n. 27. Some sense of the deme's significance as a community is conveyed by the deme lease from Aixone (see Appendix).

6. Renfrew and Wagstaff (1982) 108–10. See also Hodkinson and Hodkinson (1981) 281, and Demand (1990) 35.

7. This need not have been a source meant for domestic use, but simply for watering crops.

8. As at Platea, all of thirteen kilometers away from Thebes, or at Thebes itself. Xenophon describes exiles secretly returning to Thebes at nightfall "as if they had been working in the fields . . . just as the last of the laborers were coming in" (*HG* 5.4.3).

9. At Priene the citizens lived high up and well fortified, while passing armies burned the farmsteads in the plain below (*OGIS* 765.13–15). The man who "in a distant upland field hides the red embers of his fire under the ashes so as to save having to go to the neighbors for a light" (*Od.* 5.488–90) surely belongs to just such a rural population.

10. Cf. Snodgrass (1985).

11. Snodgrass (1985).

12. See n. 5. It remains unclear how substantial the physical center of the deme was in any instance, although we may assume the existence of a sanctuary such as is known at Icaria, for example.

13. Implied throughout the discussions of Whitehead (1986) and Osborne (1985).

14. Polystratus had an education in the city and returned to farm the land when he was grown up (Lysias 20.11–12).

15. See Lysias 1 (referred to later in the chapter).

16. The family's deme is unknown; the speaker may have belonged to this deme by ancestral right, not just through recent residence. Osborne (1985, 17–18) argues that there was no dwelling on the farm; otherwise a wall to exclude trespassers would not have been needed. This is to ignore the question of the neighborly visiting as a result of which the speaker's mother knew how small was the damage actually done to the stores in Callicles' property—where there obviously was a residence.

17. His is not an isolated dwelling, in that it stands next to a cave shrine of Pan.

18. Young (1956).

19. Langdon and Watrous (1977).

20. See Kent (1948) 299–300; *IG* XIV 645 I 138–41: farm buildings at Heraclea; Pečírka (1973).

21. Jones, Graham, and Sackett (1962) and (1973).

22. On bees, see the section on plowing and planting in chapter 3. Jones, Graham, and Sackett (1973, 418) comment on the lack of agricultural equipment about the house at Vari. Osborne (1985, 190–91) doubts that the Dema house was a farming establishment.

23. See Pečírka (1973) 124–29, for a convenient assembly of farmhouse and dwelling house plans.

24. Jones, Graham, and Sackett (1962) 82–83; cf. Osborne (1985).

25. See Pečírka (1973) on house towers, and see my section on farming in its setting in chapter 3.

26. Tod, no. 202.11–16. Cf. Tenos (*IG* XII 5, 872) and the settlements in southern Italy and Sicily.

27. Demades 14 and Dem. 18.36 refer to the bringing of farm property into the city for safety.

28. On Euphiletus (Lysias 1), see my subsequent discussion in the text; cf. Ischomachus in Xen. *Oecon.* 11.18. Jones, Graham, and Sackett (1973, 418 n. 141) cite agricultural equipment in city residences. This is not the place to enter into the debate about whether the ancient city was a "consumer city" or not but merely to point out that dependence on one's own farm could endure over great distances: for example, the philosopher Arcesilaus had supplies sent to him in Athens from his property at Pitane in Aeolis, and Strato got olive oil from his trees in Aegina for the school at Athens (Diog. Laert. 4.38 and 5.71). For recent review of the question whether the larger ancient settlements were agrotowns or consumer cities, or neither, see Jongman (1988) and Engels (1990).

29. The Spartan preoccupation with the land is suggested by Aristotle's remark, that the Guardians of Plato's Republic should not engage in agriculture, "which is exactly the rule that the Lacedaemonians are *now* trying to introduce" (*Pol.* 1264 a 10).

30. See n. 9 and the implications of Alexander's edict, discussed by Sherwin-White (1985) 80ff.

31. Austin (1981) nos. 97 and 98.

32. Cf. Pečirka (1973) 146–47.

33. Presumably the appeal of local affairs and of immediate family was equally strong in regions where the city-state had not come to full development. But how far can the known characteristics of Athenian society be taken to apply to Aetolia or Doris, Magnesia or Epirus?

34. Lysias 1 gives no hint of where anyone's land was.

35. Cf. Finley (1952) 27, quoting Wilamowitz, on the neighbors' information network. On sycophancy, see Jones (1957) 58 and n. 90; MacDowell (1978) 181–83.

36. Perhaps it would be inaccurate to draw a very close comparison with the tensions of village life in Egypt under the later Roman empire (Brown [1978] 82–85). Much petty litigation over matters of this sort was presumably brought before the demarch or some other official at the most local level.

37. See Millett (1984) 93–103.

38. But not in Attica, most likely, as will be discussed. In general it should be remembered that the order of magnitudes in the Greek economy was quite unlike those of modern economic perceptions. Thus Thucydides is concerned to mention a Spartan raid on Argive territory which netted only a few cartloads of grain (6.7.1).

39. See discussion in Hodkinson (1988) 39–40.

40. See Andreyev (1974). For Pharsalus, see Schwyzer, *DGE* 567; for Chersonesus, Pečirka (1973) 142; for Dicaeogenes' farm, Isaeus 5.22. At Metapontum a series of long parallel ditches about 220 meters apart suggests some form of land division; might the lots have been 220 meters

square (or perhaps a little longer than they were wide—no transverse lines have been observed)? If so, they would have constituted a grid of approximately fifty-*plethra* plots. (Cf. Crimean Chersonesus, where the divisions were *squares* of this size, discussed in chapter 3 in the section on causes of plants.) See Graham (1982) 185 on Metapontum.

41. Cf. K. D. White (1970) 345–47.

42. Pl. *Alc.* I 123 c, on Alcibiades' estate; Lysias 19.29, 42 on Aristophanes' purchase.

43. If it is accepted that the basic framework of land tenure, as of social and political thinking, was established during the early agonies of the Greek communities in the Dark Age, there is no need to associate such a limit with, say, the reforms of Solon, or one set by the tyrants on the holdings of their aristocratic opponents. The principle of setting a limit on land holdings could have been established early, and restated many times over. For sure, the more land a man owned in excess of requirements, the more he had to "lend" or rent out, or have worked for him by dependent labor; and some might see this as a great advantage. But at all periods others might have preferred a more restricted form of property because it would have been less complicated to manage, as well as desiring to curb the excesses of rivals.

44. See de Ste. Croix (1966).

45. Pečirka (1973) 142. See also Dufkova and Pečirka (1970) 174, for the largest farm.

46. See, e.g., Figueira (1984).

47. If the olives were the main or only planting. See the section on plowing and planting in chapter 3 for the customary density of olive trees.

48. See n. 19.

49. Cf. Dem. 20.115.

50. But see Andreyev (1974).

51. See, e.g., Mossé (1962); Michell (1957) 39; and my chapter 4, with n. 14.

52. See my section on the troubled countryside in chapter 3.

53. On the probable fate of Athenian cattle, see the section on livestock in chapter 3.

54. See Jones (1957); Finley (1952) chap. 5 on property; Davies (1971) and (1981).

55. Davies (1971) on all these men's fortunes.

56. See chapter 1, n. 77, for Adeimantus's and Oeonias's estates. For vineyard allotments at Black Corcyra, see *SIG*[3] 141.7–8.

57. See chapter 1, at the end of the section on private possession and the family estate.

58. On Thessalian agricultural wealth, see Westlake (1935).

59. On horses in the Greek world, see Anderson (1961), which is concerned more with the technicalities of horse keeping than with the economic implications.

60. Schwyzer, *DGE* 526.

61. See Cartledge (1979) 233 and (1987) 149 on Laconian horse breeding.

62. *IG* V 1, 213 = Buck (1955) no. 71. I give only a shortened version of the inscription.

63. Paus. 6.1.7–2.1. But Spartan interest in horses is well attested earlier; Euagoras won three successive Olympic victories, the only man to do so before Cimon (see my subsequent discussion in the text)—Hdt. 6.103.4.

64. Isocrates 16.1; cf. Diod. Sic. 13.74.3.

65. These were animals so cherished that they were buried opposite the place chosen for their master's burial.

66. The same difficulty arises whenever any Athenian is referred to as a cavalryman, or a *hippotrophos*. Davies (1981, appendix) shows that of forty-four entries in Olympic chariot races, twenty-five came from three families only.

67. Hodkinson and Hodkinson (1981) 278–79.

68. In the *Iliad* (2.571) Phleius (Araethyrea) is described as "lovely," probably meaning *fruitful,* just as the area is with vines today (*RE* Phleius 272). For the cavalry of Phleius, see Xen. *HG* 7.2.3–4. Other states may have decided to specialize in vines, when and where trade for other necessities that could not then be produced locally became possible. Thus a higher yield from small allotments would have been achieved, and the property qualification of poorer men would have risen. Some such arrangement as this may underlie Aristotle's enigmatic remark about Aphytis in the Chalcidice (*Pol.* 1319 a 17–19). On vines at Aphytis, see the section on plowing and planting in chapter 3.

69. See chapter 3 for further comment.

70. See chapter 3, especially the section on farming in its setting.

71. Cf. Forbes (1976); see Hodkinson (1988) on the value of beasts.

72. See the Introduction and chapter 3.

73. The Megarian tyrant Theagenes is supposed to have slaughtered the cattle of the rich as they grazed on land recently given over to other men's farming; see Ar. *Pol.* 1305 a 24.

74. Nevertheless, other considerations sometimes outweighed those of economic practicalities, as in the case of the Eleusinian *orgas,* which was deliberately left uncultivated during the fourth century (see chapter 1, n. 21).

75. Thus the use of slave labor on the land is sometimes seen as "uneconomic" because it required maintenance the year round, not just when

labor was really needed; and intensive agriculture itself is taken to be less productive than the amount of labor put in should have achieved.

76. Many matters were decided by other than strictly rational economic considerations, as for example prices for public works contracts; see Burford (1965) and (1969) 159–206.

77. See the section on plowing and planting in chapter 3.

78. See Kent (1948) 269–71 on this aspect of leasing; and Lewis (1973).

79. Cf. the section on landlord and tenant in chapter 4.

80. The concept of purchasing large areas of land for cash from another state was perhaps long-standing and widely held; cf. the Phocaeans' offer made to Chios for the Oenussae islands (Hdt. 1.165.1).

81. See Lewis (1973).

82. At 50 drachmas a *plethron* the price given for a garden of 250 drachmas suggests a plot of five *plethra* (*IG* II² 1596.18–20), which seems larger than one might expect. Perhaps garden land was valued at a higher rate than arable, and the plot was correspondingly smaller.

83. Lysias 19 gives details of Aristophanes' life. The Thetes' circumstances are, naturally, less apparent in the sources, but it is largely to them that Aristotle refers when he says that "the poor [*aporoi*] have no slaves and must depend on the help of wives and children" (*Pol.* 1323 a 5–6). See chapter 5, on poor farmers and free hired laborers.

84. Poverty in the Greek world is a somewhat neglected subject. Literary contrivances such as *Anth. Pal.* 9.149 (cf. 150) no doubt reflect reality to some degree—a man has one ewe and one cow; the ewe is killed by a wolf, the cow dies during calving, and the farmer hangs himself in a wild pear tree.

85. Theophrastus refers in passing to edible wild plants and "famine food" in *HP* and *CP.* Cf. Jameson (1983) 9.

86. See West (1978) for the correct interpretation of this passage.

87. See the first section in chapter 4 on the autourgic sense of humor.

88. Davies (1971) no. 7826, pp. 264–68.

89. Cf. the Introduction. There has been a tendency, perhaps, to underestimate Xenophon's aims in writing the *Oeconomicus*—see, e.g., Anderson (1974).

90. See chapter 4 on the landowner and the bailiff.

91. He speaks of having bought in the past.

92. What I question is the fitness of the term for Greeks who were citizens, or who had some claim on the land, and limited rights at least within the citizen body. If the *thetes* (pre-Solonian Thetes—see chapter 5) had not been in this position, rather than subject peasants of long standing, how could Solon have integrated them so successfully into the citizen body proper?

93. Millett (1984) argues in favor of this definition against Starr (1977, 123–28), who sees Hesiod as part of an upwardly mobile class of commoners aspiring to aristocracy. Neither description seems quite apt, but in other respects Millett's view of Hesiod is to be preferred. On the debate over peasants in Greek society, see further de Ste. Croix (1981) and Wood (1988).

94. It seems more a case of "When Adam delved and Eve span, who was *not* then the gentleman?"

95. See the section on dependent labor in chapter 5.

96. Here Millett's view of Hesiod and his attitudes is surely correct. On Greek peasant attitudes, see also Walcot (1971).

97. Finley (1978) 64–67: in gift exchange one should not gain; cf. p. 122—the heroes shared peasant attitudes.

98. Millett does not go so far as to make this connection, but his presentation of Hesiod's attitudes may be taken to point toward it. Thucydides' reference to Hesiod's death (3.96.1) also shows that the poet was still very much a subject of attention during the Classical period.

99. Cf. West's comment on the fact that Greeks in general disliked seafaring.

100. But cf. Austin and Vidal-Naquet (1977) 147, 150, 166–68, with references to further discussion.

101. Lysias 19.46.

102. See Davies (1971) no. 7876, pp. 264–68; cf. Cox (1989) 42–44.

103. Cratinus F328 (Edmonds).

104. See Lacey (1968) 126–27; MacDowell (1978) 93–95.

105. His son Hipponicus (once a suitor of Ischomachus's granddaughter) was himself involved in a fight with the orator Autocles *over a farm:* Autocles slapped him, and a third party was "dragged by the hair, and struck by both of them" (Hyper. fr. 36 Loeb).

106. Lacey (1968, 143) suggests that bigamy might have been practiced, and legally so, on occasion.

107. Lysias 18.14.

108. A particularly nasty family quarrel is depicted (alleged?) in Isaeus's speech on the estate of Ciron (8): when the husbands of three sisters objected to their half brother Diocles' seizure of their inheritances, he walled one of them up and then had him disfranchised, while another he had murdered in such a way that the blame for his death fell upon the wife—and so on.

109. For Alcibiades' horses, see the earlier section on landed wealth. For Nicias's dedications, see Plut. *Nicias* 3.2–6. A rich man's enemy might reproach him with not spending some of his wealth on public services or even maintaining horses—so Isaeus 5.43–44, against Dicaeogenes.

110. On visible and invisible property, see Finley (1952) 53–56.

111. For discussion and references, see Davies (1971) no. 3597.

112. Hesiod and his brother Perses provide an early example of such litigation. Justice in western Boeotia was "crooked," so Hesiod says, but perhaps no more so than that of the popular juries of the Athenian democracy, swayed as they were by peripheral considerations very often. The competence of the deme to deal with problems concerning landed property may be gauged by the tone of the lease from Aixone (Appendix).

113. L. Gernet, in his introduction to Dem. 42 (Budé edition).

114. Gernet's commentary on this speech (Budé edition) attempts no analysis of *antidosis* as it appears here. See Finley (1952) 3 and 14—this was an institution only understandable "in the absence of other ways of determining a man's wealth." Cf. MacDowell (1978) 162–64.

115. When family burial plots are mentioned, they are generally thought of as being situated within established cemeteries; so Lacey (1968) 148–49.

116. But see Dem. 55.15, quoted subsequently in the text. On the other hand, Thucydides does not mention country burial places among the things it grieved the Athenians to abandon in 431. See Humphreys (1980) on family tombs.

117. Cf. Bourriot (1976) 1151 on the shortness of family tradition in this respect.

118. The lease regulations for the estate of Dionysus at Heraclea included a prohibition against *burial* in the estate (*IG* XIV 645 I.137). If tombs were generally recognized as a mark of private ownership, then this clause would have been meant to reinforce the god's ownership over the attempts to establish private right of possession by encroachment, which had been the reason for the great reorganization of sacred land in the first place.

119. There remains the question of Deinias's burial on Timesius's farm, and the provision he made for his descendants to be buried in the same place. He seems not to have been a citizen, and in no sense an owner of the land; but whether he was a devoted bailiff or an unofficial member of Timesius's own family, is unclear. (See the section on landowner and bailiff in chapter 4, and the end of chapter 5.)

*Chapter 3 Farming the Land*

1. On Xenophon's underlying aims in the *Oeconomicus,* see the Introduction, and on Ischomachus as a historical figure see the section on social status and economic attitudes in chapter 2.

2. See especially *Birds* 229–54, 297–304, 1058–71, 1088–1101.

3. Known only from references in such sources as Theophrastus, the elder Pliny, and the Roman agronomists Varro and Columella.

4. See the Introduction for Hesiod's main interests in the *Works and Days*.

5. E.g., *WD* 609–14, 775, 795. Cicero seems to have assumed that he *was* intending to give a full review of agricultural procedure, for he mentions the omission of reference to manure (*De Senectute* 15.53–54).

6. Cf. Vernant (1969) 202–6 for agreement with Xenophon's approach; see also Vidal-Naquet (1986) 235–36. On the *techne* of craftsmen, cf. Burford (1972) 198–207.

7. On training the bailiff, see the section on landowner and bailiff in chapter 4.

8. On Theophrastus, see Einarson and Link (1976)—introduction, and comments on the text throughout; Hort (1916) has the advantage of indexes. See also Lloyd (1973) 8–15; and Hughes (1975) 64–66 and (1988).

9. See Lloyd (1970) 115–24 on Aristotle's biological works. His studies of animals (*HA, GA, PA*) include domestic types, but deal with animal life as a whole; animal husbandry is mentioned only as a part of the wider discussion.

10. If he is rightly identified with the Androtion who wrote a chronicle of Athens, and against whom Demosthenes delivered a political speech (22).

11. Einarson and Link (1976, xix-xx) remark that it was not good form to cite contemporary authorities by name.

12. He confuses date-palm pollination with the caprification of figs.

13. See Georgi (1982).

14. But Sommerstein (1987) sees here confusion on the part of the town dweller who does not share the interests of country people to the extent of understanding all the details of cultivation. See chapters 2 and 6, on the tendency to exaggerate the differences between town and country.

15. On the climate and geography of Greece, see Semple (1932); Philippson (1952); Sallares (1991) introduction and chap. 3; and for a succinct survey, Osborne (1987) 27–34.

16. Greek achievements in drainage and irrigation, modest though they may have been, deserve more attention than they have generally received in surveys of ancient technology. Richter (1968) 105–6 provides a good starting place, as may various regional studies, e.g., Tomlinson (1972) 7–14, esp. 8–11. On dry farming, see Forbes and Foxhall (1976). For the merits and drawbacks of comparisons with modern farming in Greece, as demonstrated by Forbes (1976) among others, see Halstead (1987), Halstead and Jones (1989), and Sallares (1991).

17. Kent (1948) 288.

18. As Theophrastus often implies. The basis of this survey of Greek agricultural methods is the literary texts of Hesiod, Xenophon, and The-

ophrastus; the inscribed lease regulations; archaeological material such as has already been referred to; and modern studies, the chief of which are Guiraud (1893), Jardé (1925), and Richter (1968). Useful references are included in Michell (1957). White (1970) provides many helpful parallels; but reference to Roman practices has been kept to a minimum, because this is not meant to be an exhaustive examination of agricultural techniques as such, but to provide a context, merely, in which landowners and laborers may be set for consideration.

19. See Phaenippus's estate, for instance; it is described as an *eschatia* that included woodland, as did the sacred estates of Dionysus at Heraclea (see my subsequent discussion in this chapter). Rackham (1983) points out the usefulness of scrub for grazing, and its capacity to withstand even the attentions of goats.

20. *IG* XIV 353 II 24–39 = Schwyzer, *DGE* 313.

21. On Phaenippus's inheritance, see the section on private possession and the family estate in chapter 1.

22. Or conceivably the speaker of Dem. 42 included in his reckoning of Phaenippus's property a large area of adjacent scrubland which was not actually a part of either estate. See de Ste. Croix (1966) for a decisive reduction on other grounds of the usual dimensions accorded to the estate, and for the suggestion that an irregularly shaped boundary would take in a smaller area than a regularly shaped one. Sallares (1991, 342) points out that measurement by circumference was meaningful to an ancient audience (against de Ste. Croix [1966] 111). One might therefore suppose that since the jurymen in Phaenippus's case knew that the estate was an *eschatia*, it was up to them to judge what the speaker meant by "circumference" in the context of rugged hill country. They should also have been aware of the upper limit (of about 300 *plethra* per estate), so that they could have been well aware of the true dimensions of the property.

23. So the Athenian lease, *IG* II² 1241.9–12, defines the land of the Dyaleis. Compare the way in which mining concessions are defined in the *poletai* lists, according to the surface properties over and surrounding them—e.g., *IG* II² 1582. 65–68.

24. *IG* XIV 645 I 15–20.

25. On the layout of the estates, their dimensions and the units of measure applied to them, see Uguzzoni and Ghinatti (1968) part 2, 172–218.

26. Bradford (1956) and (1957), for terracing below Mount Hymettus; on the connection between urban space and the division of the surrounding farmland, see Boyd and Jameson (1981); cf. Martin (1973); and see also site plans of western settlements in Graham (1982) 168, 176.

27. Dufkova and Pečirka (1970).

28. E.g., of Halieis—see Boyd and Jameson (1981).

29. The difficulty being that the square root of fifty is not a whole number. See Salviat and Vatin (1974) 257–59.

30. See the section on landed wealth in chapter 2, on the basic hoplite plot of 50 *plethra,* more or less.

31. Alcinous's orchard (see chapter 3 on plowing and planting) is *te-tragyas* in area, "a day's plowing in extent" (LSJ)—variable, therefore, and determined by the nature of the terrain and soil. The *gyēs* was also known at Athens—see Walbank (1983) 181, 184, 212, 215; the conclusion seems to be that the *gyēs* is an *entity,* but not a fixed measure.

32. See chapter 3 on olives; for vineyards, plots of 3 to 4 *plethra* were allotted at Black Corcyra, and of 6 *schoinoi* or more at Heraclea in southern Italy. It is not immediately apparent why a measure of 100 feet became the most widely used measure of length and area; whatever the reason, temples of that length were popular in the Archaic period, and the pavilion that Ion put up at Delphi was 1 *plethron* in area (Eur. *Ion* 1137). The modern Greek *stremma* measures about the same, and both terms are probably plowing measures derived from the "turn" that the plow animals make at the end of each furrow. Cf. Sallares (1991) 342. The plowing measure *zugon* in use on Amorgos (*SIG*³ 963.14) clearly has to do with the yoke or plow team, but the amount of work or area worked that it denoted is unknown.

33. The whole problem of Greek land measure may perhaps best be described as somewhat subjective in character and local in its determination, a little like the medieval virgate whose dimensions are notoriously hard to define.

34. Salviat and Vatin (1971, 19) discuss the etymology of *kapbolaia* and offer "handful" as a possible meaning, but they do not pursue the matter of sowing rates. There would be many variables involved in such a measure if this was its significance.

35. The subdivisions of a *schoinos* were, 1 *schoinos* = 30 paces = 4 feet.

36. Dufkova and Pečirka (1970) 152.

37. *SIG*³ 963.17–20.

38. But irrigation on the scale of Persian, Egyptian, or Mediterranean systems was of course quite unknown. See chapter 3, on plowing and planting.

39. See chapter 2.

40. The city would exercise its right to take land over for public use.

41. Cf. Osborne (1987) 75–92, on the industrial use of the land. Was agriculture quite so depressed by ancient mining and quarrying as he seems to suggest? See, however, Hughes (1975) 73–75 on the scars left by quarrying and the pollution caused by mining.

42. E.g., from the quarries of Mount Pentele to Athens and Eleusis. Roadways for large teams of draught animals would have been required,

as for any major building project, very often on routes not used by ordinary traffic or even passing armies.

43. *IG* XIV 645 I 138–41: the cattle shed to measure 22 by 18 feet, the straw barn 18 by 15 feet, and the granary 15 by 15 feet (which is about the measurement of the majority of rural towers, as it happens).

44. In many urban dwellings as in country houses—see the beginning of chapter 2.

45. Young (1956). Cf. also Osborne (1987) 63–69. The tower at Halaesa (see chapter 3) is obviously detached. But is it the remnant of a former farmstead, a defense tower, or a rural refuge and store?

46. See Young (1956), and Nowicka (1975). Hodkinson and Hodkinson (1981) 250–52 refer to a farmstead with tower in Mantinean territory. Towers have on the whole been found in comparatively treeless regions. Perhaps towers built of wood were common elsewhere; this would explain their absence from the archaeological record. (I owe this suggestion to Brian MacDonald.)

47. *IG* XII 5, 852.50–55.

48. Cf. Austin (1981) no. 50, and Hesiod *WD* 604.

49. Cf. Forbes (1976); Osborne (1987) 38–40.

50. Phaenippus's double estate came about through neighborly or indeme marriage; cf. Cox (1988), on the consolidation of estates by such means.

51. Inherent weaknesses, actual or supposed, in Greek agriculture, both of method and of the physical context in which Greek farmers operated, remain the starting points for many discussions (even though a fairer and more generous assessment has gained ground in recent years). Thus Murray (1988, 217) begins a reasonable account of farming in Attica with the comment that Attica only provides "small pockets of cultivable land, most of that suitable for olives"; Austin and Vidal-Naquet (1977, 58), speak of "inadequate" use of the soil in the early period; Rickman (1980, 26) notes the Greeks suffered from "limited territory, poor-quality soil and growth in population," among other things; according to Green (1973, 71), the danger of "soil exhaustion" increased because more and more marginal land was put under the plow. Many other such comments could be adduced. Jardé (1925) gives a not very optimistic presentation of the *results* of Greek farming, it is true, but is less disparaging of the thought and effort put into it. Certainly Thucydides speaks of Attica's poor soil being the reason why there was less quarrelsome competition for the land in the early period (1.2.5); yet Attica was also known as "an excellent land for barley" (Theophr. *HP* 8.8.2).

52. For Tod (1927, 13), referring to the period before c. 400, Greek agriculture was "backward"; Cary (1927, 57) sees agricultural advance in the fourth century. The widespread belief in a leap forward in the fourth

century is prompted by the assumption that the Peloponnesian War resulted in profound changes in the management and ownership of land, which are then seen to be demonstrated by Xenophon's *Oeconomicus*.

53. This is the impression that Theophrastus gives. Hesiod and Xenophon should be viewed as indicating not *development,* but the *nature* of farming in their time.

54. These being matters that we have largely to infer. (But see chapter 5.)

55. See the earlier section on the causes of plants.

56. Cf. Jardé (1925) 87–90.

57. Cf. Hodkinson (1988) 49–50.

58. *SIG*³ 963.20–21.

59. *IG* V 2, 3.28 = Buck (1955) no. 18 for Tegea; *Ath. Pol.* 50.2 for the *koprologoi.*

60. Cf. my comments on fertilizing vegetable gardens toward the end of this section.

61. Chinese agriculture has depended on the extensive use of well-matured human dung, for domestic animals have always been scarce, apart from pigs; the household privy would be adjacent to the pigsty, for agricultural convenience. See Bray (1984) 290–93.

62. So the deme lease of Aixone prescribes leaving half the plowland fallow (see Appendix). Cf. Hodkinson (1988) 41–42 on grazing the fallow, and 51–58 for the limited extent of transhumance, on the whole.

63. At *CP* 5.15.2–3 he warns against overmanuring.

64. Jardé (1925, 83) will only admit that they teetered on the brink of crop rotation; the implication in many discussions of the biennial-fallow system is that the Greeks *ought* to have advanced beyond it. Discussions such as Lynn White's (1962, 69–76) deny that crop rotation ever did, and by implication ever could have, come into use at all in antiquity. And see the subsequent section on livestock.

65. *IG* II² 1241.21–24—the Dyaleis phratry lease; *IG* II² 2493.8–10—a deme lease from Rhamnous. Cf. Hodkinson (1988) 42–43.

66. On the farming year, see the tabulation of Osborne (1987) 15. For Hesiod's cart and plow, *WD* 424–36; the dimensions given for the cart suggest a little gig or pony trap, not a hay wain or turnip carrier. Cf. West (1978).

67. Cf. the earlier section on the causes of plants.

68. See West (1978).

69. On the preplowing ceremony, see *IG* II² 1029.16, and Farnell (1906) vol. 3, 42–43.

70. K. D. White (1984, 29 and 59) emphasizes the simplicity and adequacy of the Greek plow for work in the kind of soil most often encountered—light and shallow.

71. Cf. Van Wersch (1972) 185—wooden plows with reinforced tips were still being used in Messenia during the 1960s.

72. As shown by *Il.* 10.351–53.

73. Ar. *HA* 575 a 31, and see West (1978).

74. See the later section on livestock for professional plow-ox trainers.

75. Cf. Menander's *Dyscolus*.

76. Cf. chapter 2, on landed wealth.

77. The record of a gift of land at Gambrium gives its dimensions in terms of the amount of seed grain it requires (*SIG*³ 302), in *kyproi*. Since neither the area to be sown nor the exact capacity of a *kypros* is known, no reliable estimate can be made of sowing rates on this particular piece of land. But see Jardé (1925) 33 n. 4.

78. Jardé (1925) remains fundamental. See Foxhall and Forbes (1982); Garnsey (1988).

79. For an underestimation of the importance of barley, see, e.g., Jones (1957) 77.

80. See Theophr. *CP* 3.21.3 and Einarson and Link (1990).

81. *IG* II² 1672, conveniently tabulated by Garnsey (1988) 98. Whether these figures can be used to calculate actual output or not, and what they might mean for grain production in general, is uncertain. The year 329/8 may have been particularly bad; and farmers may never have declared their full harvest, on principle.

82. See the section on the *autourgos* in chapter 4.

83. Millet also appears among the property of a Hermocopid (Pritchett [1956] 186–87), but it could have been purchased from elsewhere, for horse feed.

84. On alfalfa, cf. K. D. White (1970) 217.

85. See Hodkinson (1988) 45 on *kytisos*. Theophrastus mentions it only in passing.

86. Kent (1948) 288; no grazing or arable was included in the estate (other than that required by the occupants, whatever they were, of the "cattle shelter" listed).

87. Kent (1948) 289–90 shows that the same number of vines and orchard trees was maintained for decades on some Delian estates. Lease regulations elsewhere stipulated that the tenant leave the same number of trees as there had been when he entered on the lease, on pain of fine per tree or vine. (Cf. the terms of the Aixone lease in the Appendix.)

88. See the Appendix.

89. On olive tree cultivation, see Richter (1968) 134–40. See also Forbes and Foxhall (1978) on the extraction of olive oil.

90. Richter (1968) 134–40. Wright (1972, 199) concludes, on the basis of pollen analysis, that the olive was not a major crop in Messenia until after the Mycenaean period. Cf. Sallares (1991) 32–33; he also argues

that since the olive is not really suited to Attica, a conscious effort may well have had to be made (by Solon, or the tyrants?) to get it established there as a major crop. But see n. 94.

91. Rackham (1983, 313) suggests that the olive was not extensively cultivated in inner Boeotia until after 1800.

92. See Andrewes (1982) 408.

93. See the Athenian lease, *IG* I² 94.

94. Zimmern (1911, 54) supposes that since olive trees take decades to mature, they could only be cultivated on a large scale by a patient farming population under a strong central government such as did not exist until the tyrants' time. But *local* discipline and a determined interest in olives would perhaps have been enough to encourage their cultivation earlier. Bravo (1983, 17 and n. 4) argues against the proposition that olive culture only became a major specialization in the sixth century (against Murray [1980] 46).

95. See the earlier section on the causes of plants.

96. On the *ampelourgos,* see my subsequent discussion in the text.

97. Richter (1968, 144) suggests that the almond was not cultivated in Greece before the mid-fifth century.

98. *SIG*³ 963.28–31—in December.

99. He states clearly that soil makes a difference to the *plant* (*CP* 2.4.7), but he would probably attribute difference of flavor to the process of *concoction* (as it were, *ripening*).

100. See Dufkova and Pečirka (1970) pl. 5 for sketches of excavated vine holes. For Amorgos, see *SIG*³ 963.13, and 28–31.

101. *SEG* 21.644.18–20; cf. *IG* II² 2493.25–26—provision for the lessee to leave vine props behind when he vacates the lease.

102. *IG* II² 2492.17–18—see the Appendix.

103. *IG* II² 1557.44, 91.

104. Cf. Burkert (1985) 266 (mistakenly placing the incident at Methone).

105. For Zelea, see the Introduction; a freedman or metic *kepouros, IG* II² 10.7 = Tod no. 100.15; and the Athenian garden lease, *IG* II² 2494.8.

106. *IG* II² 2494.9–11. The text is poorly preserved, and restorations in *IG* are presented without comment.

107. Cf. *Il.* 21.257–62: when Achilles fights with the river Scamander he is caught by the flood like a gardener whose irrigation channels overflow.

108. Salviat and Vatin (1971) 22.

109. Cf. Watson (1983).

110. Cf. the bee garden that Aristotle recommends should be planted about hives (discussed in the section on livestock).

111. See the comments toward the end of this chapter on Heracles and Apollo as slayers of insects.

112. On Apollo as banisher of rust, see the later section on a troubled countryside.

113. See the section on chattel slaves in chapter 5.

114. Wells (1989). Cf. Pollux 4.53.

115. See Pollux 4.53; and Athen. 14.618 c, on work songs of various kinds.

116. Here Xenophon seems almost to parody his own Socratic style. Cf. *Il.* 5.499–502, on winnowing.

117. See the earlier section on farming in its setting.

118. *IG* II² 1672.292; I² 76.10–12.

119. See the Introduction.

120. See Aristoph. *Acharnians* 255, with Sommerstein (1980) on domestic ferrets. Mousetraps were known to Callimachus (*Aetia* 177), but they may have been an Alexandrian refinement unknown in the Greek world proper. Apart from Hdt. 2.66–67 on the treatment of cats in Egypt, there is virtually no reference to cats of any kind in Greek literature. Herodotus's account shows that the Egyptians' attitude toward them was remarkable and quite unlike the Greeks'; why cats should not have gained respect (if not affection) as efficient vermin catchers in the Greek world is not at all clear. (Aristotle's remarks refer to feral and big cats only.)

121. Scarcely any records survive which contain both area and number of laborers employed. *IG* XII 3, 349, of the Roman period from Thera is, like others of its kind, too incomplete to provide any basis for comparison.

122. Meiggs–Lewis no. 79.64–73. The absence of patronymic suggests that he was a metic.

123. On bees, see Richter (1968) 84–87; and Jones, Graham, and Sackett (1973) 397–414, 443–52.

124. Cf. Hesiod *WD* 233—wild bees in trees.

125. See the section on landed wealth in chapter 2 on horses, for instance, and the Introduction for reference to the question whether there was a major transformation by the end of the Dark Age from a largely pastoral (and meat-eating) society to one much more dependent on cereals.

126. Cf. *HA* 558 b 10–27 for the laying habits of poultry. The Delian records show that pigeon dung was a commercial commodity there (Michell [1957] 54 n. 7).

127. Davies (1971) 329–30.

128. Jameson (1988) 105.

129. On pig keeping and the use of pigs for sacrifice, see Jameson (1988) 98–99. The Hippocratic corpus refers to pork as the best meat to eat (cf. Sallares [1991] 226).

130. Pataecus of Eleusis sold two pigs to the sanctuary in 329—hardly big business, but sufficient for the cult's immediate needs (Davies [1971] no. 11678). Cf. Vial (1984) 320 on small-scale pig keeping at Delos.

131. Probably all that can be said is that the statue was dedicated by a certain Rhombus, son of Palus, c. 570–560, on the Athenian acropolis.

132. No evidence survives of grants made to outsiders of the right to graze in Athenian pasture—not because Attica lacked grazing altogether, but because domestic demand left none to spare.

133. Admiration for fine cattle is apparent in the Panathenaic frieze of the Parthenon, and in the wealth of literary references to Myron's cow and other superrealist sculptures of animals (Pollitt [1965] 63–64).

134. Sallares (1991, 312) suggests that oxen were borrowed quite freely, so that the ox population (and the supply of manure) was proportionately smaller than some would suppose.

135. Who does Thucydides mean, when he speaks at this point of "the Athenians?" That *all* Athenians owned land and beasts? Or is it, *only* those who owned these things? Or were there some Athenians *who could not afford* to send their animals across the water?

136. See Rackham (1983) and Hodkinson (1988) on the usefulness of woodland and scrub for grazing.

137. Sallares (1991, 312) points out the bare adequacy of winter feed for stalled animals; cf. Hesiod *WD* 559–62, recommending reduction by half.

138. On Panaetius, see n. 122.

139. *IG* II² 351. Jameson (1988, 96) acknowledges the existence of large numbers of Athenian draft animals but sees this inscription as evidence of a *need* for more. As for the timing of the project, it is worth bearing in mind that when Dionysius I commandeered men and oxen from the countryside for public works (sixty thousand men and six thousand oxen—Diod. Sic. 14.18), they were detained for no more than three weeks.

140. *SIG*³ 636 and 826 G.

141. Schwyzer, *DGE* 526. On marsh plants as fodder, see Theophr. *HP* 4.10.1–7.

142. Diels, II 416, ii 11 (Anon. Sophist.). For horses on Thessalian coinage, see Kraay (1963) nos. 466–68.

143. On Panaetius, see n. 122; Dem. 47.52: 50 sheep; Isaeus 11.41: 60 sheep and 100 goats; Isaeus 6.33: 1,300 drachmas-worth of goats with their shepherd, perhaps 80 to 100 animals, judging by goat and slave prices in the "Attic Stelai" (Pritchett [1956] 258–59 and 276–78). Hodkinson (1988, 63) indicates that a single shepherd could manage flocks of these dimensions.

144. His own estate at Scillus included pigs, goats, and horses (*Anab.* 5.3.11).

145. Aelian, *Char. An.* 16.32, quoting Aeschylides of Ceos.

146. *IG* II² 2498.

147. Tegea, *IG* V 2, 3; Orchomenus, Schwyzer, *DGE* 526.

148. But see Hodkinson (1988) 51–54, showing that there is much to be said for the attachment to a home base.

149. Hodkinson (1988) 51–54. Cf. Georgoudis (1974).

150. See Osborne (1987) 51 for a large scale map of the kind of terrain concerned.

151. Georgoudis (1974).

152. Cf. Hodkinson (1988) 56–57.

153. *Il.* 4.433–35—the sheep of a rich man are milked in the farmyard.

154. See Jameson (1983). Cf. Xen. *Mem.* 3.6.13: "No doubt you have reckoned how long the grain grown in the country will maintain the population and how much is needed annually."

155. The law quoted in Dem. 43.71 forbids the uprooting of any olive tree without good reason, not only sacred trees. See chapter 2 on Solon's laws concerning the use of the countryside (in the section on residence and neighborhood) and on some of the collective decisions that may have been taken on how the land should be exploited (in the section on landed wealth).

156. So Bloch (1967) 174; cf. Jongman (1988) 85 on the persistence of the biennial system in Roman Italy.

157. For criticism of the plow, see Richter (1968) 103—the plow's feeble efforts *had* to be supplemented by digging. But the plow did what it should; digging was regarded as the proper treatment for finishing the job (as noted in the section on plowing and planting).

158. There was, to be sure, no wholesale alteration in the basis of agricultural practice; things *continued,* including the number of fruit trees in a plantation. See comment on this "lack of improvement" in Finley (1973) 108–9. But see also Sallares (1991) 313–16 on the effects of "evolutionary biology."

159. This is certainly not to argue that yields were generally good, but that the fault lay less with Greek farmers than some would allow. See Jardé (1925), and now Garnsey (1988), for conservative estimates of productivity.

160. What we need to be able to say is, how many men did what work, how carefully, and for how long. The evidence does not permit such estimates. Was it inefficient for someone to be busy making lettuce-stalk trellises, for instance? Was it less economic to keep labor on permanently, "under employed," or to find oneself without workers at the busy seasons of the year?

161. See chapter 1, on the city-state's authority as owner in chief.

162. On territorial disputes as causes of war, see the Introduction. Famine itself, not merely the fear of future shortages, could provide a compelling reason for attacking a neighbor (Demand [1990] 173ff.).

163. See Hanson (1983).

164. See Thuc. 2.19.1 and 3.1.1 for two of many comments on the state at which crops were when the enemy moved into another city's territory.

165. Perhaps the most damaging effect was, to encourage the flight of slaves (see chapter 5, the section on chattel slaves).

166. A view typified by Michell (1957) 85–86.

167. Theophrastus's reference to the way vines are pruned at Acanthus helps to confirm their importance to the Acanthian economy (*CP* 3.15.5).

168. *IG* II² 834.7–8.

169. Some would argue that the frequent changes of owner and tenants indicate the unsatisfactory nature of Athenian agriculture in the aftermath of war. They could also be seen as evidence of considerable interest in getting back to the land by whatever means possible in those years—and in that sense may not be typical of land tenure once the countryside had settled down.

170. Chios: Pleket (1964) no. 40 B 41; cf. Clazomenae: Pleket (1964) no. 46.1; Athens: *IG* II² 2492.12–14 (see the Appendix); *SEG* 21, 644.11–16; Heraclea: IG XIV 645 I 151—the rent was cut.

171. Austin (1981) nos. 98 and 50. Anxiety about the harvest in wartime, common to all societies after all, is indicated by Aeneas Tacticus's reference to "men in the city hanging about nearby, eager to save the crops. These persons must be gathered into the city" (7.1–2).

172. Lacey (1968, 149) refers to the festivals designed to promote fertility and prosperity, celebrated by the city and by individual families, often enough on their own land. See Osborne (1987) chap. 8, esp. 172–74, on the close links between city and territory and its cultivation, as they appear in the cults of the Greek communities. This closeness is certainly demonstrated by the agricultural character of the Athenian religious calendar, for example.

173. In fact the calendar also illustrates the point that agriculture was only a part of or subordinate to the social and political concerns of Greek religion; the natural rhythm of the agricultural year was disregarded by the calendar, so that the "harvest festival" of the Thesmophoria did not necessarily take place at the time of the actual harvest. Nor does the calendar reflect *all* the stages of the farmer's year. Cf. Burkert (1985) 226.

174. *IG* I² 76. Cf. Burkert (1983) 248–97 on the Eleusinian cult.

175. Pan and the Nymphs were especially associated with the concerns of country people; see Borgeaud (1988) 140.

176. See Burkert (1985) 264–66 and the many myths that mention drought as a cause or result of the action—in Euboea (Plut. fr. 157), or at Delphi (Plut. *Mor.* 293 C–F), for example. Cf. Vernant (1969) 137–38 for rituals dealing with hunger and its expulsion, and Jardé (1925) 67 n. 3 for measures taken against hail damage.

177. See Burkert (1979) 78–98 for discussion of Heracles' many competences.

178. Tod no. 204.

179. Damia may have connections with Demeter—so How and Wells (1912). Auxesia is the equivalent of the Athenian Auxe of the ephebic oath.

180. Austin (1981) no. 91.

181. See chapter 1.

182. For what follows, cf. Borgeaud (1988) 16–19.

183. Cf. Sommerstein (1987) 2 on the theme of the animals' rebellion against human domination, which appears in the *Birds* and some other plays of Old Comedy. The main interest may have been in the inversion of the normal order of things rather than in arguing in favor of animal rights. Even so the sense is expressed that the natural world should not be trampled underfoot.

184. See Hughes (1975) 53, 61, 68.

## Chapter 4  Management of the Land

1. Cf. the discussion near the end of chapter 2.

2. There has been a tendency to think of owner farmers as invariably poor.

3. Menander, *Georgus* 35–39: "it pays back fair and square."

4. In commenting on the deserved fate of Cynaetha at the hands of the Aetolians, Polybius says that they had abandoned the cultivation of music, which the Arcadians had instituted to alleviate the nastiness of their climate and the harshness of their lives as *autourgoi* (4.21.1). It is not clear whether he means that all Arcadians were hardworking owner farmers *and poor* or simply that farming, with or without assistance, is a toilsome business.

5. Strauss (1987, 52) relates this passage to Thuc. 1.143.4–5, and takes the contrast to be between those who have other lands overseas to draw on (such as the cleruchies), and the Peloponnesians who have only their own territories. This would be to make the emphasis "working their *own* land," not "working their land *themselves.*"

6. There are *autourgoi* with and without resources, with and without assistants. Some own property big enough to make it worthwhile to use oxen (see chapter 2, in the section on landed wealth), and others work smaller plots without the help of animals. On the question how far

down the scale slave owning went, and what Ar. *Pol.* 1252 b 12 means ("the ox is the poor man's slave"), see the section on chattel slaves in chapter 5.

7. What he actually says is that the *lack* of such allegations supports his case that he did not destroy the tree: what he suggests here was probable but impossible.

8. Polystratus's experience is compared with that of the oligarch Phrynichus, who spent his youth as a herdsman, and then turned to the worser side of politics—informing and oligarchy.

9. The farmer envisioned by the composer of *Anth. Pal.* 7.321 (quoted at the end of the Introduction) is surely an *autourgos*.

10. But it seems that he employed several *epitropoi* on more than one estate (*Oecon.* 12.2). How much attention did he pay to them all?

11. Vial (1984, 336–37) suggests that Delian lessees who also held office must have employed bailiffs. Distances would of course have been quite small enough to make it possible for them to check on their employees frequently, even despite the press of official Delian business.

12. Glotz (1926) 251.

13. Cf. the discussion of Audring (1973).

14. Cf. the section on landed wealth in chapter 2: farming continued along much the same lines after the war as before it, and evidence for the large-scale dispossession of smallholders is absent (except by the accident of war—casualty figures are reckoned to have been high among the Thetes, according to Strauss [1987] 71–73, 179–82).

15. Cf. Audring (1973) 110 n. 2.

16. Cf. Osborne (1987) 23, for the limited nature of the innovation.

17. His job would have been simplified if Pericles had turned his farm over to monoculture—either vines, or olives, or cereals. Otherwise, the single sale of produce once a year which Plutarch says was the basis of Pericles' system would have meant storing a variety of harvested crops until the time chosen to sell; and prices might not have been as favorable then for some commodities as for others. Plutarch's account raises more questions than it answers. De Ste. Croix (1981, 132) suggests that the whole story is an invention of Hellenistic biographers.

18. Langdon and Watrous (1977).

19. *SEG* 32 (1982) no. 313. See chapter 2, n. 119, and the close of chapter 5 for the possibility that Deinias was a freedman, and constitutes a rare example of (more or less) hereditary tied labor in Attica.

20. See chapter 5, in the section on hired free labor, for the possibility that citizens did take up such work.

21. Cf. workshop slaves, *misthophorountes,* in Garlan (1988) 70–71.

22. Hesiod recommends the thirtieth day of the month for handing out rations and inspecting work (*WD* 766–67). It rather sounds as if he

has not the resident *autourgos* in mind here, but the employer of a bailiff, or semi-independent laborers, at least. (Cf. West [1978].)

23. See Audring (1973) 116.

24. See the section on the community and the land in chapter 1.

25. See chapter 1 on the alienation of land. That tenancy and hired labor were closely connected is implicit in the root of the terms for "rent," *misthosis, misthoma,* and "wages,"—*misthos;* cf. MacDowell (1978) 140–42.

26. A clause in the Salamis decree, c. 500, may have forbidden *klerouchoi* to lease their holdings to anyone other than a kinsman (Meiggs–Lewis no. 14.3–6). But otherwise evidence for private tenancy is scarce enough at Athens, and virtually nonexistent elsewhere.

27. Zimmern (1911) 234; cf. Mossé (1969) 54. Renting houses was common enough, by contrast; thus Xen. *Mem.* 2.7.2 mentions the absence of *rent* from houses as a result of the occupation of Decelea, but of *profit* (not rent) from the land.

28. The previous owner, Anticles, who had bought the property from Apollodorus, had also rented it out.

29. It does not necessarily mean that farming was depressed, rather the contrary, in that there were men willing to buy and wanting to rent.

30. Hereditary leases, or leases in perpetuity, may only have existed for public tenancies; the Lepreans probably held their land from Elis thus (Thuc. 5.31.2). Tenants at Heraclea rented from Dionysus "forever." And various leases in Attica were perpetual (*IG* II² 2496, 2497, 2501; *SEG* 21.644, 24.151 = Pleket [1964] no. 41). Cf. Aetolia: Pleket (1964) no. 47. The purpose of such leases presumably was to ensure a regular return for the owner; the advantage to the lessee lay in security of tenure at a lower rent than was usually paid for short-term tenancies.

31. These suspiciously round figures have been used innumerable times to argue that rents were customarily set at or about 8 percent of the land's overall value (see, e.g., Jones [1957] 139 n. 72). This is *the only* surviving example of a rent equal to 8% of the total value. Cf. Burford-Cooper (1977) 169 n. 38 for an attempt to challenge the usual argument.

32. MacDowell (1978, 93–94) refers to the guardian's duties in this respect. Isaeus (fr. 11 Loeb) may refer to a tenant farmer whose rent is to go toward what the guardian owes to his ward.

33. *IG* II² 1553.24–25 (not included in Whitehead [1977]). Tenant farmers may number among the metic *georgoi* honored by the restored democracy in 403 (*IG* II² 10; see Whitehead, 99 n. 8).

34. His former owner was now dead, so that he would presumably have been an independent agent (unless bound in some way to the heirs).

35. Lysias 7.9–10: Callistratus, Demetrius, and Proteas.

36. Jane Austen, *Persuasion,* chap. 18. Nevertheless, Theophrastus's Pretentious Man pretends that the house he is renting was inherited from his father (*Char.* 23.9).

37. Delian tenancies started at different seasons, from one period to another (Kent [1948] 268). Athenian records show considerable variation during the same period (the fourth century).

38. The rent for the Raria: *IG* II² 1672.253–54; at Heraclea: *IG* XIV 645 I 181–85, and II 36, 41, 50, etc. See also Schwyzer, *DGE* 419, a barley rent at Olympia.

39. Thus Xen. *Sympos.* 8.25: "The one who pays attention to [the beloved's] appearance is like a man who takes a lease on a plot of land. For he is not concerned that it become worth more, but that he himself may harvest the largest possible crop."

*Chapter 5 The Laborers on the Land*

1. The very persistence of dependent labor and slavery is proof enough. What follows derives from the debate generated by many studies, in particular those of Finley (1980) and (1981 b, c, d, e); de Ste. Croix (1981); Jameson (1977); Garlan (1988); Wood (1988); Lotze (1959).

2. See chapter 2, in the section on residence and neighborhood, concerning the viability of very small farms.

3. Also see Millett (1984).

4. No attempt is made here to estimate numbers, or the proportion of free to unfree among those who worked on the land. See Garlan (1988) 55–60 for the problems and to some degree the pointlessness of such calculations.

5. Cf. the *laoi agroiotai* who followed the ruler of Elis in war (*Il.* 11.671–76).

6. The situation is complicated by the fact that, at Athens, those who before the sixth century were among the unfree, economically and practically speaking, became full citizens thereafter; see the section on the alienation of land in chapter 1, and the comments in this chapter on Solon and the *thetes*/Thetes.

7. No figures of any kind for chattel slavery at Sparta are known.

8. Cf. Hodkinson and Hodkinson (1981) 279–80.

9. The father was perhaps a cleruch who stayed on after the formal collapse of the Athenian Empire in 404.

10. But if Euthyphro was really so concerned about his hired man, why had he not rescued him from the ditch where he died? Whether or not this is a remotely true story, Plato was surely trying to represent a lifelike situation.

11. E.g., Isaeus 5.39: "those who have been obliged to become

hired workers"; but Pindar *Isthm.* 1.47–49 shows no special scorn for hired work.

12. See also the tradition connected with the ancestors of the Macedonian kings (Hdt. 8.137.2–4).

13. Solon also refers to agricultural laborers hiring by the year (Diels fr. 1.47–48).

14. Cf. Wender (1973) and de Ste. Croix (1981) 185.

15. Menander *Hero* 20–30 indicates that debt bondage was back informally in Athens after the suppression of democracy in 322. (See de Ste. Croix [1981] 163; Finley [1981b] 99 on the persistence of debt bondage outside Athens.)

16. There is little on which to base calculations of the *thetes'* numbers or their demographic habits before the Classical period.

17. On Solon's reforms, see n. 6.

18. Cf. Gallant (1982).

19. Wood (1988, 76–77) sees elements of tenancy here.

20. See Wood (1988) 68, against de Ste. Croix (1981) 181.

21. See the discussion of de Ste. Croix (1981) 79–204.

22. Cf. Garlan (1988) 38–39.

23. See Whitehead (1977) 99, and references in n. 8; *IG* II² 10.

24. *IG* II² 1553.24; 1554.19; 1556.37; 1557.44, 91; 1558.65; 1559.52; 1566.22, 40; 1570.69.

25. Cf. Socrates' argument put to Eutherus (in chapter 4).

26. *IG* II² 1672.119. A slave would have been known to and in some sense valued by his owner.

27. Meiggs–Lewis no. 20.44–45.

28. See Garlan (1988); Cartledge (1979) chap. 10 and appendix 4; Lotze (1959) 26–47.

29. The closest parallel in Athenian tradition is provided by the story of the Pelasgians, the indigenous inhabitants of Attica: they had contended with the Athenians over poor farmland, which had been given to the Pelasgians in return for building the walls of Athens. This land they had "improved beyond all recognition" (Hdt. 6.137); the Pelasgians then departed from Attica and so did *not* become a dependent population.

30. The *perioikoi* of Laconia and Messenia were subordinate to but not directly ruled by Sparta. They controlled their own territories, and as far as we know had no direct connection with the Spartan system of helotage—although they may have had dependent laborers of their own. Elsewhere *perioikos* came to have the meaning of "dependent."

31. Pausanias, book 4, throughout.

32. Cartledge (1979) chap. 9.

33. The fullest study remains that of Jeanmaire (1913).

34. See chapter 2, with n. 29, for the possibility that Spartans took some active interest in their estates.

35. Naupactus became a base for a Messenian government-in-exile, after the great rebellion of the 460s.

36. Plut. *Mor.* 239 e: "they paid a return which was regularly settled in advance. There was a ban against letting for a higher price, so that the helots might make some profit and work willingly for their masters." This sounds like tenancy of a kind.

37. Cartledge (1979, 165–66) shows that this is a vexed question.

38. Cartledge (1979) 163–77; see also his article (1985).

39. Garlan (1988) 96–97.

40. At the time of Cinadon's so-called conspiracy of 397 it was said that the underprivileged would rise up, disfranchised Spartiates, helots and all, armed with the weapons most readily to hand—agricultural tools (Xen. *HG* 3.3.5–7).

41. In the 220s Cleomenes III emancipated all helots who could find five hundred drachmas each, and six thousand of them were able to do so (Plut. *Cleomenes* 23.1).

42. This may have been a story put about by Sparta's enemies, which gained such credence that even Thucydides accepted it.

43. See Lotze (1959) 48–53; Garlan (1988) 101–2.

44. Theocritus, *Idyll* 16, speaks of "monthly wage earners" working for the great families of Thessaly. If the prosperity of some *penestai* came about at the expense of their masters, this might help to explain the decline in the prosperity of the Thessalians as a whole, which is commented on during the fourth century.

45. Critias's ally has generally been understood to be a Thessalian (see *RE* vol. 23, 1 *Nachträge*: Prometheus no. 3, 1287), but the name Prometheus is scarcely known except as that of the Titan. It may have been a nickname of Jason of Pherae, possibly an ally of Critias in his youth. But Theramenes was perhaps referring disparagingly to some now lost political treatise of Critias's which had the title of *Prometheus,* something on the lines of his known work *Sisyphus,* a fragment of which contains the edifying argument that the state rests on fraud, not force (Diels 88 Kritias 25).

46. On the younger Menon's temperament, see Xen. *Anab.* 2.6.21–29.

47. Cf. Garlan (1988) 102.

48. Callistratus (Athen. 6.263 e). See Garlan (1988) 99–101; Lotze (1959) 4–26. Garlan comments on the reasons for the variety of terms in the ancient sources for tied and slave labor in Crete.

49. Reference to "those of the *klaros*" getting property if there are no other relatives left to inherit has been interpreted as allowing the *klarotai* to inherit within the household to which they have been attached; this is

surely incorrect. *Klaros* must mean here not the land lot or estate, but something like "fellow clan members," or relatives outside the *anchisteia*. See Meiggs–Lewis, p. 98, for comment.

50. See also Lotze (1959) 53–54.

51. Can Tiryns, so close to Argos, have been not yet fully incorporated into the Argive state? It was only in the late 470s that Mycenae was subdued, but Mycenae lay some miles farther north.

52. See Asheri (1975) 35–39 for references and discussion.

53. Dependent labor would have been a familiar enough concept in central Greece; there were *woikiatai* "who went with the land" in Locris, after all. But attempts to interpret the name Kylikranos as either a derogatory epithet, or showing slave-connotations, or ethnic associations have so far failed.

54. The Kragalidai of Crisa were "enslaved" after an attempt to take over Delphi and the sacred land of Apollo was defeated in the early sixth century (in the first Sacred War). Who employed them and under what conditions is another question. See Asheri (1975) 38.

55. Garlan (1988) 102–3; Asheri (1972); Pippidi (1973).

56. Hdt. 3.90.2, 7.72.

57. Mariandynian nationalism received some expression in the farm laborers' song on the death of Borimos, a son of the Mariandynian king; see Pollux 4.53 (and see chapter 3, in the section on plowing and planting).

58. Pippidi (1973) 72–75.

59. Pippidi (1973) 73–74.

60. Pippidi (1973) 75.

61. Austin (1981) nos. 98 (Istria) and 97 (Olbia).

62. Garlan (1988) 95, 102; Finley (1968, 76) refers to their probable fate.

63. *I Priene* 3 = *SIG*³ 282. The Pedieis had become so long associated with producing grain for their employers that they had taken their name (or had it given to them) from the grain-growing district or "plain" (*pedion*) itself. Cf. the *pedion* cultivated by the Tauroi at Chersonesus.

64. Sherwin-White (1985).

65. A situation most clearly exemplified at Sparta.

66. Athen. 12.523 f–524 b: the Milesians' revenge included tarring and feathering their enemies. See Robertson (1987) 374–75.

67. Sherwin-White (1985).

68. Garlan (1988) 106–112. Cf. the resident working population that accompanied the grant of land at Zelea (quoted in the Introduction).

69. This leaves open the size of the slave labor force in agriculture. Jameson (1977) and de Ste. Croix (1981) have argued in support of a comparatively large number of slaves within the farm population of Attica. Wood (1988) takes the view that much farming, in particular of the

small and scattered segments of which many richer landowners' estates are presumed to have consisted, was carried on by tenants, poor citizens (Thetes), for whom this was the only means of access to the land and who would not have employed slaves. All that the evidence really seems to show is that some tenancy certainly existed; but metics and freedmen might have made up much of the tenant population. The evidence for extensive small holding is slight enough, but not so as to militate against the assumption that there were still many small farmers in the fourth century. The terminology used for slaves and other laborers in the sources is far more varied, and makes for a much more complex topic than I indicate here, but this is the aspect of most relevance to the matter in hand.

70. See earlier in this chapter (the section on hired free labor) on the effect of Solon's reforms with regard to the labor hitherto (assumed to have been) available.

71. Garlan (1988) 38, with reference to Finley's discussion of the connection between democracy and the development of chattel slavery, as seen in Athens and Chios.

72. A connection surely exists between Chios's being the first to employ chattel slavery and subsequently doing so on a larger scale than any other community, and the development of intensive viticulture (Wiedemann [1988] 78). Whether the same connection existed in Thasos and other communities heavily committed to vines, there is not enough evidence to argue. Exactly what sort of transformation Elis may have undergone is also not revealed by the sources, except that, having become a loosely federated (if one dare use the term) city-state c. 470, it was possible thereafter for "very many slaves" to be captured by the Spartans (Xen. *HG* 3.2.26); cf. Polybius's comments on the later "abundance of slaves and farm stock" (4.73.5, 75.1–2). The terminology of the sources does not indicate what kind of enslavement was involved, whether debt bondage, chattel slavery, or what.

73. See Garlan (1988) chap. 3, esp. 119–26; the ancient debate on whether slavery was a natural or unnatural institution may only have begun in the late fifth century.

74. See de Ste. Croix (1981) 227 and 585 n. 1 on the cheapness of slaves.

75. There is another problem, in that Hesiod's meaning is unclear. The line, "a chattel woman, not wedded, one who could follow the herds," is widely considered to be spurious, but the context suggests that Hesiod's brother Perses, admonished for inefficiency and indebtedness, is not at this point considered to be in a position to marry. This line may perhaps be taken as Hesiod's own amplification of what he means by "woman" in line 405, or a later addition to the text that follows Hesiod's own, not fully

expressed thinking. See West (1978) on the difficulties of this passage.

76. Garlan (1988) 197.

77. The best evidence in support of this statement comes from the building accounts for the Erechtheum at Athens; see Randall (1953).

78. Cf. Garlan (1988) 23.

79. See now Cartledge (1985).

80. See Garlan (1988) 195–97.

81. Thuc. 7.27.5: "more than twenty thousand *cheirotechnai* fled." The question hotly debated by Jameson, de Ste. Croix, and Wood, to mention some of the most recent contributors to the discussion, concerns, first, the nature of the runaways' skills: Were only craftsmen and miners included among them, or did a fair proportion consist of agricultural workers too? Second, what if anything does the figure twenty thousand imply for the size of the slave population as a whole? As to the first problem, Alcibiades' remark at Sparta, when he first suggested the occupation of Decelea, may be relevant (Thuc. 6.91.7). He said that "much of the property with which the land is equipped will come over to you . . . *partly of its own volition.*" Alcibiades might naturally have supposed that farm workers had quite as much economic value for the Spartans and the slaves' purchasers as craftsmen or miners; at the same time, mine-slaves would have been the most eager of all the slaves in Attica to give up their occupation for almost any other form of labor. (The loss of *field* slaves would in any case have depended partly on the speed with which the Athenians evacuated the countryside as the Spartan occupying force rolled up in 412, and how willing or able they were to give them shelter in the city—not very, presumably).

As for the figure twenty thousand it has long been pointed out that neither Thucydides himself nor any other competent recorder was standing on the Athenian frontier as runaway slaves passed by. Even if this figure were correct, *we* still would not know how big the total slave population had been; probably no one knew within a few thousands how many had run off or otherwise vanished—certainly not Thucydides. Perhaps his penchant for making grand statements all the more startling by their seeming precision may have led him into throwing in a generously rounded figure of "more than twenty thousand" at this disastrous moment in his narrative. There are other examples of what might be called superlative emphasis in his history—Antiphon's was "the best defense speech," the Sicilian expedition "the greatest force sent out," the defeat in Sicily the "greatest action" and "the most calamitous defeat," the disaster at Mycalessus "more complete, more sudden, and more horrible" than any other, and so on.

82. See my previous comments on the advance of slavery and democracy in Chios.

83. See Cartledge (1985) on Drimacus.

84. The concern here is for the master's frame of mind, not for the slave who may suffer because of it.

85. Cf. Dem. 53.16—a farmer was legally entitled to beat another man's slave if he caught him stealing his crops.

86. Cf. Cato *De Agricultura* 57–58 and 104 recommending sour wine and rough relishes for inclusion in the field hands' diet.

87. See chapter 3 (the section on use of the land) on barley and wheat.

88. Cf. Cato *De Agricultura* 2.3, on *repairing* patched cloaks.

89. See chapter 3.

90. The *misthotoi* (hired workers) cannot therefore have been citizens, entitled to attend the assembly themselves; they might have been metics or freedmen, or perhaps have belonged to that part of the Athenian population which had been disfranchised in 322 when democracy was curtailed.

91. See my comments early in chapter 2.

92. West (1978) suggests that shelters for the laborers, not barns, are meant here.

93. See Kent (1948) 298–99 on the living accommodation of the Delian and Rhenean estates. Cf. Columella *De Re Rustica* 1.8.5 on the advisability of allowing the bailiff a female companion.

94. See chapter 4, the section on landowners and bailiffs.

95. On slaves as agents for their masters, see Garlan (1988) 66–68. Arethusius's slaves whom he hired out did not act on their own responsibility (Dem. 53.21).

96. This is the implication of Xen. *Oecon.* 13.10–12.

97. Cf. Columella *De Re Rustica* 1.8.15 on the need for the master to chat and joke with his farm workers, and to take them into his confidence concerning new projects on the estate.

98. Westermann (1955) 23.

99. How he would have applied this precept to the training of slaves by a slave or freedman bailiff is not made clear.

100. Would slaves have been entrusted with flocks in far distant regions? Running away was not in itself a very satisfactory alternative for the slave; and from the owner's point of view, a slave who had proved himself reliable might be considered a good security risk. But there were always risks involved in herding for one reason or another, whatever the status of the herdsman.

101. The standard work on manumission remains A. Calderini, *La Manomissione e la Condizione dei Liberti in Grecia* (Milan, 1908).

102. *SEG* 32 (1982) no. 313.

103. See Pritchett (1953), "Attic Stelai" 1.28 for Pistus; 6.54 for Aristomachus. The fact that they are named suggests "professional" status; in these records slaves are otherwise identified by ethnicity only.

104. Cf. Garlan (1988) 199 for similar comment.

105. Sadly, no indication is given of what they were. Cf. Aristotle's dream of automata in the workshop (*Pol.* 1253 b 35–39).

## Chapter 6 *The Farmers and the Rest of Society*

1. The self-styled *kakodaimonistai*, about the time of the mutilation of the Hermae, who liked to dine on unlucky days, might be taken as an extreme example of this kind of grouping and naming (Lysias fr. 53 Th.; Dodds [1951] 188).

2. For analysis of this point of view, see Strauss (1987) 59–63. Heitland (1921), still a useful collection of sources, might be added to Strauss's list of studies that subscribe to the view under scrutiny here.

3. Thucydides speaks only of "the Athenians" and their reactions to the order to evacuate in 431 (2.13.2, 14.1–16.2). The Acharnians in their country town and district are specified, but only because of the Spartans' stand nearby and their threat to the region (2.19–23); they are not a separate *rural* pressure group, but simply that part of the Athenian people which happens to be under attack at this stage. Cf. Aristophanes' *Acharnians*.

4. On the Ellopieis, see Hesych. Ellopes, and Asheri (1975) 48–49 n. 28.

5. On Cleisthenes of Sicyon, see Hdt. 5.67.1–68.2.

6. Wells (1989). In his introduction and an appendix, Wells discusses the realism of Theocritus's rural scene, and the nature of the link between the shepherd and the development of music and poetry.

## Appendix *A Lease for Land Belonging to the Deme of Aixone in South Attica, 345/4*

1. *IG* II² 2492. See Pleket (1964) no. 42 for an improved text and further references. Cf. the comments of Whitehead (1986) 154–59.

# Bibliography

Anderson, J. K. (1961) *Ancient Greek Horsemanship.* Berkeley.

―――. (1974) *Xenophon.* London.

Andrewes, A. (1982) *Cambridge Ancient History,* 2nd ed. Vol. III, pt. 3. Cambridge.

Andreyev, V. N. (1974) "Some Aspects of Agrarian Conditions in Attica in the Fifth to Third Centuries B.C." *Eirene* 12:5–46.

Asheri, D. (1963) "Laws of Inheritance, Distribution of Land and Political Constitutions in Ancient Greece." *Historia* 12:1–21.

―――. (1966) *Distribuzioni di terre nell'antica Grecia.* Memorie dell' Accad. d. Scienze di Torino, Cl.d.sc.mor., stor., e fil., ser. 4, no. 10.

―――. (1972) *Über die Frühgeschichte von Herakleia Pontike.* Vienna.

―――. (1975) "Eracle, Eraclea e i Cylicranes: mitologia e decolonizzazione nella Grecia del IV sec. a.C." *Ancient Society* 6:33–50.

Audring, G. (1973) "Über den Gutsverwalter (*epitropos*) in der attischen Landwirtschaft des 5. und des 4. Jhs. v.u.Z." *Klio* 55:109–16.

Austin, M. M. (1981) *The Hellenistic World from Alexander to the Roman Conquest.* Cambridge.

Austin, M. M., and Vidal-Naquet, P. (1977) *Economic and Social History of Ancient Greece.* Cambridge.

Bloch, M. (1967) *Land and Work in Medieval Europe—Selected Papers.* London.

Borgeaud, P. (1988) *The Cult of Pan in Ancient Greece.* Chicago.

Bourriot, F. (1976) *Recherches sur la nature du génos: Étude d'histoire sociale athénienne—périodes archaïque et classique.* Lille.

Boyd, T. D. (1988) "Urban Planning." In Grant and Kitzinger (1988), vol. 3, 1691–1700.

Boyd, T. D., and Jameson, M. H. (1981) "Urban and Rural Land Division in Ancient Greece." *Hesperia* 50:327–42.

Bradford, J. (1956) "Ancient Field Systems on Mt. Hymettos, near Athens," *Antiquaries journal* 36, 172–80.

———. (1957) *Ancient Landscapes*. London.

Bravo, B. (1983) "Le commerce des céréales chez les Grecs de l'époque archaïque," In Garnsey and Whittaker (1983) 17–29.

Bray, F. (1984) *Science and Civilisation in China*. Vol. VI, pt. 2, sec. 41: *Agriculture*. Cambridge.

Brown, P. (1978) *The Making of Late Antiquity*. Cambridge, Mass.

Buck, C. D. (1955) *The Greek Dialects*. Chicago.

Burford, A. (1965) "The Economics of Greek Temple Building." *Proceedings of the Cambridge Philological Society* 191 (n.s. no. 10):21–34.

———. (1969) *The Greek Temple Builders at Epidauros*. Liverpool.

———. (1972) *Craftsmen in Greek and Roman Society*. Ithaca, N.Y.

Burford-Cooper, A. (1977) "The Family Farm." *Classical Journal* 73:162–175.

Burkert, W. (1979) *Structure and History in Greek Mythology and Ritual*. Berkeley.

———. (1983) *Homo Necans*. Berkeley.

———. (1985) *Greek Religion*. Cambridge, Mass.

Cantarella, E. (1987) *Pandora's Daughters*. Baltimore.

Cartledge, P. (1979) *Sparta and Lakonia: A Regional History 1300–362 B.C.* London.

———. (1985) "Rebels and Sambos in Classical Greece." In Cartledge and Harvey (1985) 16–46.

———. (1987) *Agesilaos and the Crisis of Sparta*. London.

Cartledge, P., and Harvey, F. D., eds. (1985) *CRUX: Essays presented to G. E. M. de Ste Croix on His 75th Birthday*. Exeter.

Cary, M. (1927) *Cambridge Ancient History*. Vol. VI Cambridge.

Chisholm, M. (1968) *Rural Settlement and Land Use*. London.

Coldstream, J. N. (1977) *Geometric Greece*. London.

Cole, T. (1967) *Democritus and the Source of Greek Anthropology*. Cleveland.

Cox, C. A. (1988) "Sisters, Daughters and the Deme of Marriage." *Journal of Hellenic Studies* 108:185–88.

———. (1989) "Incest, Inheritance and the Political Forum in Fifth-century Athens." *Classical Journal* 85:34–46.

Davies, J. K. (1971) *Athenian Propertied Families*. Oxford.

———. (1981) *Wealth and the Power of Wealth in Classical Athens*. New York.

Demand, N. (1990) *Urban Relocation in Archaic and Classical Greece.* Norman.

de Ste. Croix, G. E. M. (1966) "The estate of Phaenippus." In *Ancient Society and Institutions: Studies Presented to Victor Ehrenberg,* ed. E. Badian, 109–14 Oxford.

————. (1972) *The Origins of the Peloponnesian War.* Ithaca, N.Y.

————. (1981) *The Class-struggle in the Ancient Greek World.* Ithaca, N.Y.

Dodds, E. R. (1951) *The Greeks and the Irrational.* Berkeley.

Dufkova, M., and Pečirka, J. (1970) "Excavations of Farms and Farmhouses in the Chora of Chersonesos in the Crimea." *Eirene* 8:123–74.

Dunbabin, T. J. (1948) *The Western Greeks.* Oxford.

Einarson, B., and Link, G. K. K. (1976, 1990) *Theophrastus, de causis plantarum.* Vols. 1–3. Cambridge, Mass.

Eliot, C. J. (1962) *The Coastal Demes of Attica.* Toronto.

Engels, D. (1990) *Roman Corinth: An Alternative Model for the Classical City.* Chicago.

Fairclough, H. R. (1930) *Love of Nature among the Greeks and Romans.* Repr. 1963. Lanham, Md.

Farnell, L. R. (1906) *The Cults of the Greek States.* London. Repr. 1971. Chicago.

Feyel, M. (1936) "Études d'épigraphie béotienne." *Bulletin de Correspondances Helléniques* 60:175–83, 389–415.

Figueira, T. J. (1984) "Mess Contributions and Subsistence at Sparta." *Transactions of the American Philological Association* 114:87–109.

Fine, J. V. A. (1951) *Horoi: Studies in Mortgage; Real Security and Land Tenure in Ancient Athens.* Hesperia, Suppl. IX. Princeton.

Finley, M. I. (1952) *Studies in Land and Credit in Ancient Athens 500–200 B.C.* New Brunswick, N.J.

————. (1968) *Ancient Sicily.* New York.

————. (1973) *The Ancient Economy.* Berkeley.

————. (1975) "The Alienability of Land in Ancient Greece." In *Use and Abuse of History,* 153–60. New York.

————. (1978) *The World of Odysseus,* 2nd. ed. New York.

————. (1980) *Ancient Slavery and Modern Ideology.* New York.

————. (1981a) *Economy and Society of Ancient Greece.* London.

————. (1981b) "Was Greek Civilisation Based on Slave Labour?" In Finley (1981a) 97–115.

————. (1981c) "Between Slavery and Freedom." In Finley (1981a) 116–32.

————. (1981d) "The Servile Statuses of Ancient Greece." In Finley (1981a) 133–49.

————. (1981e) "Debt-bondage and the Problem of Slavery." In Finley (1981a) 150–66.

————. (1983) *Politics in the Ancient World*. Cambridge.

Finley, M. I., ed. (1973) *Problèmes de la terre en Grèce ancienne*. Paris.

Flacelière, R. (1965) *Daily Life in Greece at the Time of Pericles*. New York.

Forbes, H. A. (1976) "'We have a little of everything': The Ecological Basis of Some Agricultural Practices in Methana, Trizinia." In *Regional Variations in Modern Greece and Cyprus: Towards a Perspective on the Ethnography of Greece,* ed. M. Dimen and E. Friedl, 236–50. *Annals of the New York Academy of Sciences* 268. New York.

Forbes, H. A., and Foxhall, L. (1976) "The 'thrice-ploughed field': Cultivation Techniques in Ancient and Modern Greece." *Expedition* 19, no. 1:5–11.

————. (1978) "The Queen of All Trees." *Expedition* 21, no. 1:37–47.

Forrest, W. G. (1968) *History of Sparta*. New York.

Fox, R. Lane. (1985) "Aspects of Inheritance," In Cartledge and Harvey (1985) 208–32.

Foxhall, L., and Forbes, H. A. (1982) "*Sitometreia*: The Role of Grain as a Staple Food in Classical Antiquity." *Chiron* 12 (1982) 41–90.

Gallant, T. W. (1982) "Agricultural Systems, Land Tenure, and the Reforms of Solon." *Annual of the British School at Athens* 77:111–24.

Garlan, Y. (1988) *Slavery in Ancient Greece*. Ithaca, N.Y.

Garland, R. (1990) *The Greek Way of Life*. Ithaca, N.Y.

Garnsey, P. (1988) *Famine and Food Supply in the Graeco-Roman World: Responses to Risk and Crisis*. Cambridge.

Garnsey, P., and Whittaker, C. R., eds. (1983) *Trade and Famine in Classical Antiquity*. Cambridge Philological Society suppl. no. 8. Cambridge.

Gauthier, P. (1966) "Les clérouques de Lesbos et la colonisation athénienne au Vᵉ siècle." *Revue des Études Grecques* 79:64–88.

————. (1973) "À propos des clérouques athénienne du Vᵉ siècle." In Finley, ed. (1973) 163–78.

Georgi, L. (1982) "Pollination Ecology of the Date Palm and Fig Tree: Herodotus I 193.4–5." *Classical Philology* 77:224–28.

Georgoudis, S. (1974) "Quelques problèmes de la transhumance dans la Grèce ancienne." *Revue des Études Grecques* 87, 155–85.

Glotz, G. (1926) *Ancient Greece at Work*. London.

Graham, A. J. (1971) *Colony and Mother-city*. Manchester.

————. (1982) *Cambridge Ancient History,* 2nd ed. Vol. III, pt. 3. Cambridge.

Grant, M., and Kitzinger, R., eds. (1988) *Civilization of the Ancient Mediterranean*. New York.

Green, P. (1973) *Ancient Greece*. London.

Grote, G. (1888) *History of Greece,* 3rd ed. London.

Guiraud, P. (1893) *La propriété foncière en Grèce jusqu'à la conquête romaine.* Paris.

Halstead, P. (1987) "Traditional and Ancient Rural Economy in Mediterranean Europe: Plus ça change?" *Journal of Hellenic Studies* 107: 77–87.

Halstead, P., and Jones, G. (1989) "Agrarian Ecology in the Greek Islands: Time Stress, Scale and Risk." *Journal of Hellenic Studies* 109:41–55.

Hanson, V. D. (1983) *Warfare and Agriculture in Ancient Greece.* Ann Arbor, Mich.

Heitland, W. E. (1921) *Agricola.* Cambridge.

Higgs, E. S. (1972) *Papers in Economic Prehistory.* Vol. I. Cambridge.

Hodkinson, S. (1986) "Land Tenure and Inheritance in Classical Sparta." *Classical Quarterly* 36:378–406.

———. (1988) "Animal Husbandry in the Greek Polis." In Whittaker (1988) 35–74.

Hodkinson, S., and Hodkinson, H. (1981) "Mantineia and the Mantinike: Settlement and Society in a Greek Polis." *Annual of the British School at Athens* 76:239–96.

Hort, A. (1916) *Theophrastus, Enquiry into Plants.* Cambridge, Mass.

How, W. W., and Wells, J. (1912) *Commentary on Herodotus.* Oxford.

Hughes, J. D. (1975) *Ecology in Ancient Civilizations.* Albuquerque.

———. (1988) "Theophrastus as Ecologist." In *Theophrastean studies: On Natural Science, Physics and Metaphysics, Ethics, Religion, and Rhetoric,* ed. W. W. Fortenbaugh and R. W. Sharples 67–75. New Brunswick, N.J.

Humphreys, S. C. (1980) "Family Tombs and Tomb Cults in Ancient Athens: Tradition or Traditionalism?" *Journal of Hellenic Studies* 100: 96–126.

Jameson, M. H. (1977) "Agriculture and Slavery in Classical Times." *Classical Journal* 73:122–45.

———. (1982) "The Leasing of Land in Rhamnous." *Hesperia* suppl. 19, 66–74.

———. (1983) "Famine in the Greek World." In Garnsey and Whittaker (1983) 6–16.

———. (1988) "Sacrifice and Animal Husbandry in Classical Greece." In Whittaker (1988) 87–119.

Jardé, A. (1925) *Les céréales dans l'antiquité grecque.* Paris.

Jeanmaire, H. (1913) "La crytie lacédémonienne." *Revue des Études Grecques* 26:121–50.

Jones, A. H. M. (1957) *Athenian Democracy.* Oxford.

Jones, J. E., Graham, A. J., and Sackett, L. H. (1962) "The Dema House in Attica." *Annual of the British School at Athens* 57:75–114.

————. (1973) "An Attic House below the Cave of Pan at Vari." *Annual of the British School at Athens* 68:355–452.

Jongman, W. (1988) *The Economy and Society of Pompeii.* Amsterdam.

Kent, J. H. (1948) "The Temple Estates of Delos, Rheneia and Mykonos." *Hesperia* 17:243–338.

Kraay, C. (1963) *Greek Coins.* London.

Lacey, W. K. (1968) *The Family in Classical Greece.* London.

Langdon, M. K., and Watrous, L. V. (1977) "Farm of Timesios: Rock-cut Inscriptions in South Attika." *Hesperia* 46:162–77.

Leach, E. W. (1988) *Literary and Artistic Representation of Landscape in Republican and Augustan Rome.* Princeton.

Lewis, D. M. (1973) "The Athenian *rationes centesimarum.*" In Finley, ed. (1973) 187–212.

Littman, R. J. (1988) "Greek Taxation." In Grant and Kitzinger (1988), vol. 2, 795–808.

Lloyd, G. E. R. (1970) *Early Greek Science: Thales to Aristotle.* London.

————. (1973) *Greek Science after Aristotle.* London.

Lloyd-Jones, H. (1971) *The Justice of Zeus.* Berkeley.

Lotze, D. (1959) *Metaxy eleutheron kai doulon.* Berlin.

McDonald, W. A., and Rapp G. R., eds. (1972) *The Minnesota Messenia Expedition: Reconstructing a Bronze Age Environment.* Minneapolis.

MacDowell, D. M. (1978) *The Law in Classical Athens.* Ithaca, N.Y.

Martin, R. (1973) "Rapports entre les structures urbaines et les modes de division et d'exploitation du territoire." In Finley, ed. (1973) 98–112.

Michell, H. (1957) *Economics of Ancient Greece,* 2nd ed. Cambridge.

Millett, P. (1984) "Hesiod and His World." *Proceedings of the Cambridge Philological Society* 210 (n.s. 30):84–115.

Morris, I. (1987) *Burial and Ancient Society: The Rise of the Greek City-state.* Cambridge.

Mossé, C. (1962) *La fin de la démocratie athénienne.* Paris.

————. (1969) *The Ancient World at Work.* London.

Murray, O. (1980) *Early Greece.* Atlantic Highlands, N.J.

————. (1988) "Life and Society in Classical Greece." In *The Oxford History of the Classical World I,* ed. J. Boardman, J. Griffin, and O. Murray. Oxford.

Nowicka, M. (1975) *Les maisons à tour dans le monde grec.* Institut d'histoire de la culture matérielle, *Biblioteca antiqua* 15, Wroclaw Académie polonaise des sciences. Warsaw.

Osborne, R. (1985) *Demos: The Discovery of Classical Attica.* Cambridge.

————. (1987) *Classical Landscape with Figures.* London.

Pečirka, J. (1966) *The Formula for the Grant of Enktesis in Attic Inscriptions.* Prague.

————. (1970) "Country estates of the *polis* of Chersonesos in the Crimea." In *Ricerche storiche ed economiche in memoria di Corrado Barba-gallo I*, 459–77. Naples.

――――. (1973) "Homestead Farms in Classical and Hellenistic Hellas." In Finley, ed. (1973) 113–47.

Philippson, A. (1948) *Das Klima Griechenlands*. Bonn.

――――. (1952) *Die griechischen Landschaften*. Frankfurt.

Pippidi, D. M. (1973) "Le problème de la main d'oeuvre dans les colonies grecques de la mer Noire." In Finley, ed. (1973) 63–82.

Pleket, H. (1964) *Epigraphica I*. Leiden.

Pollitt, J. J. (1965) *The Art of Greece 1400–31 B.C.* Englewood Cliffs, N.J.

Pritchett, W. K. (1953) "The Attic Stelai, Part I." *Hesperia* 22:225–99.

――――. (1956) "The Attic Stelai, Part II." *Hesperia* 25:178–328.

Rackham, O. (1983) "Observations on the Historical Ecology of Boeotia." *Annual of the British School at Athens* 78:291–351.

Randall, R. H. (1953) "The Erechtheum Workmen." *American Journal of Archaeology* 57:199–210.

Renfrew, C., and Wagstaff, M., eds. (1982) *An Island Polity: The Archaeology of Exploitation in Melos*. Cambridge.

Richter, W. (1968) *Die Landwirtschaft im homerischen Zeitalter*. Göttingen.

Rickman, G. E. (1980) *The Corn Supply of Ancient Rome*. Oxford.

Robertson, N. (1987) "Government and Society at Miletus." *Phoenix* 41:356–98.

Sallares, R. (1991) *The Ecology of the Ancient Greek World*. Ithaca, N.Y.

Salmon, J. B. (1984) *Wealthy Corinth*. Oxford.

Salviat, F. (1984) "Le vin de Thasos: Amphores, vins et sources écrites." In *Recherches sur les amphores grecques*, 145–96. *Bulletin de Correspondances Helléniques* suppl. 17. Paris.

Salviat, F., and Vatin, C. (1971) *Inscriptions de Grèce centrale*. Paris.

――――. (1974) "Le cadastre de Larissa." *Bulletin de Correspondances Helléniques* 98:247–62.

Schaps, D. M. (1979) *Economic Rights of Women in Ancient Greece*. Edinburgh.

Semple, E. C. (1932) *The Geography of the Mediterranean Region and Its Relation to Ancient History*. London.

Sherwin-White, S. N. (1985) "Ancient Archives: The Alexander Edict." *Journal of Hellenic Studies* 105:69–89.

Smithson, E. (1968) "The Tomb of a Rich Athenian Lady." *Hesperia* 37:77–116.

Snodgrass, A. (1971) *The Dark Age of Greece*. Edinburgh.

――――. (1980) *Archaic Greece: The Age of Experiment*. Berkeley.

――――. (1985) "The site of Askra." *La Béotie antique*, ed. G. Argoud and P. Roesch, 87–96. Paris.

――――. (1987) *Archaeology of Greece*. Berkeley.

Sokolowski, F. (1969) *Lois sacrées des cités grecque.* Paris.

Sommerstein, A. H. (1980) *Aristophanes, Acharnians.* Warminster.

———. (1987) *Aristophanes, Birds.* Warminster.

Starr, C. G. (1961) *The Origins of Greek Civilisation.* New York.

———. (1977) *The Economic and Social Growth of Early Greece 800–500 B.C.* Oxford.

———. (1982) *Cambridge Ancient History,* 2nd ed. Vol. III, pt. 3. Cambridge.

Strauss, B. S. (1987) *Athens after the Peloponnesian War.* Ithaca, N.Y.

Thomson, G. (1949) *Studies in Ancient Greek Society.* London.

Tod, M. N. (1927) *Cambridge Ancient History.* Vol. V. Cambridge.

Tomlinson, R. A. (1972) *Argos and the Argolid.* London.

Traill, J. S. (1975) *The Political Organisation of Attica: A Study of the Demes, Trittyes, and Phylai, and Their Representation in the Athenian Council. Hesperia* suppl. 14. Princeton.

Uguzzoni, A., and Ghinatti, F. (1968) *Le tavole greche di Eraclea.* Rome.

Van Wersch, H. J. (1972) "The Agricultural Economy." In McDonald and Rapp (1972) 177–87.

Vernant, J.-P. (1969) *Mythe et pensée chez lec Grecs.* Paris.

Vial, C. (1984) *Delos indépendante (314–167 av. J-C): Étude d'une communité civique et de ses institutions. Bulletin de Correspondances Helléniques* suppl. 10. Paris.

Vidal-Naquet, P. (1986) *The Black Hunter.* Baltimore.

Walbank, M. B. (1983) "Leases of sacred properties in Attica." *Hesperia* 52:100–35, 177–231.

Walcot, P. (1971) *Greek Peasants, Ancient and Modern.* Manchester.

Watson, A. M. (1983) *Agricultural Innovation in the Early Islamic World.* Cambridge.

Wells, R. (1989) *Theocritus: The Idylls.* London.

Wender, D. (1973) *Hesiod and Theognis.* London.

West, M. L. (1978) *Hesiod: Works and Days.* Oxford.

———. (1988) *Hesiod: Theogony, Works and Days.* Oxford.

Westermann, W. L. (1955) *Slave Systems of Greek and Roman Antiquity.* Philadelphia.

Westlake, H. D. (1935) *Thessaly in the Fourth Century.* London.

White, K. D. (1970) *Roman Farming.* London.

———. (1984) *Greek and Roman Technology.* London.

———. (1988) "Farming and Animal Husbandry." In Grant and Kitzinger (1988), vol. 1, 211–45.

White, L. (1962) *Medieval Technology and Social Change.* Oxford.

Whitehead, D. (1977) *Ideology of the Metic. Cambridge Philological Society* suppl. no. 4. Cambridge.

————. (1986) *The Demes of Attica*. Princeton.

Whittaker, C. R. (1988) *Pastoral Economies in Classical Antiquity*. Cambridge Philological Society suppl. no. 14. Cambridge.

Wiedemann, T. (1988) *Greek and Roman Slavery*. London.

Wood, E. M. (1988) *Peasant-citizen and Slave: the Foundations of Athenian Democracy*. London.

Wright, H. E. "Vegetation History." (1972) In McDonald and Rapp (1972) 188–94.

Young, J. H. (1956) "Studies in South Attica: Country Estates at Sounion." *Hesperia* 25:122–46.

Zimmern, A. (1911) *The Greek Commonwealth*. Oxford.

# Index

279

# ANCIENT SOCIETY AND HISTORY

The series Ancient Society and History offers books, relatively brief in compass, on selected topics in the history of ancient Greece and Rome, broadly conceived, with a special emphasis on comparative and other nontraditional approaches and methods. The series, which includes both works of synthesis and works of original scholarship, is aimed at the widest possible range of specialist and nonspecialist readers.

*Published in the Series:*

Eva Cantarella, *Pandora's Daughters: The Role and Status of Women in Greek and Roman Antiquity*

Alan Watson, *Roman Slave Law*

John E. Stambaugh, *The Ancient Roman City*

Géza Alföldy, *The Social History of Rome*

Giovanni Comotti, *Music in Greek and Roman Culture*

Christian Habicht, *Cicero the Politician*

Mark Golden, *Children and Childhood in Classical Athens*

Thomas Cole, *The Origins of Rhetoric in Ancient Greece*

Maurizio Bettini, *Anthropology and Roman Culture: Kinship, Time, Images of the Soul*

Suzanne Dixon, *The Roman Family*

Stephen L. Dyson, *Community and Society in Roman Italy*

Tim G. Parkin, *Demography and Roman Society*

Alison Burford, *Land and Labor in the Greek World*

Alan Watson, *International Law in Archaic Rome: War and Religion*

Sokolowski, F. (1969) *Lois sacrées des cités grecque.* Paris.

Sommerstein, A. H. (1980) *Aristophanes, Acharnians.* Warminster.

———. (1987) *Aristophanes, Birds.* Warminster.

Starr, C. G. (1961) *The Origins of Greek Civilisation.* New York.

———. (1977) *The Economic and Social Growth of Early Greece 800–500 B.C.* Oxford.

———. (1982) *Cambridge Ancient History,* 2nd ed. Vol. III, pt. 3. Cambridge.

Strauss, B. S. (1987) *Athens after the Peloponnesian War.* Ithaca, N.Y.

Thomson, G. (1949) *Studies in Ancient Greek Society.* London.

Tod, M. N. (1927) *Cambridge Ancient History.* Vol. V. Cambridge.

Tomlinson, R. A. (1972) *Argos and the Argolid.* London.

Traill, J. S. (1975) *The Political Organisation of Attica: A Study of the Demes, Trittyes, and Phylai, and Their Representation in the Athenian Council. Hesperia* suppl. 14. Princeton.

Uguzzoni, A., and Ghinatti, F. (1968) *Le tavole greche di Eraclea.* Rome.

Van Wersch, H. J. (1972) "The Agricultural Economy." In McDonald and Rapp (1972) 177–87.

Vernant, J.-P. (1969) *Mythe et pensée chez lec Grecs.* Paris.

Vial, C. (1984) *Delos indépendante (314–167 av. J-C): Étude d'une communité civique et de ses institutions. Bulletin de Correspondances Helléniques* suppl. 10. Paris.

Vidal-Naquet, P. (1986) *The Black Hunter.* Baltimore.

Walbank, M. B. (1983) "Leases of sacred properties in Attica." *Hesperia* 52:100–35, 177–231.

Walcot, P. (1971) *Greek Peasants, Ancient and Modern.* Manchester.

Watson, A. M. (1983) *Agricultural Innovation in the Early Islamic World.* Cambridge.

Wells, R. (1989) *Theocritus: The Idylls.* London.

Wender, D. (1973) *Hesiod and Theognis.* London.

West, M. L. (1978) *Hesiod: Works and Days.* Oxford.

———. (1988) *Hesiod: Theogony, Works and Days.* Oxford.

Westermann, W. L. (1955) *Slave Systems of Greek and Roman Antiquity.* Philadelphia.

Westlake, H. D. (1935) *Thessaly in the Fourth Century.* London.

White, K. D. (1970) *Roman Farming.* London.

———. (1984) *Greek and Roman Technology.* London.

———. (1988) "Farming and Animal Husbandry." In Grant and Kitzinger (1988), vol. 1, 211–45.

White, L. (1962) *Medieval Technology and Social Change.* Oxford.

Whitehead, D. (1977) *Ideology of the Metic.* Cambridge Philological Society suppl. no. 4. Cambridge.

mea." In *Ricerche storiche ed economiche in memoria di Corrado Barba-gallo I*, 459–77. Naples.

———. (1973) "Homestead Farms in Classical and Hellenistic Hellas." In Finley, ed. (1973) 113–47.

Philippson, A. (1948) *Das Klima Griechenlands.* Bonn.

———. (1952) *Die griechischen Landschaften.* Frankfurt.

Pippidi, D. M. (1973) "Le problème de la main d'oeuvre dans les colonies grecques de la mer Noire." In Finley, ed. (1973) 63–82.

Pleket, H. (1964) *Epigraphica I.* Leiden.

Pollitt, J. J. (1965) *The Art of Greece 1400–31 B.C.* Englewood Cliffs, N.J.

Pritchett, W. K. (1953) "The Attic Stelai, Part I." *Hesperia* 22:225–99.

———. (1956) "The Attic Stelai, Part II." *Hesperia* 25:178–328.

Rackham, O. (1983) "Observations on the Historical Ecology of Boeotia." *Annual of the British School at Athens* 78:291–351.

Randall, R. H. (1953) "The Erechtheum Workmen." *American Journal of Archaeology* 57:199–210.

Renfrew, C., and Wagstaff, M., eds. (1982) *An Island Polity: The Archaeology of Exploitation in Melos.* Cambridge.

Richter, W. (1968) *Die Landwirtschaft im homerischen Zeitalter.* Göttingen.

Rickman, G. E. (1980) *The Corn Supply of Ancient Rome.* Oxford.

Robertson, N. (1987) "Government and Society at Miletus." *Phoenix* 41:356–98.

Sallares, R. (1991) *The Ecology of the Ancient Greek World.* Ithaca, N.Y.

Salmon, J. B. (1984) *Wealthy Corinth.* Oxford.

Salviat, F. (1984) "Le vin de Thasos: Amphores, vins et sources écrites." In *Recherches sur les amphores grecques,* 145–96. *Bulletin de Correspondances Helléniques* suppl. 17. Paris.

Salviat, F., and Vatin, C. (1971) *Inscriptions de Grèce centrale.* Paris.

———. (1974) "Le cadastre de Larissa." *Bulletin de Correspondances Helléniques* 98:247–62.

Schaps, D. M. (1979) *Economic Rights of Women in Ancient Greece.* Edinburgh.

Semple, E. C. (1932) *The Geography of the Mediterranean Region and Its Relation to Ancient History.* London.

Sherwin-White, S. N. (1985) "Ancient Archives: The Alexander Edict." *Journal of Hellenic Studies* 105:69–89.

Smithson, E. (1968) "The Tomb of a Rich Athenian Lady." *Hesperia* 37:77–116.

Snodgrass, A. (1971) *The Dark Age of Greece.* Edinburgh.

———. (1980) *Archaic Greece: The Age of Experiment.* Berkeley.

———. (1985) "The site of Askra." *La Béotie antique,* ed. G. Argoud and P. Roesch, 87–96. Paris.

———. (1987) *Archaeology of Greece.* Berkeley.